MCSD Test Success: Visual Basic 6 Distributed Applications

MCSD Test Success™: Visual Basic® 6 Distributed Applications

Michael Gellis
Yair Alan Griver

San Francisco • Paris • Düsseldorf • Soest • London

Associate Publisher: Richard Mills
Contracts and Licensing Manager: Kristine O'Callaghan
Acquisitions & Developmental Editor: Tracy Brown
Editor: Grace Wong
Project Editor: Gemma O'Sullivan
Technical Editor: Ed Larkin
Book Designer: Bill Gibson
Electronic Publishing Specialist: Franz Baumhackl
Project Team Leader: Lisa Reardon
Proofreaders: Catherine Morris, Susan Berge, Richard Ganis, and Bonnie Hart
Indexer: Ted Laux
Cover Designer: Design Site
Cover Illustrator/Photographer: Jack D. Myers, Design Site

Library of Congress Card Number: 99-62994
ISBN: 0-7821-2434-8

Manufactured in the United States of America

10 9 8 7 6 5 4 3 2 1

To our colleagues at Flash who keep pushing us to higher achievements, and to our wives and families who understand the time we spend without pulling us back.

Acknowledgments

Michael Gellis

Thanks to my wife Nechama for holding down the fort while I typed around the clock. Thanks to Tracy Brown and the rest of the staff at Sybex for their help. Last but not least, thanks to my brother Akiva for getting me started by teaching me how to use a mouse.

Yair Alan Griver

Thanks to everyone who helped free up some of my time to work on this book. Thanks to everyone at Sybex who finally convinced me to work on a fourth one (it's only because you're all so nice). To everyone at Microsoft, old friends and new, thank you for developing interesting (and occasionally fun) development tools. Finally, I have to mention Kasey and Chush—because it's tradition.

Contents at a Glance

Table of Contents

Introduction

Corporate America is facing a major challenge in finding information workers to handle all of the computer-related tasks that are critical to almost every business. Part of the challenge is ensuring that the people who are hired are well qualified for the job. One of the methods of determining an individual's qualifications is through certification. There are a variety of certifications for different types of computer-related jobs.

For developers, one of the most significant certifications is the Microsoft Certified Solution Developer (MCSD) certification. This certification, the first of its kind in the industry, gives developers the opportunity to showcase their skills and familiarity with Microsoft platforms and development tools. The industry response has been significant. MCSD certification provides a way for developers to prove their skills, adding credibility to their job applications and promotions.

To achieve MCSD certification, you need to pass Exam 70-100, "Analyzing Requirements and Defining Solution Architectures," as well as an exam on Desktop Applications Development and an exam on Distributed Applications Development. For the Distributed Applications Development, you can choose either Visual Basic, which this book covers, or Visual C++.

Your Key to Passing Exam 70-175

This book provides you with the key to passing Exam 70-175, "Designing and Implementing Distributed Applications with Microsoft Visual Basic 6.0." Inside, you'll find information relevant to this exam together with practice questions, all designed to make sure that, when you take the exam, you are ready.

Understanding the Exam Objectives

To help you prepare for certification exams, Microsoft provides a list of exam objectives for each test. This book is structured according to the objectives for Exam 70-175, which is designed to measure your understanding of using Visual Basic in the distributed environment.

Review sections and over 300 study questions allow you to quickly learn the information that you need for each objective and for the exam itself. This enables you to prepare for the exam efficiently and effectively. However, to be truly prepared for the exam and for real-world programming, you should study Visual Basic in-depth and have some hands-on programming experience.

Getting Ready for the Real Thing

More than 200 sample test questions prepare you for the test-taking experience. These are multiple-choice questions that resemble actual exam questions. If you can pass the Sample Tests at the end of each unit and the Final Review at the end of the book, you'll know you're ready.

Determining If This Book Is for You

If you are interested in preparing for the Visual Basic Distributed Applications exam, this book is for you. The exams are written at a survey level, discussing many different topics in general terms and a few topics in specific terms. This book is designed to give you the information you need to pass the exam and to complement your understanding without overburdening you with unnecessary detail.

NOTE

Many of the objectives for the Visual Basic Distributed Applications exam overlap with the objectives for the Visual Basic Desktop Applications exam. However, all objectives for the Distributed Applications exam are covered in their entirety in this book.

Understanding Microsoft Certification

Microsoft offers several levels of certification for anyone who has or is pursuing a career as a network professional working with Microsoft products:

- Microsoft Certified Professional (MCP)
- Microsoft Certified Solution Developer (MCSD)

- Microsoft Certified Systems Engineer (MCSE)
- Microsoft Certified Systems Engineer + Internet (MCSE+I)
- Microsoft Certified Professional + Internet
- Microsoft Certified Professional + Site Building
- Microsoft Certified Trainer (MCT)

The one you choose depends on your area of expertise and your career goals.

Microsoft Certified Professional (MCP)

This certification is for individuals with expertise in one specific area. MCP certification is often a stepping stone to MCSD and/or MCSE certification. By passing one certification exam, you become an MCP.

Microsoft Certified Solution Developer (MCSD)

The MCSD certification identifies developers with experience working with Microsoft operating systems, development tools, and technologies. To achieve the MCSD certification, you must pass four exams:

1. Analyzing Requirements and Defining Solution Architectures
2. Desktop Applications Development (either Visual Basic or Visual C++)
3. Distributed Applications Development (either Visual Basic or Visual C++)
4. Elective

Possible electives include the following:

- Application Development with Microsoft Access for Windows 95
- Implementing a Database Design on Microsoft SQL Server 7.0
- Developing Applications with C++ Using the Microsoft Foundation Class Library
- Designing and Implementing Web Solutions with Microsoft Visual InterDev 6.0
- Designing and Implementing Web Sites with Microsoft FrontPage 98

Microsoft Certified Systems Engineer (MCSE)

The MCSE certification identifies network professionals with significant experience working with Microsoft operating systems, and BackOffice tools. You need to complete all of the steps required for certification. Passing the exams shows that you meet the high standards that Microsoft has set for MCSEs.

NOTE: The following list applies to the NT 4.0 track. Microsoft still supports a track for 3.51, but 4.0 certification is more desirable because it is the current operating system.

To become an MCSE, you must pass a series of six exams:

1. Networking Essentials (waived for Novell CNEs)
2. Implementing and Supporting Microsoft Windows NT Workstation 4.0 (or Windows 95)
3. Implementing and Supporting Microsoft Windows NT Server 4.0
4. Implementing and Supporting Microsoft Windows NT Server 4.0 in the Enterprise
5. Elective
6. Elective

Possible electives include the following:

- Internetworking with Microsoft TCP/IP on Microsoft Windows NT 4.0
- Implementing and Supporting Microsoft Internet Information Server 4.0
- Implementing and Supporting Microsoft Exchange Server 5.5
- Implementing and Supporting Microsoft SNA Server 4.0
- Implementing and Supporting Microsoft Systems Management Server 1.2
- Implementing a Database Design on Microsoft SQL Server 6.5
- System Administration for Microsoft SQL Server 6.5

Microsoft Certified Trainer (MCT)

As an MCT, you can deliver Microsoft certified courseware through official Microsoft channels. The number of exams you are required to pass depends on the number of courses you want to deliver. Certification is granted on a course-by-course basis.

In addition to passing exams for the courses that you want to deliver, you must also attend a trainer skills course that is approved by Microsoft. You must also demonstrate that you have prepared adequately for each new class. This can be done by either attending the class or completing a self-study checklist and sending it to Microsoft.

TIP

For the most up-to-date certification information, visit Microsoft's Training & Certification Web site at `http://www.microsoft.com/train_cert`.

Preparing for the MCSD Exams

To prepare for the MCSD certification exams, you should try to work with the products as much as possible. In addition, a variety of resources from which you can learn about the products and exams are available:

- You can take instructor-led courses.
- Online training is an alternative to instructor-led courses. This is a useful option for people who cannot find any courses in their area or who do not have the time to attend classes.
- If you prefer to use a book to help you prepare for the MCSD tests, you can choose from a wide variety of publications. These include study guides, such as the *MCSD Study Guide* series, which cover the core MCSD exams and key electives.

NOTE

For more MCSD information, point your browser to the Sybex Web site, where you'll find information about the MCP program, job links, and descriptions of other quality titles in the Sybex line of MCSD-related books. Go to `http://www.sybex.com` and click the MCSD logo.

Scheduling and Taking an Exam

Once you think you are ready to take an exam, contact Sylvan Prometric Testing Centers at (800) 755-EXAM (755-3926) or Virtual University Enterprises at `http://www.vue.com/ms`. They'll tell you where to find the closest testing center. Before you call, get out your credit card because each exam costs $100 at time of writing.

You can schedule the exam for a time that is convenient for you. The exams are downloaded from Prometric to the testing center, and you show up at your scheduled time and take the exam on a computer.

Once you complete the exam, you will know right away whether you have passed. At the end of the exam, you will receive a score report. It will list the areas that you were tested on and how you performed. If you pass the exam, you don't need to do anything else—Prometric uploads the test results to Microsoft. If you don't pass, you must pay again in order to schedule to take the exam again. But at least you will know from the score report where you did poorly, so you can study that particular information more carefully.

Knowing What to Expect

If you know what to expect, your chances of passing the exam are much greater. The following are some tips that can help you achieve success.

Getting There Early and Being Prepared

This is your last chance to review. Bring your book and review any areas about which you feel unsure. If you need a quick drink of water or a visit to the restroom, take the time before the exam. Once your exam starts, it will not be paused for these needs.

When you arrive for your exam, you will be asked to present two forms of ID. You will also be asked to sign a piece of paper verifying that you understand the testing rules and that you will not disclose the content of the exam to others.

Before you start the exam, you will have an opportunity to take a practice exam. It is not related to Visual Basic and is simply offered so that you will have a feel for the exam-taking process.

Bringing Items with You

These are closed-book exams. The only thing you can take in is scrap paper provided by the testing center. Use this paper as much as possible to diagram the questions. Many times, diagramming questions will help make the answer clear. You will have to give this paper back to the test administrator at the end of the exam.

Many testing centers are very strict about what you can take into the testing room. Some centers will not even allow you to bring in items like a zipped purse. If you feel tempted to take in any outside material, beware that many testing centers use monitoring devices such as video and audio equipment (so don't swear, even if you are alone in the room!)

Prometric Testing Centers take the test-taking process and the test validation very seriously.

Executing Test Strategy

As you take the test, if you know the answer to a question, fill it in and move on. If you're not sure of the answer, mark your best guess, then "mark" the question.

At the end of the exam, you can review the questions. Depending on the amount of time remaining, you can then view all of the questions again, or you can view only the questions about which you were unsure. Double-check your answers, just in case you misread any of the questions on the first pass. (Sometimes half of the battle is in trying to figure out exactly what the question is asking you.) You may find that a related question provides a clue for a troublesome question.

Be sure to answer all questions. Unanswered questions are scored as incorrect and will count against you. There is no penalty for guessing. Also, make sure you keep an eye on the remaining time so that you can pace yourself accordingly.

If you do not pass the exam, note everything that you can remember while the exam is still fresh on your mind. This will help you prepare for your next try. Although the next exam will not be exactly the same, the questions will be similar, and you don't want to make the same mistakes.

After Becoming Certified

Once you become an MCSD, Microsoft kicks in some goodies, including the following:

- A one-year subscription to the Microsoft Beta Evaluation program, which is a great way to get your hands on new software. Be the first kid on the block to play with new and upcoming software.
- Access to a secure area of the Microsoft Web site that provides technical support and product information. This certification benefit is also available for MCP certification.

- Permission to use the Microsoft Certified Professional logos (each certification has its own logo), which look great on letterhead and business cards.
- An MCP certificate (you will get a certificate for each level of certification you reach), suitable for framing, or sending copies to Mom.
- A one-year subscription to *Microsoft Certified Professional Magazine*, which provides information on professional and career development.

How to Use This Book

The Visual Basic exams are mostly conceptual, rather than applied. However, the exercises in this book are designed to reinforce some of the important topics on this exam, especially those topics where implementation detail will be tested. To address the wide range of topics on this exam, many Microsoft applications and development tools have been referenced in this book. To do all of the examples in this book, you must have the following software installed:

- Windows Operating System selected from the following configurations:
  - Windows 95/98
  - Windows NT workstation
- An ODBC database, preferably SQL Server with the Sample Pubs database installed.
- Microsoft Visual Basic 6 at a default installation.
- Microsoft Internet Explorer 4. Note that all exercises and screen shots in this book assume that the Active Desktop is not installed with IE 4.

All of the examples in the book assume that products have been installed according to the defaults and no consideration is given for additional customizations that you have made on the installation.

As you work through this book, you may want to follow these general procedures:

1. Review the exam objectives as you work through the unit. (You should check the Microsoft Training & Certification Web site to make sure the objectives haven't changed.)

2. Study a unit carefully, making sure you fully understand the information.
3. Complete all examples in the unit, referring to the text so that you understand every step you take.
4. Answer the study and sample test questions at the end of the unit. (You will find the answers to these questions in Appendix A.)
5. Note which questions you did not understand and study those sections of the book again.

To learn all of the material covered in this book, you will need to study regularly and with discipline. Try to set aside the same time every day to study and select a comfortable and quiet place in which to do it. Good luck!

About the Authors

Michael Gellis

Michael Gellis is a senior consultant at Flash Creative Management (`http://www.flashcreative.com`), a Hackensack, New Jersey-based consulting firm that works with businesses to jointly map their strategies and build the supporting technology and processes to achieve their growth and profit objectives. Flash is a Microsoft Solution Provider at the Partner level and a Microsoft Authorized Technical Education Center.

Flash Creative Management has been recognized as an *Inc.* 500 Company for three straight years and *Upside* magazine's 'Emerging Star' company in the field of technology. Flash was also recognized as the ninth-ranked 1995 Deloitte, Touche, Tohmatsu New Jersey Fast 50 Technology company and nationally as one of its Fast 500 companies.

Michael is a Microsoft Certified Professional in Visual Basic 5 and 6. He has lectured at Microsoft's Teched conference on Visual Basic topics and is also the VB Pro at Fawcette's *Ask The Pro* Web site. You can submit questions to him and view articles written by him at `http://www.inquiry.com` as well as at Flash's site. He can be reached at `mikeg@flashcreative.com`.

Yair Alan Griver

Yair Alan Griver is a principal and the chief information officer at Flash Creative Management. Alan is responsible for overseeing the development of Flash's methods and development frameworks. He has received the Most Valuable Professional award from Microsoft for his expertise in applying Microsoft technology to real-world applications and for sharing that knowledge with other software developers. He is the author of *The Visual FoxPro 3 Codebook* also published by Sybex and his third book in the popular Codebook series, which covers advanced development techniques and includes a comprehensive enterprise development methodology. Fortune 500 companies throughout the world have adopted his approach and methodologies. Together with his partner David Blumenthal, Alan was a finalist in Ernst and Young's 1994 Entrepreneur of the Year program.

A Microsoft Certified Solutions Developer and Certified Trainer, Alan has written articles that have been published in many leading publications and has lectured throughout the world on computer systems and software design. He can be reached at (201) 489-2500, ext. 202, or at `alang@flashcreative.com`.

Matthew Arnheiter

Matthew Arnheiter contributed material on Visual SourceSafe and Visual Component Manager. Matthew is a consultant at Flash Creative Management. He has been developing software for seven years. Over the years he has worked with FoxPro, Visual FoxPro, Visual Basic, and Java.

Prior to joining Flash, Matthew worked as a consultant at Survey Data Securities Corp. in Long Beach, New York. He designed and implemented many applications for social service organizations throughout the country. Matthew received his B.S. in pure mathematics from Fordham University. He can be reached at `matta@flashcreative.com`.

Contacting Sybex

Technical Support (e-mail): `support@sybex.com`

NOTE To find information on this book on the Sybex Web site, click Catalog, then type **2434** in the search field and press Enter.

UNIT 1

Developing the Conceptual and Logical Design

Test Objective:

- **Given a conceptual design, apply the principles of modular design to derive the components and services of the logical design.**

NOTE

Exam objectives are subject to change at any time without prior notice and at Microsoft's sole discretion. Please visit Microsoft's Training & Certification Web site (`www.microsoft.com/Train_Cert`) for the most current exam objectives listing.

This unit discusses developing design models of a distributed application and translating the models into physical implementations. It also discusses how to design the model in order to optimize performance.

Designing a Database

Designing a database involves two steps: the logical design and the physical creation of the database. *Logical design* involves describing the things about the system that is being created and how they relate to each other. *Physical design* involves turning that description into a data structure that exists on disk.

Creating a Logical Design

When you create a logical design, also known as 'entity-relationship modeling,' you go through four phases:

- Identify the entities by reviewing the requirements.
- Document an entity identifier for each entity.
- Identify each entity's attributes.
- Identify the relationships between entities.

Identifying the Entities

In this phase you look for the nouns that describe things that store information. For example, you might have a 'customer' and an 'invoice' entity. There are three basic types of entities (see Table 1.1).

TABLE 1.1: The Basic Entity Types

Entity Type	Description	Example(s)
Kernel	A base table that neither describes other entities nor is used for a relationship between them.	Customer, Order
Associative	An entity used to join two entities together in a many-to-many relationship.	CompanyContact that links one company to many contacts or one contact to many companies.
Characteristic	An entity used to describe another entity, typically when that entity's information changes over time.	LineItemDetail that duplicates the cost of an item so that an invoice history of the changing cost of the item can be retained.

Documenting an Entity Identifier

In the first phase, each entity is given a unique identifier, such as CustomerID. The unique identifier is maintained by the system, not by the user.

Identifying an Entity's Attributes

In the second phase, you describe an entity by its attributes. These attributes are typically nouns that are found in the requirements. For instance, a Customer entity might have the attributes of name, address, and phone number.

Identifying the Relationships between Entities

In the third phase, you describe how one entity is related to another by adding the main entity's identifier to the subordinate entity. For instance, since one customer has many orders, the CustomerID identifier would also appear in the Order entity. In a model, you would draw a line between the two CustomerID attributes and add a few words to describe the relationship, as in, "A Customer *places* Orders."

There are three types of relationships: one-to-one, one-to-many, and many-to-many. They are described in Table 1.2.

TABLE 1.2: The Three Types of Relationships

Relationship Type	Description	Example
One-to-one	One entity in the first table is related to one entity in the second table. This relationship is rare.	A system may have Customer and CustomerPassword tables. Each customer has one password, but the tables are split up so that different security can be set for the CustomerPassword table.
One-to-many	An entity in the first (often called a parent) table is related to zero or more entities in the second (child) table. This is the most common relationship.	A system may have Customer and Invoice tables in which each customer may have zero to *n* invoices.
Many-to-many	This relationship is created through the use of an associative entity, which consists of copies of the identifiers from both entities in the many-to-many relationship. This relationship allows you to create two one-to-many relationships to the associative entity.	A system may have Customer, Contact, and CustomerContact tables. The CustomerContact table has the CustomerID and ContactID identifiers from the other two tables. In this manner, you can look up all contacts for a customer and all customers for a contact.

Creating a Physical Design

Once you have set up your logical model, you must move it into a physical database schema. When you do this, the following rules apply:

- Each entity typically becomes a table.
- Each attribute becomes a column in a table (also known as a field).
- Each instance of an attribute becomes a row in a table (also known as a record).
- Each identifier becomes a primary or foreign key column in a table. It is a *primary key* if it is the identifier for that table; it is a *foreign key* if it has been migrated from another table to be used in a relationship.
- Each relationship also becomes a relationship in the database schema; the primary and foreign keys are used to enforce the relationship.

Once you have followed the above rules, you should perform the following actions:

- Assign each column a data type and size.

TIP: Unless you can do math on the column, you should create it as a character column, even if it only contains numbers.

- Assign column constraints that force a column to adhere to certain rules. These constraints can include those that tell a column that it cannot include nulls (NOT NULL), cannot have duplicates (UNIQUE), can only allow certain values (CHECK), among others.

TIP: Different databases support different features, and it pays to know what your database supports before creating the schema.

- Check if any of the columns should be broken into more than one column. For instance, you may have a logical model with a Contact Name attribute. In the physical database schema, you may want to break that down into LastName and FirstName columns.

Designing Services

Designing a distributed system involves breaking down the requirements of the business into a series of 'services' that your application will use. It is convenient to think of these services as existing in three tiers:

Data tier This tier is used to provide access to data. It may be made up of stored procedures as well as a physical database schema.

Business services tier This tier (also known as the middle tier) is used to provide access to a logical view of the business. It is composed of two types of components: data components that provide a standardized way of accessing the data tier and business components that implement most rules of the business and are accessed by the front end.

User interface (UI) tier This tier is used to orchestrate access to the middle-tier business components. It ensures that users access information in a logical order.

Reviewing Distributed Systems

Before we go into the details of the three tiers, we should review what is meant by a 'distributed system'. In order to do that, let's take a look at a little history.

Application development has gone through four phases:

1. mainframe database development
2. network database development
3. client/server development
4. distributed (or three-tier) development

In mainframe development, all of the application logic, data access, and screen writing occurred on one machine, the mainframe, which controlled everything. As more users were added, the mainframe had to be upgraded at great expense in order to handle the load. This was a single-tier solution.

Network databases (like Microsoft Access and Microsoft Visual FoxPro) put the logic on the PC, which handled the screen drawing (allowing for richer front ends) as well as the logic and database access. The databases could be shared on a network file server, but the logic for the requests happened on the user's PC. This solution allowed the network to handle some of the file access issues, but most of the work was done on the client. Let's call this the 1.5-tier solution.

Client/server databases (like Microsoft SQL Server) allowed the data access to occur on the database server. The client simply sent a string to the server that requested data or requested that a stored procedure be run. In this model, the client handled the user interface processing, the server handled the database processing, and business rules were either on the client or on the server. This is known as a two-tier solution.

Distributed solutions break the business rules onto their own server, allowing scaling to occur at any level: client, business rule, or database server. This is called a three-tier solution because each of the tiers of a typical application can be placed on its own server(s) and updated independently of the rest.

With this knowledge, let's take a closer look at each of the three tiers in a distributed system.

Understanding the Data Tier

The data tier is comprised of a database server (like Microsoft SQL Server) that provides access to permanent data storage on disk. The data is typically accessed in one of two ways: direct access or through stored procedures. Table 1.3 describes each approach.

TABLE 1.3 Accessing Data through a Server

Approach	Description
Direct access	The middle tier issues an SQL statement that accesses the data directly.
Stored procedures	Access is coded into the database, which allows the database to precompile the query, resulting in some speed gains.

Understanding the Business Tier

The business tier is physically made up of COM DLLs, which live on their own server or set of servers. This tier is composed of two types of components, data and business, which work together to provide access to data and the rules that run the business.

Understanding Data Components

Data components mediate between the server database and the business components to provide a standardized 'view' into the database, regardless of the physical structure. For instance, a business component may call a method of a data component that creates an ADO command that accepts the customer's ID and returns her current credit limit as an ADO recordset. The business component doesn't care if the credit limit is an actual column in the customer table or if it is a stored procedure that subtracts the amount owed by the customer from some arbitrary number. The business component simply sees that there is a credit limit it can request.

This capability of masking the physical structure is very important in a distributed system where your applications may be asked to access data of various formats and in various database systems. A change in the physical structure only requires a change to data components, not to the system as a whole.

Understanding Business Components

Business components implement the rules that run a business. They mediate between the data components and the user interface. The user interface typically calls on the business component to perform a function such as saving an invoice, at which time the business component might check the customer's credit limit, ask a data component to do the physical save, then send out an e-mail confirmation of the credit to the client.

Business components typically provide properties that are made up of the columns of a database, as well as properties that are calculated but provide easier access to front end developers. In other words, a business component called Customer would typically include LastName and FirstName properties, but it may also have a calculated property called FullName that combines the two. In this way, the business component provides easier access to the front-end developer, who doesn't have to write code to combine FirstName and LastName into FullName.

When implementing a business component, it is often helpful to begin by looking at the core entities of your business and asking, What information do I need to access for each of these? and What services should each of these be able to provide? For instance, in an accounts receivable application, you might have components called Customer and Invoice. Invoice might contain a collection of LineItems that are only accessible through the Invoice object. The Customer and the Invoice objects might have a Save method that calls into the CustomerData and InvoiceData objects to do the actual writing to the database. While this approach is not always the proper one for every given circumstance, it does provide a good starting point for implementing business components.

Understanding the User Interface

The user interface (UI) is what users run in their day-to-day operations. It typically consists of either a Win32 front end (written in a language like VB) or sets of Active Server Pages serving up a Web page (in HTML or DHTML) to a user. In either case, the front end simply functions as a means to direct the user through the steps necessary to perform a task and calls the proper business components to perform any rule validation and calls to data components for accessing or saving data.

The front end selection that you make depends on whether the client's hardware can run a Win32 application, how rich the application's interface has to be, and whether you need to access non-Windows hardware, among other things. Generally, Web pages have the greatest reach because they can be run on Windows, Macintosh, and Unix clients (among others), while Win32 front ends are richer because they can provide such things as drag-and-drop capabilities and exact placement of design elements.

Keeping Tabs on Performance Issues

When designing a distributed system, you should:

Keep the rules at the proper location. For example, if you have a rule that requires access to most of the data in your database, implementing it as a stored procedure will reduce any network traffic, and typically, enhance the speed of your application. On the other hand, if the rule relies on only a few rows of data, implementing it in a business component will allow you the most flexibility in maintenance.

Keep transactions short. If you are going to be implementing a number of rules that validate data before a save, have them run before the transaction begins. A transaction takes up many system resources and can keep other users waiting.

Think about network traffic. This is a corollary to the first rule. When transferring data between physical servers that contain the various logical tiers, plan for how that data will be transferred and when communication will take place. For instance, in a WAN (wide area network) application, communication is slow and expensive, so sending a disconnected recordset to the client may often make the most sense. This allows the client to work with the data as long as it needs to and to reconnect and update the data when it is ready. In a case like this, having the UI access data as properties of a server-based COM object would require too many roundtrips to the server.

STUDY QUESTIONS

Designing a Database

1. What are the two main phases of designing a database?

____

____

2. What do entities typically become when moving from a logical to a physical design?

____

3. What are the three basic entity types?

____

____

____

4. What are the three types of relationships?

____

____

____

5. Three examples of column constraints are __________, __________, __________.

6. What is a column typically shown as in a logical model?

____

STUDY QUESTIONS

Designing Services

7. Name the three tiers in a distributed system.

____

____

____

8. What kind of components mediate between the physical data and the rest of the distributed system?

____

9. ______________ and ______________ are two methods that can be used to access data.

10. What kinds of front ends typically comprise the user interface tier?

____

____

11. What physical packaging mechanism typically comprises the business tier?

____

Keeping Tabs on Performance Issues

12. Which data manipulation approach keeps processing closest to the database?

____

STUDY QUESTIONS

13. What should you do in order to keep transactions as short as possible?

____

14. True or False. In a WAN, minimizing communication will typically be the greatest issue in performance tuning.

SAMPLE TEST

1-1 What is the relationship that is *least* used in a database schema?

A. one-to-many

B. one-to-one

C. one-to-zero

D. many-to-many

1-2 Which column constraint allows you to force a column to contain only specific values?

A. UNIQUE

B. CHECK

C. SPECIFIC

D. NOT NULL

1-3 What is the relationship that requires an intermediary table?

A. one-to-many

B. one-to-one

C. intermediary

D. many-to-many

1-4 If you are accessing a large amount of data to implement a rule, how should the rule be coded?

A. as a method in a business component

B. as a function in the front end

C. as a stored procedure

D. as a data warehouse

SAMPLE TEST

1-5 Which of the following are valid column constraints?

A. NOT NULL

B. BETWEEN

C. UNIQUE

D. CONSTRAINTOF

1-6 If you are accessing a small amount of data to implement a rule, how should the rule be coded?

A. as a method in a business component

B. as a function in the front end

C. as a stored procedure

D. as a data warehouse

1-7 If you are changing the database underlying your application, the only components that you should need to change are:

A. recordsets.

B. business components.

C. data components.

D. UI dropdowns.

1-8 What is an entity that is used to join two entities together in a many-to-many relationship?

A. general

B. kernel

C. joinative

D. associative

SAMPLE TEST

1-9 If you need to write an application that can be run from Macintosh computers as well as Windows 98 machines, you should code the front end using:

A. Visual Basic, Enterprise Edition.

B. Active Server Pages serving up Web pages.

C. Active Server Pages and Visual Basic active documents.

D. pixel addressing.

1-10 The data and business components are part of which logical tier?

A. business

B. user interface

C. data

D. user data

UNIT 2

Deriving the Physical Design

Test Objectives:

- **Assess the potential impact of the logical design on performance, maintainability, extensibility, scalability, availability, and security.**
- **Design Visual Basic components to access data from a database in a multi-tier application.**
- **Design the properties, methods, and events of components.**

NOTE

Exam objectives are subject to change at any time without prior notice and at Microsoft's sole discretion. Please visit Microsoft's Training & Certification Web site (`www.microsoft.com/Train_Cert`) for the most current exam objectives listing.

This unit complements the previous unit by focusing on how the logical design and the tools and technology used for its physical implementation impact performance, maintainability, extensibility, scalability, availability, and security. We will examine each tier of a distributed application and assess the impact of its logical and physical design.

Choosing a Data Tier

Data is at the heart of any business application, and most business applications deal with sensitive data. Therefore, it is vital that data be highly accessible and secure. There are two basic types of databases:

Relational database management system (RDBMS) These systems include Microsoft SQL Server and Oracle, and they have the following capabilities:

- Server-side data storage and processing—SQL statements are processed on the server and only the requested data is returned to the client.
- The ability to handle many simultaneous users.
- A sophisticated security schema—Some RDBMS security can be integrated with Windows NT security.
- Many relational database management systems support the OLETX or XA standards, which allow a database to take part in MTS transactions.

Desktop/network databases These databases include Microsoft Access and Microsoft Visual FoxPro. Compared to an RDBMS they have the following capabilities and limitations:

- Data storage that can be networked—The database engine running on the user's machine must perform the SQL processing, which can require that more data be sent across the network to be processed.

- A limited number of simultaneous users.
- Little or no security functionality on some desktop databases.
- No support for the OLETX or XA standard—They cannot take part in MTS transactions.

In summary, using an RDBMS as the data tier of an application allows the application to scale to many users by providing superior performance and robust security. But a poorly designed application and unqualified SQL statements can bring even the most robust RDBMS to its knees.

Designing the Middle Tier

As described in the previous unit, the middle tier of a distributed application consists of COM DLLs that perform business functionality and data access. The section "Designing and Creating Components that Will Be Used with MTS" in Unit 5, "Creating and Managing COM Components," explains the necessity of an application infrastructure for the middle tier and how MTS can be used to provide it. This section discusses advantages of using business and data components in the middle tier.

Designing Business Components

Mixing the business functionality with the presentation layer, such as enforcing a business rule behind the Click event of a command button, is ultimately difficult to maintain. Several steps can be taken to abstract the business functionality that will enhance your ability to maintain and scale an application.

1. Centralize the business functionality by separating it from the presentation layer to allow for easier modification and maintenance, which in turn, will allow the application to change and grow with the business.
2. Design components that mimic business rules and functionality and you will be able to translate business requirements more easily into component functions and enhance component reuse.

3. Maintain the business components on a separate physical tier to make maintenance even easier and scalability greater. As a result, when you issue a component update, you will only have to reinstall the server component instead of redistributing the revised component to all the users. In addition, you can take advantage of MTS security that allows you to map users to business components as opposed to database entities.

Although it is ideal to maintain business rules on the middle tier, there will be times when, for the sake of performance, it will make sense to enforce business rules on the front end or on the data tier. All situations are different and require careful analysis to determine what is the most practical approach. Here are some guidelines:

- Rules that are related to user input validation may make sense to enforce on the front tier if the user expects immediate validation. Weigh this against the probability that the validation rule will change, which can be too expensive to maintain on the front end.
- Rules that require a lot of data access may be more efficiently enforced in stored procedures.

Designing Data Components

As described in the Unit 1 section "Understanding the Business Tier," the middle tier also includes data components that perform the data access for business components. Abstracting data access code such as SQL statements into these separate components provides the following advantages:

- Provides a standardized way for business components to access data regardless of whether it is stored in one SQL Server database or in multiple relational and nonrelational data stores. This leads to greater extensibility.
- Masks the physical structure of the database. Changes to the database entities will not require revisiting all the business components that access data. This allows for easier development and maintenance.
- Allows for the pooling of database connections. As described in the "Designing and Creating Components that Will Be Used with MTS" section of Unit 5, "Creating and Managing COM Components," in order for Microsoft Transaction Servers to pool connections, they must have the same connection settings. By centralizing the data access code, it is easier to ensure the use of uniform connections.

Choosing a Front Tier

After removing business functionality from the presentation layer, you are left with less front-end code to write, and this gives you greater flexibility in choosing a front end. The following sections discuss the front-end options and their impact on extensibility and maintainability.

Using a Win32 User Interface

A Win32 UI, such as those created with VB forms, has the following pros and cons:

Pros:

- Easy creation of a rich user interface.
- Finer control over user interaction with the application—Control is better than browser-based applications in which the user can navigate to and from the application at whim.

Cons:

- Client machine must have DCOM support and special Registry settings—Communication with the middle tier is typically done through DCOM, which requires the client machine to have DCOM support. Also, every user machine must have special Registry settings that point to the components on the middle tier. This can hinder maintenance and scalability.
- Users must install the program using a setup program—Therefore the program cannot be accessed from any machine. In addition, the setup program typically copies and registers many DLLs on the user's machine, which can lead to version conflicts and other problems that prevent successful setup.
- Changes to the UI require the program's EXE to be recompiled and redistributed to all the users.

Using an HTML User Interface

A browser-based UI that accesses business components via a Web server is low in maintenance, high in scalability, but also may be low in performance.

There are several variations of browser-based front ends: Active Server Pages, DHTML, and client-side components and scripting.

Using HTML and Active Server Pages (ASP)

Plain HTML served to browsers by ASP has the following pros and cons:

Pros:

- Widest distribution—Distribution is not limited to location or machine configuration as long as a machine has a browser and a connection to the Internet. To run the application, the user simply has to access the HTML or ASP page and does not have to go through the troublesome process of installing DLLs.
- Easy to modify UI—Changes to the UI are simply done by modifying the HTML page on the Web server; no compiling or redistribution is necessary.
- Special Registry settings are not needed—Communication with the middle tier is done through HTTP and it does not require special client-side Registry settings.

Cons:

- Limited user interface—Plain HTML does not allow for the creation of rich user interfaces.
- Slow performance—All dynamic changes to the UI require a trip to the server to refresh the entire page, which may result in unacceptable performance.
- Limited control over user interaction—A user can navigate away from the application and return at will. The application must be carefully designed to deal with this.

Using DHTML

Dynamic HTML solves some of the limitations of HTML:

- The UI can be dynamically changed without making a trip to the server.
- It allows for the creation of a rich user interface.

However, distribution is limited to browsers that support DHTML, namely Internet Explorer 4 and above and Netscape Navigator 4 and above. To complicate matters further, supporting browsers do not implement the same DHTML standard. Therefore, DHTML is typically used for intranet applications in which the user base can be limited to using a specific browser.

Using Client-Side Components and Scripting

In addition to displaying HTML, browsers can also run scripts such as VBScript and JScript to perform client-side processing. Some browsers are also able to download and install components, such as ActiveX controls and DLLs that are referenced by an HTML page. This results in a thicker client and its associated issues, such as component installation and browser dependency.

Visual Basic's DHTML project type is an example of a thick client. The application code is compiled into DLLs that are downloaded to the user's machine. In addition, if the user does not have the VB runtime DLLs, it must also download and install them.

STUDY QUESTIONS

Choosing a Data Tier

1. What are four reasons to use RDBMS for a distributed application as opposed to a desktop database?

Designing the Middle Tier

2. How does maintaining business components on a middle tier allow for easier overall maintenance?

3. Under what circumstances would it make sense to enforce a business rule on the front tier?

4. Under what circumstances would it make sense to enforce a business rule on the data tier?

STUDY QUESTIONS

5. How would you design the business components of an application that must access data from multiple data sources of different formats?

____

Choosing a Front Tier

6. Which kind of user interface has the most inexpensive maintenance, and why?

____

7. Why is a traditional Win32 front end that accesses the middle tier through DCOM more difficult to scale than an HTML application?

____

____

8. Which type of front end is the easiest to distribute, and why?

____

9. How does DHTML provide better performance than HTML?

____

10. Why is a VB DHTML application not a *thin* front end?

____

SAMPLE TEST

2-1 What is the benefit of abstracting business functionality into components that are maintained on the middle tier?

A. wider distribution

B. easier maintenance

C. better security

D. all of the above

2-2 Which one of the following technologies is typically used only within a corporate intranet?

A. DHTML

B. ASP

C. DCOM

D. MTS

2-3 A business rule states that a customer can only spend over her line of credit if she has been buying with the company over five years, the purchases total over $10,000, and it is the holiday season. Where should you enforce this rule, and why?

A. on the front tier because it is subject to change

B. on the business tier because it is a business based on complex logic

C. on the data tier in a stored procedure because it requires extensive data access

2-4 What are two advantages of using an HTML front end?

A. better performance

B. richer UI

C. easier maintenance

D. wider distribution

SAMPLE TEST

2-5 What are two ways to enhance data access performance in a distributed application?

A. Integrate database security with Windows NT security.

B. Abstract data access code into separate components on the middle tier.

C. Be careful to properly qualify SQL statements.

D. Use a database that processes SQL on the server side.

UNIT 3

Establishing the Development Environment

Test Objectives:

- **Establish the environment for source-code version control.**
- **Install and configure Visual Basic for developing distributed applications.**
- **Configure a server computer to run Microsoft Transaction Server (MTS).**
  - Install MTS.
  - Set up security on a system package.
- **Configure a client computer to use an MTS component.**
  - Create packages that install or update MTS components on a client computer.

NOTE

Exam objectives are subject to change at any time without prior notice and at Microsoft's sole discretion. Please visit Microsoft's Training and Certification Web site (`www.microsoft.com/Train_Cert/`) for the most current listing of exam objectives.

This unit discusses configuring and working in a development environment used for team development of distributed applications.

Establishing the Environment for Source-Code Version Control

In team-based development, where many developers have access to source code, it is necessary to have some way of organizing and controlling who has ownership of specific pieces of code. This section discusses using Visual SourceSafe for source code control.

Using Visual SourceSafe

Visual SourceSafe (VSS) is a project-oriented tool used to control and manage source code and other files among teams of developers. It provides two important functions: source code control and version tracking.

VSS is described as a project-oriented tool because it uses the concept of a project to maintain links between files. VSS projects are similar to VB projects. A project within VSS is a collection of interrelated files. It provides a hierarchy that allows developers to easily organize files within VSS. VSS provides source code control by allowing only one developer to make changes to a file at a time. This restriction guarantees that changes made by one developer do not overwrite the changes made by another developer. VSS contains a setting for allowing multiple users to make changes to a file at the same time, but this can result in conflicts that have to be resolved.

Version tracking allows a developer to track changes to files over the lifetime of the project with the ability to restore any prior version. This is accomplished through the *reverse delta* technique. This technique stores the latest version of each file in the VSS database along with enough information to restore prior versions. This allows VSS to limit the amount of storage space used, while quickly accessing the latest version when needed.

There are three different interfaces for working with VSS:

Graphical user interface (GUI) This includes VSS Explorer and the VSS Administrator. All of the functions described next can be performed using these tools.

Command line interface This interface can perform all of the VSS functions, as well as run batch files and macros from a command prompt.

VSS add-in VSS provides an interface that can be launched from within the development environment. This add-in interface allows you to perform most of the VSS user functions except for the administrative operations.

Administering VSS

Administrators for VSS need to manage the user list, grant access rights, and perform routine maintenance. The routine maintenance tasks include performing backups, analyzing the data integrity, and cleaning up the VSS data. The VSS Administrator and the command line interface can be used to perform the administrative tasks.

Managing User Lists The user list is managed in the VSS Administrator. Users can be added, edited, and deleted through the VSS Administrator. Passwords are also controlled through this program. The administrator can change any user's password, but cannot retrieve an old password.

Each user also can be assigned a default security level. The two levels that can be assigned are:

Read-only Users can view all files in all projects.

Read-write Users can view and change all files in all projects.

Security can also be set up for each project in VSS, as described next.

Providing Security The default levels of security may not be sufficient for all development environments. VSS provides a more restrictive level of security based on projects. When security is enabled by project, rights can be assigned to each user for each project. There are four levels of security that can be assigned to each user:

Read Allows the user to view files within a project.

Check Out/Check In Allows the user to view and modify files within a project.

Add/Rename/Delete Allows the user to view and modify files and also add, rename, and delete files within the VSS project. A deleted file is recoverable.

Destroy Grants the user all of the above rights while also allowing the user to roll back, destroy, and purge files from the VSS project. A destroyed or purged file is not recoverable.

The VSS Administrator displays the security in two views:

Rights By Project Displays all users who have rights to the selected project.

Assignments For Users Displays the projects and assigned rights by user.

Managing and Controlling Source Code

Managing and controlling source code are the primary functions of VSS. Source code files are stored within the Data subdirectory of VSS. This subdirectory is like a database. Whenever a developer wants to work on a file, the file is copied to the developer's working folder. Working folders can be created for each user by project. All modifications to the source code are made on the files that have been copied to the working folder. No modifications can be made to the source code files stored in the VSS database. Once all of the modifications are complete, the file is then copied back to the database.

VSS provides four functions for moving files between the database and the working folder:

Check Out Copies a file from VSS into the working folder so modifications can be made.

Check In Copies a file from the working folder back into VSS, thereby storing the modifications that have been made.

Undo Check Out Reverts a file back to its prior state before it was checked out and deletes all modifications made.

Get Latest Version Copies a read-only file from VSS into the working folder so that the file can be compiled or viewed.

By default, VSS allows one developer to modify a file at a time. Administrators can change this functionality and allow multiple developers the right to change the file at the same time, but this can result in conflicts that have to be merged.

VSS offers three functions to help manage source code among multiple projects:

Sharing *Sharing* within VSS allows a file to be linked to multiple projects. Each project contains a pointer to the file within the VSS database. Since there is only one copy of the file, modifications made to a shared file within a project are immediately propagated to the shared files within other projects. This process helps to promote code reuse among development projects.

Branching *Branching* is the process of taking the file down two different paths or branches. Branching is similar to sharing except that the dynamic link is not maintained. Changes within one project are not propagated to the other projects. VSS stores multiple copies of the file within the database, but maintains a link between the files by storing the path. Branching can be used to create a specialized version of the source code; for instance, the source code could be specialized for different platforms. Each branch would represent the code for a different platform.

Branches can also be merged within VSS. Internally, VSS compares the files with the differences to the original file and creates a new file with all of the changes. This process is known as a *three-way merge*. If conflicts arise during the process, VSS displays the Visual Merge window, which allows the developer to decide how to resolve the conflict.

Pinning *Pinning* is the process of freezing a file so that changes cannot be made to it. It is useful when used in conjunction with sharing. If a file is shared between two projects and one of the projects pins the files, then that project cannot make changes to the file. However, changes made to the file from the second project will be seen by the first project. When a file is pinned and then shared, both files are still pinned and no changes can be made.

Tracking Versions

Tracking changes made to source code over time is the other main function of VSS. Whenever changes are made to files or projects, VSS stores information about these changes. By storing this information, VSS can perform many functions, including:

- tracking the history of a change, when it was changed, who changed it, and any comments recorded about the change
- rolling back files and projects to previous versions
- comparing two versions of a file and determining the changes that have been made
- viewing the complete history of a file, including its creation and any modifications made to the file

VSS uses three properties to track versions: version numbers, date/time stamps, and labels.

VSS automatically generates a new version number whenever a change is made to a file. The version number is always a whole number. The date/time stamp is also recorded automatically when a change is made. VSS also allows the developer to label each version with a descriptive name. Typical labels are 'Beta Version' or 'Release v2.0'.

Storing Different File Types within VSS

The types of files that can be stored within VSS are not limited. VSS groups files into two categories: text and binary. Text files are files that contain only characters. Binary files are all the others. To determine file type, VSS scans the file for a NULL character (bytes with a value of 0). If it finds one it identifies the file as binary.

VSS imposes several restrictions on binary files:

- VSS cannot show the differences between binary files, it can only show that the file has been changed.
- Binary files cannot be merged.
- Multiple checkouts on a binary file are not permitted.

Since there is no limit on the types of files, VSS can be used to control Word documents, HTML files, VB source code, or anything else that requires versioning and control.

Installing and Configuring VB for Developing Distributed Apps

Installing VB is simple. All you have to do run the setup program from the CD and click Next a couple of times. However, you should be aware that there are minimum system requirements and certain add-ins that integrate the VB environment with other development tools.

Meeting System Requirements

The minimum system requirements for installing Visual Basic 6 are:

- Windows 95 or higher, or Windows NT workstation 4 or higher (service pack 3 recommended)
- 486DX/66 processor (Pentium or higher recommended)
- 16MB RAM for Windows 95, 32MB of RAM for NT workstation

Using Add-Ins

Add-ins typically provide functionality otherwise not available in the VB environment or integrate VB with other tools. When you install an add-in, it usually appears in the Add-In menu so you can easily launch it.

To install an add-in in the VB environment, follow these steps:

1. In the Add-Ins menu, choose Add-In Manager.
2. Locate and select the desired add-in.
3. Check the desired load option. The options are:
   - Loaded/Unloaded—when checked it loads the add-in; when unchecked it unloads the add-in
   - Load On Startup—loads the add-in when the environment is started up; it does not load it into the current VB session
   - Command Line—loads the add-in when VB is started from the command line

Add-ins that help integrate the VB environment with other team-oriented tools and distributed application tools include:

Visual SourceSafe This add-in allows you to integrate source code control using Visual SourceSafe. You may perform the user (not the administrative) functions of VSS such as checking in or checking out source code.

Visual Component Manager This add-in allows you to share project components and documentation using the services of Visual Component Manager. See "Using Visual Component Manager to Manage Components," in Unit 5.

Visual Modeler This add-in allows you browse and reverse-engineer class diagrams created with Visual Modeler.

Microsoft Transaction Server (MTS) This add-in is used to maintain special settings for MTS components being developed with VB. More discussion of MTS can be found in Unit 5, "Creating and Managing COM Components."

Configuring a Computer to Run Microsoft Transaction Server

Microsoft Transaction Server 2 is available as part of the Windows NT 4 Option Pack. In order for a machine to run MTS, it should:

- have Windows NT server with service pack 3, Windows NT workstation, or Windows 95 with DCOM support, which can be downloaded from Microsoft's Web site.
- be an I386-compatible computer with 32MB of RAM.
- have SQL Server service pack 3 installed if MTS will be used with SQL Server 6.5.

Once you've installed MTS, you should set up administrative security. By default, anybody can create, install, modify, delete, shut down and export MTS packages. You can set computer-wide security by setting security on the System package (MTS automatically creates a package called 'System' that contains components it uses internal processing). The System package has two default roles:

Administrator Users assigned to this role have full control over all the packages on the computer.

Reader Users assigned to this role can only view objects in the MTS Explorer; they cannot create, install, modify, delete, shut down, or export MTS packages.

To enforce the security settings check the Enable Authorizing Checking option on the Security tab of the System package's property page.

WARNING

If you check the Enable Authorizing Checking option without first assigning at least one user to the Administrator, then MTS Explorer will become practically unusable.

Configuring DCOM on a Client Computer and on a Server Computer

See the "Installing and Registering DCOM Components" section of Unit 8, "Deploying an Application," for coverage of this topic.

STUDY QUESTIONS

Establishing the Environment for Source-Code Version Control

1. What are the two basic functions provided by Visual SourceSafe?

____

____

2. What are the two basic security levels provided by VSS?

____

3. What happens when a user checks out a file in VSS?

____

4. In VSS, what is the difference between sharing and branching?

____

5. If you have a VSS file that is being shared by Project A and Project B and the file is pinned by Project A, what is the effect on both projects?

____

6. What are three ways to identify a file version in VSS?

____

____

____

STUDY QUESTIONS

7. What are three restrictions of working with binary files in VSS?

____

____

____

Installing and Configuring VB for Developing Distributed Apps

8. Which service pack is recommended for running VB on a Windows NT workstation?

____

9. What functionality does the MTS add-in provide?

A. It allows you to set transactional properties of components developed with VB.

B. It maintains special settings for MTS components being developed with VB.

C. It allows you to reverse-engineer compiled MTS components into VB project files.

D. It allows you to export VB components into MTS packages from the VB environment.

10. What functionality does the Visual Modeler add-in provide?

____

11. Which service pack should you install to use MTS with SQL Server 6.5?

____

STUDY QUESTIONS

12. What are the two default roles of the System package?

A. Administrator

B. Reader

C. Developer

D. Creator

13. What must you do to enforce the security settings of the System folder?

____

14. How do you control who can modify MTS packages?

____

SAMPLE TEST

3-1 What access rights do you need in order to roll back a file or a project?

A. Read

B. Check In/Check Out

C. Add/Rename/Delete

D. Destroy

3-2 Which of the following are two restrictions imposed by VSS on working with binary files?

A. Files cannot be shared.

B. Files cannot be merged.

C. Files cannot be rolled back.

D. Multiple checkouts are not permitted.

3-3 Which of the following is a requirement for running MTS on Windows NT server?

A. DCOM support (must be separately installed)

B. SQL Server

C. service pack 3

D. Internet Information Server

3-4 You have a class module file that needs to be used by Project A and Project B. Project B will use the file but will not do any of the development work on it. How should you set up the file in Visual SourceSafe?

A. Share the file between Projects A and B, and pin the file within Project B.

B. Share the file between Projects A and B, and branch the file within Project A.

C. Grant Project B read-only rights to the file.

D. Branch the file to Projects A and B, and pin it within Project A.

SAMPLE TEST

3-5 Which of the following is *not* a minimum or recommended requirement to run VB?

A. 32MB for Windows NT workstation

B. 16MB for Windows 95

C. service pack 3 for Windows NT workstation

D. DCOM support

3-6 How do you restrict developers from modifying MTS packages?

A. Set security on the System package.

B. Set security on the Computer node of the MTS Explorer.

C. Use the Permission settings on a package's property page.

UNIT 4

Creating User Services

Test Objectives:

- **Given a conceptual design, apply the principles of modular design to derive the components and services of the logical design.**
- **Implement navigational design.**
  - Dynamically modify the appearance of a menu.
  - Add a pop-up menu to an application.
  - Create an application that adds and deletes menus at run time.
  - Add controls to forms.
  - Set properties for controls.
  - Assign code to a control to respond to an event.
- **Create data input forms and dialog boxes.**
  - Display and manipulate data by using custom controls. Controls include **TreeView**, **ListView**, **ImageList**, **Toolbar**, and **StatusBar**.
  - Create an application that adds and deletes controls at run time.
  - Use the **Controls** collection to manipulate controls at run time.
  - Use the **Forms** collection to manipulate forms at run time.
- **Write code that validates user input.**
  - Create an application that verifies data entered at the field level and the form level by a
  - Create an application that enables or disables controls based on input in fields.
- **Write code that processes data entered on a form.**
  - Given a scenario, add code to the appropriate form event. Events include Initialize, Terminate, Load, Unload, QueryUnload, Activate, and Deactivate.
- **Add an ActiveX control to the toolbox.**
- **Create dynamic Web pages by using Active Server Pages (ASP) and webclasses.**
- **Create a Web page by using the DHTML Page Designer to dynamically change attributes of elements, change content, change styles, and position elements.**

- **Use data binding to display and manipulate data from a data source.**
- **Instantiate and invoke a COM component.**
  - Create a Visual Basic client application that uses a COM component.
  - Create a Visual Basic application that handles events from a COM component.
- **Create call-back procedures to enable asynchronous processing between COM components and Visual Basic client applications.**
- **Implement online user assistance in a distributed application.**
  - Set appropriate properties to enable user assistance. Help properties include **HelpFile**, **HelpContextID**, and **WhatsThisHelp**.
  - Create HTML Help for an application.
  - Implement messages from a server component to a user interface.
- **Implement error handling for the user interface in distributed applications.**
  - Identify and trap run-time errors.
  - Handle inline errors.
  - Determine how to send error information from a COM component to a client computer.
- **Use an active document to present information within a Web browser.**

NOTE

Exam objectives are subject to change at any time without prior notice and at Microsoft's sole discretion. Please visit Microsoft's Training & Certification Web site (`www.microsoft.com/Train_Cert`) for the most current exam objectives listing.

This unit discusses creating user services for a distributed application. *User services* are the front tier of a distributed application. It includes the graphical user interface (GUI) and help for the user. This unit covers creating several types of front ends, such as Win32, ASP, and DHTML. It also covers creating HTML Help files and implementing help in an application.

Implementing Navigational Design

This section discusses creating the user interface that allows the user to interact and navigate through the application. The discussion focuses on menus and assumes you are familiar with adding controls to a form, setting its properties, and handling its events.

Menus are a useful and familiar way to organize and categorize the functionality of an application. This section covers creating and modifying standard menus and pop-up menus. In Visual Basic (VB), you add menus to forms using the Menu Editor. To access the Menu Editor, set your focus on the desired form and then open the Menu Editor by clicking one of the following:

- Tools ➢ Menu Editor
- Ctrl+E
- Menu Editor icon on the toolbar

NOTE: If the focus is not on a form, then the Menu Editor will not be available.

The Menu Editor organizes menus hierarchically based on how you indent them in the dialog. All top-level (nonindented) menus will be displayed on the menu bar of the form. Indented menus will be displayed as *submenus* of the menu item above. A submenu itself can contain up to five submenus. A submenu is displayed indented to the right of the parent menu. A parent menu item indicates that it has a submenu by displaying a right arrow. The level of indentation of a menu can be changed using the arrow keys of the Menu Editor dialog (see Figure 4.1).

FIGURE 4.1

In the Menu Editor dialog, the indented items are submenus.

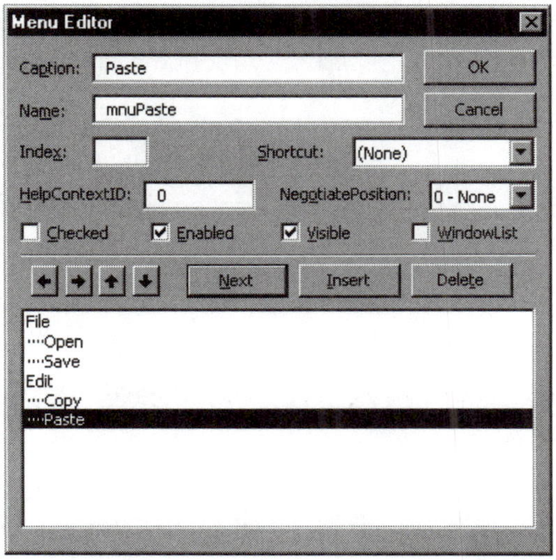

Menus are objects just like other controls on the form, and each menu item is its own object. Menu objects have a Name property by which they are referenced in code. Each menu has its own Click event that is triggered when the menu is clicked.

Modifying the Appearance of a Menu

You can change how a menu item is displayed by changing several of its properties. Some of these properties can be changed at runtime, as shown in Table 4.1.

TABLE 4.1

Menu Properties

Property	Description	Available at Runtime?
Caption	Sets text displayed on the menu.	✔
Checked	Boolean. Sets whether a check is displayed to the left of the caption. Used for options that can be toggled.	✔

TABLE 4.1 *(cont.)* Menu Properties

Property	Description	Available at Runtime?
Enabled	Boolean. Sets whether the menu is enabled. If disabled, it appears grayed-out in the menu list.	✔
Shortcut	Sets a key combination that serves as a shortcut to the menu. Alternately, you can set an accelerator key by placing an ampersand (&) before the desired letter in the caption menu.	
WindowList	Indicates that the menu will automatically list the open windows in an MDI application.	
Visible	Boolean. Sets whether a menu is visible. If set to False, the menu and all its submenus are invisible and the menu following it replaces it in the menu list.	✔

Adding a Pop-up Menu to an Application

Pop-up menus are those nifty little menus that sometimes pop up when you right-click in the Windows environment. A pop-up menu in VB is actually a regular menu that is activated with the PopupMenu method of the form:

```
Form.PopupMenu MyMenu
```

Although pop-up menus are commonly activated by right-clicking a window, the PopupMenu method can actually be called from anywhere in the code. A menu must have at least one submenu to qualify as a pop-up menu, and *only* its submenus will be displayed. After the PopupMenu method is called, subsequent code is not executed until the user responds to the menu.

Creating an Application that Adds and Deletes Menus at Runtime

Similar to other controls, menus can be arrays and can have items added and removed from the array at runtime (see the "Adding and Deleting Controls at Runtime" section later in this unit for more information). There are two restrictions that regulate which menus can be included in the same array at design time:

- The menus must be on the same level in the menu hierarchy.
- The menus must be adjacent to each other; they cannot be separated by a menu that is not part of the array.

To create a menu array, follow these steps:

1. Open the Menu Editor.
2. Create two menus with the same name.
3. Set the Index properties of the menus included in the array.

Creating Data Input Forms and Dialog Boxes

This section discusses creating standard Win32 GUIs. It covers using common Windows controls, working with forms, and working with the Controls collection.

Displaying and Manipulating Data by Using Custom Controls

This section focuses on several custom controls that are part of the Microsoft Windows Common Controls 6 component. The following controls are commonplace in the Windows environment:

- TreeView
- ListView
- Toolbar

- StatusBar
- ImageList

These controls are part of MSCOMCTL.OCX. They can be added to the Toolbox by following these steps:

1. Open the Components dialog in one of the following ways:
   - Click Project ➢ Components.
   - Click Ctrl+T.
   - Right-click the Toolbox and choose Components.
   - Click the Toolbox icon on the toolbar.
2. Choose Microsoft Windows Common Controls 6.

These controls have some common functions which are explained next.

Displaying Images

The TreeView, ListView, and Toolbar controls all have properties that allow you to display different graphics depending on the state of the element. For instance, the TreeView control has a Node object that can have two states, expanded and collapsed. The Node object's properties for those two states are Image and ExpandedImage.

These controls simplify managing icons by allowing you to store icons in an ImageList control and to point to the ImageList control through the ImageList property of the respective control. Each image in the ImageList has an index and key that can be used as the value of a property (such as the Image and ExpandedImages mentioned before). The following code illustrates this point:

```
Set TreeView1.ImageList=ImageList1
TreeView1.Nodes(1).Image=1
TreeView1.Nodes(1).ExpandedImage=2
```

Using the Add Method

The TreeView, ListView, Toolbar, StatusBar, and ImageList controls all have an Add method that allows you to add members to their respective collections.

The Add method has several parameters that allow you to set values for properties of the newly added item. These properties can also be set individually as properties of the item. For instance, the Add method of the TreeView control:

```
TreeView.Add([relative], [relationship], [key], [text],
[image], [selectedimage])
```

is equivalent to:

```
TreeView.Add([relative], [relationship], [key])
Treeview.Nodes(Key).Text=Text
Treeview.Nodes(Key).image=Index
Treeview.Nodes(Key).selectedimage=Index
```

The Add method can be used as displayed above or it can return a reference to the newly added item:

```
Set NewNode=TreeView.Add([relative], [relationship])
NewNode.Text=Text
NewNode.image=Index
NewNode.selectedimage=Index
```

Using the ImageList Control

The ImageList control serves as a repository for graphical files to be used in your application. Many controls have properties that are graphical in nature, such as MouseIcon (for the mouse pointer when it moves over the control) and Picture (bitmap to be displayed by the control). These properties can be set to an image from the ImageList control. In addition, some of the Windows Common Controls can be bound directly to the ImageList control as described earlier in the "Displaying Images" section.

The ImageList control supports the following types of graphics:

- bitmap (`.bmp`)
- cursor (`.cur`)
- icon (`.ico`)
- JPEG (`.jpg`)
- GIF (`.gif`)

Images are usually added to the ImageList during design time using the ImageList's property page (see Figure 4.2). The property page allows you to insert an image and specify its Index and Key properties.

Images can also be added during runtime using the Add method of the ListImages collection:

```
ImageList.ListImages.Add [index], [key], picture
```

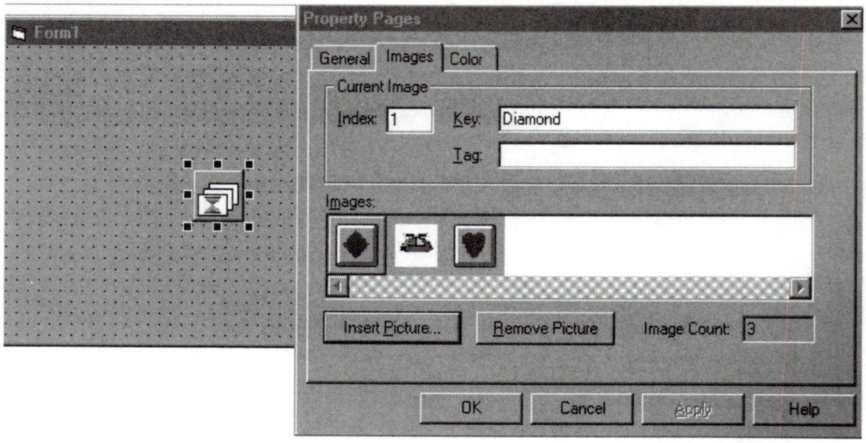

FIGURE 4.2 The ImageList property page

The Picture parameter is the picture to be added and must be an actual picture, not just its filename. You can reference a picture either by referencing a property of an object that returns a picture or using the LoadPicture function:

```
Object.Picture
```

or

```
LoadPicture(FileName)
```

Using the TreeView Control

Most people know the TreeView control as the left pane of the Windows Explorer. It displays information in a hierarchical format using a treelike structure (see Figure 4.3). You navigate the hierarchy by clicking the plus (+) and minus (–) signs to expand and collapse the ‘branches’ of the ‘tree.’

Populating and Depopulating the TreeView You have full control over the population and depopulation of the TreeView control through the Nodes collection. The Nodes collection allows you to add new nodes to any level of the hierarchy through the use of the Add method and its parameters. The Add method accomplishes this by allowing you to add a new node in relation to an existing node, as explained next in Table 4.2.

```
TreeView.Nodes.Add([relative], [relationship], [key],
[text], [image], [selectedimage])
```

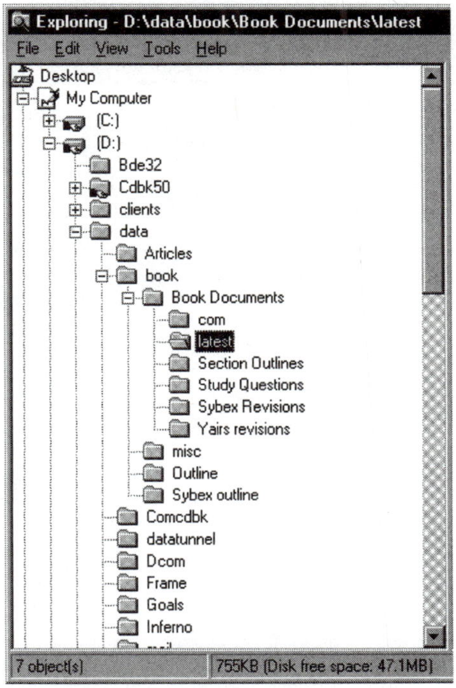

FIGURE 4.3
The TreeView control

TABLE 4.2: Arguments of the Nodes Collection's Add Method

Arguments	Description	
Relative	Index or Key of an existing node. If a relative node is not specified then the new node is added as the last node on the top level of the hierarchy.	
Relationship	Indicates where to position the new node in relation to the node specified in the Relative parameter.	
	tvwFirst	First on the same level as the node specified in the Relative parameter.

TABLE 4.2: Arguments of the Nodes Collection's Add Method *(continued)*

The depopulation of the TreeView is done using the Remove method: `TreeView.Remove Index`

Arguments	Description	
Relationship	tvwLast	Last on the same level as the node specified in the Relative parameter.
	tvwPrevious	One before the node specified in the Relative parameter.
	tvwNext	One after the node specified in the Relative parameter.
	tvwChild	Added as a child of the node specified in the Relative parameter. The new node is added as the last of the children nodes.
Key	String that uniquely identifies the node.	
Text	Text displayed as the node's caption.	
ImageZ	Integer indicating the Index of an image in the ImageList control specified in the ImageList property. This image will be displayed when the node is *not* selected.	
SelectedImage	Integer indicating the Index of an image in the ImageList control specified in the ImageList property. This image will be displayed when the node *is* selected.	
Index	May be either the Index or Key of a node.	

NOTE The Index of a node does not change as nodes are added and removed from the Nodes collection; therefore, it is valid to store the Index of a node in a variable and use it at a later time.

Navigating the TreeView There are several properties that allow you to navigate the TreeView hierarchy. They allow you to move forward, back, up, and down from a specific node. However, you must first position yourself at the desired node. (You are always positioned at the currently selected node.) The two properties used to set and determine the selected node are listed in Table 4.3. The properties used for navigating are listed in Table 4.4.

TABLE 4.3 Properties Used to Set and Determine the Currently Selected Node

Property	Object	Description
SelectedItem	TreeView	Returns (read-only) the currently selected node.
Selected	Node	Boolean. Returns or sets whether or not a node is selected.

TABLE 4.4 TreeView Navigational Properties

Property	Description
Previous	Moves to the previous node on the same level.
Next	Moves to the next node on the same level.
Parent	Moves to the parent node. This property can also be used to set the parent node.
Child	Moves to the first child node.
FirstSibling	Moves to the first node on the same level.
LastSibling	Moves to the last node on the same level.
Root	Moves to the root node of the current node.

Displaying Data The TreeView control has several display styles. The properties and settings listed in Table 4.5 determine how data is displayed.

TABLE 4.5: TreeView Display Settings

Property	Description and Enumerations
Style	Determines if: • parent nodes have plus (+) or minus (–) symbols. • nodes have text or images. • nodes are visibly connected with branches. tvwTextOnly tvwTreelinesText tvwPictureText tvwPlusMinusText tvwPlusPictureText tvwTreelinesPictureText tvwTreelinesPlusMinusText tvwTreelinesPlusMinusPictureText
Linestyle	Determines whether branches are displayed between root nodes. This property only shows if the Style property is set to a setting that displays lines. tvwTreeLines Lines connecting nodes only. tvwRootLines Lines connecting both root nodes and regular nodes.
Image SelectedImage ExpandedImage	Determines the image displayed for a node in its various states. These properties can be set either as the Index or Key of an image in the TreeView's ImageList control.

Using the ListView Control

Most people know the ListView control as the right side of the Windows Explorer and as the Open/Save dialogs commonly seen in the Windows environment. The ListView control allows you to display sets of information graphically (see Figure 4.4).

The ListView control has two main views: Icon and Report.

Displaying in Icon View When the ListView is set to Icon view (lvwIcon) it is fairly simple to use. There is one collection to deal with, the ListItems

FIGURE 4.4

The ListView control in Icon view

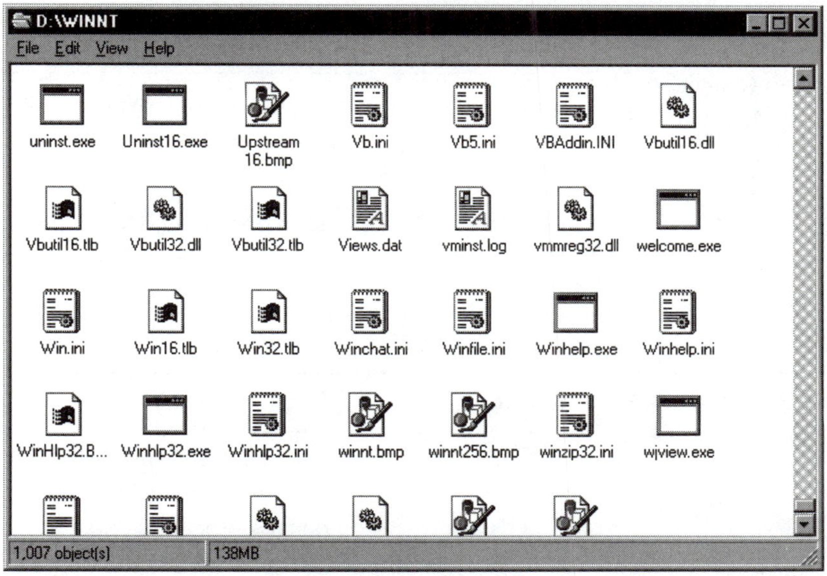

collection, which contains the items that are displayed in the ListView. Use the Add method to populate the ListItems collection. Table 4.6 explains the arguments of the Add method.

```
ListView.ListItems.Add [index], [key], [text], [icon],
[smallIcon]
```

Information can be displayed in several styles in ListView. Table 4.7 lists the valid settings for the View method.

TABLE 4.6

ListItem Collection's Add Method

Property	Description
Index	Sets or returns the position of the new item in the collection.
Key	String that uniquely identifies the new item.

TABLE 4.6 *(cont.)* ListItem Collection's Add Method

Property	Description
Text	Text to be displayed as the caption.
Icon	Icon displayed when View is set to Icon view.
SmallIcon	Icon displayed when View is set to SmallIcon view.

TABLE 4.7 Valid Values of the ListView's View Property

Setting	Description
lvwIcon	Each item is displayed as a full-sized icon with a caption underneath. The item can be moved around the display area.
lvwSmallIcon	Each item is displayed as a small icon with a caption displayed to the right of the icon. The item can be moved around the display area.
lvwList	Items are displayed as small icons arranged in rows and columns, with the captions displayed to the right of the icons. The items *cannot* be moved around the display area.

Displaying in Report View When the ListView's Style property is set to Report view (lvwReport), it displays information in a table-like fashion, with the first column displaying the main piece of information and subsequent columns displaying attributes of the main item. It works just like the Windows Explorer, which lists a file as the main piece of information and its attributes (such as size, type, date modified) as details in subsequent columns when in Report view (see Figure 4.5). Table 4.8 describes how the ListView's objects and properties correspond to elements of the report.

The ColumnHeaders collection has an Add method that allows you to add items to the collection:

```
ListView.ColumnHeaders.Add index, key, text, width,
alignment, icon
```

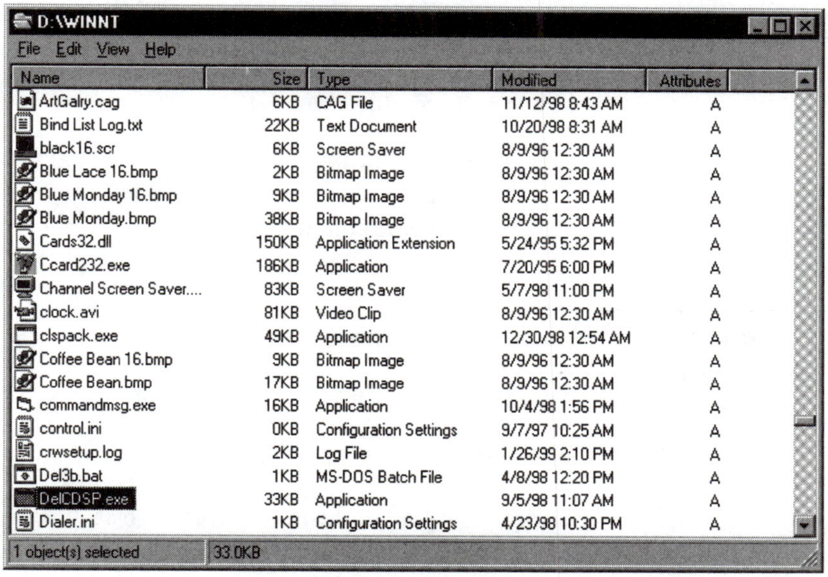

FIGURE 4.5

ListView control in Report view

TABLE 4.8

ListView's Objects and Properties and their Corresponding Display Elements

Report Element	Corresponding ListView Element	Description
Column	ColumnHead object	A new column is displayed in ListView for each ColumnHead appended to the ColumnHeads collection.
Main item	ListItem object	The ListItem is displayed in the first column and may include both text and an icon.
Attributes of the main item	ListSubItem object	The ListItem object has a ListSubItems collection that corresponds to its attributes. There must be a ColumnHeader for each SubItem to be displayed.

The ListSubItems collection also has an Add method that allows you to add items to the collection:

```
ListView.ListItems(1).ListSubItems.Add index, key, text,
ReportIcon, ToolTipText
```

Table 4.9 lists the primary properties of the ListView control. Note that the three sort properties work together to allow you to sort the ListView control based on a specific column.

TABLE 4.9 ListView Properties

Property	Description
SelectedItem	Returns (read only) the currently selected ListItem.
MultiSelect	Allows for multiple ListItems to be selected.
Sorted	Boolean. When set to True, the ListView will sort based on the settings of the SortKey and SortOrder properties.
SortKey	Integer. The Index of the ColumnHeader upon which the sort is based.
SortOrder	Indicates whether to sort ascending or descending. lvwDescending lvwAscending

Using the Toolbar Control

The Toolbar needs no introduction—it is well known to all Windows users. You have great flexibility in setting the Toolbar's style and the style of its buttons.

The Toolbar control's Style property has the settings listed in Table 4.10.

TABLE 4.10 Toolbar's Style Property Settings

Setting	Description
tbrStandard	Buttons have the standard three-dimensional look.
tbrFlat	Buttons are two-dimensional (flat), but when the mouse moves over them, they have a three-dimensional look.

Using the Buttons Collection Buttons can be added to the Toolbar both at design time and runtime. When the user clicks a button, the Toolbar's ButtonClick event is fired; the individual button that was clicked is referenced by the *Button* parameter. Buttons are added to the Toolbar during runtime using the Buttons collection:

```
Toolbar.Buttons.Add index, key, caption, style, image
```

The arguments of the Add method are described in Table 4.11.

TABLE 4.11: Arguments of the Buttons Collection's Add Method

Property	Description	
Index	Integer indicating the position of the button.	
Key	String uniquely identifying the button.	
Caption	String displayed as the caption.	
Style	Determines the style of the button:	
	tbrDefault	Regular push button.
	tbrCheck	Button remains depressed when clicked until it is clicked again.
	tbrButtonGroup	A button that belongs to a group of buttons that has its Style set to tbrButtonGroup. The group is delimited by buttons with the Style property set to tbrSeparator. Only one button in the group may be pressed at a time.
	tbrSeparator	This button is displayed as a fixed space of 8 pixels. It cannot be clicked. It can be used to group buttons visually and to delimit a ButtonGroup (see tbrButtonGroup).
	tbrPlaceholder	This button is displayed as a space and its width is adjustable with the Width property. It is used to provide space for a control on the Toolbar. The control must be manually sized and aligned to fit the space.
	tbrDropDown	This button appears and behaves like a menu. Use the ButtonMenus collection to add ButtonMenu objects that correspond to items on the menu.

Using the StatusBar Control

The StatusBar control is the panel at the bottom of many Windows applications, such as MS Word and Internet Explorer, and it displays status information for the user. The StatusBar has two styles in which it displays information: Simple and Normal.

Using Simple Style When the StatusBar's Style property is set to Simple (sbrSimple) it only displays one large panel that extends along the bottom of the form. The text displayed is set and returned from the SimpleText property.

Using Normal Style When the StatusBar's Style property is set to Normal (sbrNormal) it can display multiple panels, each with its own unique information. Panels are added to the Panels collection using the Add method:

```
StatusBar.Panels.Add [index], [key], [text], [style],
[picture]
```

The Text argument is the text that is displayed on the panel. The Style argument can take the predefined styles listed in Table 4.12. When a style is specified, the value of the Text property is ignored.

TABLE 4.12
Valid Settings of the Style Argument (StatusBar.Panels.Add)

Value	Description
sbrText	Allows for the text displayed to be set with the Panels text property.
sbrCaps	Displays CAPS when caps lock is on.
sbrNum	Displays NUM when num lock is on.
sbrIns	Displays INS when insert functionality is enabled.
sbrScrl	Displays SCRL when scroll lock is on.
sbrTime	Displays the current time.
sbrDate	Displays the current date.

Using the Controls Collection to Manipulate Controls at Runtime

All VB forms have a Controls collection that contains all the controls on the form. The Controls collection has the standard Item and Count properties. The Item method's Index argument can take either a numeric value indicating the position of the control in the collection or the name of the control as a string.

A common use of the Controls collection is to traverse all the controls on the form. This allows you to do things like change the font of all the controls:

```
For each ctl in Controls
 ctl.Font.Bold=True
Next ctl
```

NOTE The Controls collection of the current form does not have to be prefixed with the form's name.

Using the TypeOf Keyword

In order to determine what type of control is contained in the Controls collection you may use the TypeOf keyword together with an If statement. The TypeOf keyword checks if a control is of the specified object type:

```
If TypeOf Controls(6) Is TextBox Then
 Controls(6).Text=""
End If
```

This is useful if you want traverse all controls of a specific type on the form.

Adding and Deleting Controls at Runtime

There are two ways to add controls to and delete controls from a form during runtime. The older method is to create a control array in design time and add controls to the array during runtime. The new method in VB 6 is to use the Add method of the Controls collection to add controls from scratch. The Controls collection also has a Remove method that allows you to remove dynamically added controls.

Creating Control Arrays

A *control array* can be created by setting the Index property of a control to a numeric value. If you name a control the same name as an existing control, VB will automatically create a control array.

Controls can be added and removed from the array during runtime. Suppose you have an array of command buttons called `cmds( )` that contains one control during design time. You can add controls by using the Load statement as follows:

```
Load cmds(1)
```

You must specify an index that is not being used by an existing control.

> **NOTE** The indexes do not have to be in sequential order. It is possible to start off an array with an index of any integer.

Newly loaded controls:

- are initially invisible; you must set their Visible property to True.
- are placed on the same container as the first control in the array.
- have the same Height, Width, Caption, Top, and Left as the first control in the array.

To remove a control, use the Unload statement on the specific element of the array:

```
Unload cmds(1)
```

> **NOTE** Only controls added during runtime may be removed with the Unload statement.

Adding to the Controls Collection

A new feature of VB 6 is the ability to add nonarray controls to the Controls collection during runtime. You can add any control, even if the control is not in the Toolbox. Controls are added using the Controls collection's Add method with the following arguments:

```
Set NewControl=Controls.Add (ProgID, name, [container])
```

Argument	Description
ProgID	The ProgID of the control being added. For standard VB controls the ProgID is `VB.Control`.
Name	Identifier of the control in the collection; not used for referencing in code.
Container	The container on the form, such as a Frame or PictureBox, upon which the new control should be placed. The default container is the form itself.

You can reference the new control in code by the variable that it is set to:

```
Set NewTextBox=Controls.Add ("VB.TextBox", "txt", Frame1)
NewTextBox.Visible=True
```

or by using the Controls collection:

```
Controls.Add ("VB.TextBox", "txt", Frame1)
Controls("txt").Visible=True
```

Handling Events of New Controls When a control is added to a form during design time, VB automatically adds the control's event routines to the code window. Even when adding a control to a control array during runtime, you can write code to handle the events of new controls in the event routines of the control array. However, a control that is added during runtime to the Controls collection doesn't have any event routines in the code window during design time that you can use to handle events. The solution to this problem depends on whether the control is in your project's Toolbox. The Toolbox is the mechanism by which your project references controls.

If your project contains a reference to the control, then all you need to do is declare the variable that will contain the control as the control's type using the WithEvents keyword. VB will automatically add event routines for the control to the code window:

```
Dim WithEvents NewTextBox as TextBox
Set NewTextBox=Controls.Add ("VB.TextBox", "txt", Frame1)

Private Sub NewTextBox_Change()

End Sub
```

If a control is not referenced, then it can only be declared as Object. Variables declared as Object cannot use the WithEvents keyword. The solution to this problem is to declare nonreferenced controls as VBControlExtender. Once again, VB will add event routines to the code window. However, it will only add basic events such as GotFocus and DragDrop. In order to handle the control's custom events, VB provides an event called ObjectEvent:

```
ObjectEvent(Info As EventInfo)
```

This event is raised for all custom events. The Info parameter (a variable of EventInfo type) provides information about the specific custom event that was raised. The EventInfo object has the properties listed in Table 4.13.

TABLE 4.13 EventInfo Properties

Property	Description
Name	Name of the custom event.
EventParameters collection	Collection with information about any parameters that may have been passed into the event. The collection has the standard Item and Count properties. There is one EventParameter object for each parameter passed into the event. It has two properties: Name — Name of the parameter. Value — Value of the parameter.

Using the Forms Collection to Manipulate Forms at Runtime

A VB form created at design time is essentially a class that can have multiple instances. If you have a form called Form1, you can instantiate instances of Form1 as follows:

```
Dim NewForm as Form1
Set NewForm=New Form1
NewForm.Show
```

The tricky thing to understand is that when you refer to the design time form, let's say Form1, without instantiating a new instance of it, VB instantiates an instance of it behind the scenes and stores it in a variable identical to the form name, Form1. Therefore, only the design time form can be referenced by its name (Form1). All the other instances of the form must be referenced by the variable that is set to reference it; in the example, it is NewForm. All the loaded forms in an application are contained in the Forms collection. This includes regular forms, MDI forms, and MDI child forms. So if your application has one standard form loaded and an MDI form with two of its children loaded, then the Forms collection will contain four forms. The Forms collection has the standard Item and Count properties. The Item method, which is the default method (and therefore doesn't have to be spelled out), returns the form in the collection based on the numeric Index argument:

```
Forms(2).Visible=False
```

New instances of a form are also added to the Forms collection. The problem is that all instances of a particular form have the same value for the Name property, and therefore, you will be unable to determine which instance of a form you have retrieved from the Forms collection by checking its name. In order to mitigate this problem you should give a unique value to either the Caption or Tag properties of all newly instantiated forms.

Writing Code that Validates User Input

Business rules ideally should be enforced in the business tier. However, the following rules should also be enforced on the front end by validating user input:

- nonbusiness rules, such as valid dates and Social Security number format
- simple nonchanging business rules that you don't want to enforce by making a network trip to the business tier

The next section reviews several ways to validate user input on the front end.

Validating User Input on the Field Level

Field-level validation is enforced by not allowing a user to leave a control if the data entered is invalid. It can be performed in two ways: by restricting input and by validating input.

Restricting Input

If the input into a text box must be restricted to a certain set of characters, then you can restrict the user's data entry by using the KeyPress event:

```
Private Sub KeyPress(KeyAscii As Integer)
```

The KeyAscii parameter contains the key pressed by the user. This parameter is passed ByRef, and therefore, can be changed to any value you choose or it can be set to zero, which effectively cancels the user's input. For example, the following code restricts the user from entering non-numeric characters:

```
If KeyAscii < Asc("0") Or KeyAscii > Asc("9") Then
 KeyAscii=0
End If
```

NOTE The Asc function returns the Ascii value of a character and the Chr function returns the character represented by the Ascii value.

Validating Input

If the validation is more complex than the previous scenario, in VB 6 you can use the *CausesValidation* property together with the *Validate* event to prevent a user from leaving a control if validation fails. If the CausesValidation property is set to True, then when the user attempts to leave a control, the Validate event is raised. You can write validation code in the Validate event routine, and depending on whether the validation fails, set the Cancel parameter to True. This will keep the focus in the control and effectively stop the user from leaving the control until a valid value is entered. A sample validation routine that ensures that a date is entered into the text box looks like this:

```
Text1.CausesValidation=True

Private Sub Text1_Validate(Cancel as Boolean)
```

```
If IsDate(Text1.Text)=False Then
 Cancel=True
End If
End Sub
```

Validating User Input on the Form Level

Locking a user into a control until a valid value is entered may be annoying to your users. Therefore, you may choose to perform validation only when the user has completed all the data entry on the form. The code for such validation should be executed when the user attempts to save the form, as discussed later in the section on "Writing Code that Processes Data Entered on a Form."

Enabling/Disabling Controls to Restrict Input

You may need to restrict data input based on certain options the user chooses. Let's say you only want to allow the user to move to the next screen if they accept the end user agreement. This is done by simply setting the initial value of the Next button's Enabled property to False and setting it to True when the user chooses 'I Agree.'

Writing Code that Processes Data Entered on a Form

During the course of your application you will very likely need to perform certain actions as forms open and close. For instance, you may need to initialize controls to display certain data before the form opens, or you may want to prompt the user to save changes before the form closes. In order to properly manage the forms in your application, you must understand the form lifecycle. The following events occur in a form's lifetime:

- Form is first loaded into memory.
    - Initialize
    - Load

- Form is displayed.
  - Activate
  - GotFocus (occurs only if there aren't any controls on the form that can currently receive the focus)
- Form loses the focus.
  - LostFocus (occurs only if there aren't any controls on the form that can currently receive the focus)
  - Deactivate
- Form is unloaded.
  - QueryUnload
  - Unload
- Form is removed from memory.
  - Terminate (only occurs if there aren't any valid references to the form or any of its controls)

Let's take a closer look at each of these events in the form lifecycle.

Form Is First Loaded into Memory

There are several things that can cause a form to load into memory. Some of them trigger both the Initialize and Load event, while others only trigger the Initialize event (see Table 4.14).

TABLE 4.14 Reasons for a Form to Load into Memory

Reason	Event
The Load statement is used to load the form.	Initialize Load
The form's Show method is called.	Initialize Load
A property of a control on the form is referenced.	Initialize Load
A procedure of the form is called from another module.	Initialize

The Initialize and Load events are where you should put initi
code that must execute before the form is loaded. As you can
Table 4.14, if a procedure of a form is called from another module then the Initialize event is raised, but not the Load event. Therefore, any initialization needed for procedures to run should be put in the Initialize event. Initialization related to the controls of the form should be put in the Load event.

Form Is Displayed

Loading a form using the Load statement does not display the form. A form is either displayed because it is the start-up form (as specified in Project Properties) or because its Show method is called. When a form is displayed, the Activate event fires first and then the GotFocus event. The Activate event is fired every time the form becomes the active form, and therefore, is not typically a good place for initialization code. You will, however, want to use the Activate event for initialization when:

- the initialization code executes graphical functions that aren't valid unless the form is displayed.
- some data-bound controls may not be fully initialized in the Load event.

Remember, if the initialization should only happen when the form is first displayed and not every time it gets activated, then you should use a static variable in the Activate event that signifies that the form has already been initialized.

The GotFocus is rarely used for initialization because it only occurs if there are no controls on the form that are capable of getting the focus.

Form Loses the Focus

When a form loses focus, it may need cleanup code, validation, or the entered data to be saved.

The LostFocus and Deactivate events fire when a different form in the *same* application becomes the active form, thereby deactivating the current form. These events do not fire when the focus is shifted to a different application.

Since the shifting of focus from a form does not signal that the form is being closed, it is not usually the place for cleanup code, for validation, or for saving information. However, in some applications, it may make sense to validate and save in the Deactivate event.

As with the GotFocus event, the LostFocus event only fires if there aren't any controls on the form capable of currently receiving the focus.

Form Is Unloaded

A form is unloaded from memory when one of the following occurs:

- Unload statement is used
- user closes the form
- operating system is shutting down and attempting to close the application
- Task Manager is closing the application
- parent MDI form is closing
- owner form is being closed

TIP

The *owner form* is a new concept in VB 6, in which a form has another form as its owner. The owned form is always displayed on top of its owner and is minimized, restored, and closed with its owner. The second argument of the form's Show method allows you to set the form's owner.

Using the QueryUnload and Unload Events

Before a form is actually removed from memory it goes into an unloaded state. When it enters this state it is not a window, and therefore, all of its properties and controls are reset to their default values. However, it does maintain its memory resources, and therefore, modular variables retain their values.

A form is destroyed (removed from memory) when there are no more valid references to it or any of its controls. A commonly overlooked reference is the default instance of a form. Since it has global scope, it never goes out of scope and must be explicitly set to Nothing.

Both the QueryUnload and Unload events fire before the form unloads, allowing you to cancel the unload by setting the Cancel parameter to True. However, the QueryUnload has two things the Unload event doesn't have:

- A parameter that indicates why the form is being closed.

- A Cancel parameter that when set to True aborts the entire unload process. Aborting in the Unload event only cancels the unload of the current form and all subsequent forms. Table 4.15 describes how aborting the unload in the QueryUnload and Unload events affects the entire unload process.

TABLE 4.15: Aborting in QueryUnload Vs. Unload

Cause for Unload	Effect of Aborting in the QueryUnload	Effect of Aborting in the Unload
Application is being closed either by the Task Manager or Windows.	The shutdown of the application is stopped, and the 'Program is not responding dialog' prompts the user to decide whether to kill the program.	Same as QueryUnload.
The MDI parent form is being closed and the unload is being aborted from within a child form.	The MDI parent and all its child forms are not unloaded.	All child forms that are still loaded are not unloaded. The parent form is not unloaded.
The owner form is being closed and the unload is being aborted from within the owned form.	Both the owner form and the owned form are not unloaded.	Same as QueryUnload.

In an MDI application (owner forms behave the same as the MDI parent form), when the user attempts to close the MDI parent form, the events fire in the following order:

1. QueryUnload of the MDI parent form
2. QueryUnload of all MDI child forms
3. Unload of all MDI child forms
4. Unload of the MDI parent form

The QueryUnload event has the following syntax:

```
Form_QueryUnload (Cancel as Boolean UnloadMode as Integer)
```

The UnloadMode parameter may have the values listed in Table 4.16.

TABLE 4.16 Possible Values of the UnloadMode Parameter Query-Unload Event

Values	Description
vbFormControlMenu	The user clicked the Close button on the form.
vbFormCode	The Unload statement was invoked on the form.
vbAppWindows	The operating system is attempting to shut down.
vbAppTaskManager	The Task Manager is attempting to close the application.
vbFormMDIForm	The parent MDI form is being closed.
vbFormOwner	The owner form is being closed.

Both the QueryUnload and Unload events can be used for prompting the user to decide whether they want to close or whether they want to save changes. Use the QueryUnload event if you want to determine why the form is being closed or if you want to abort the entire unload process as explained earlier.

The Unload event is the place for cleanup code and saving information.

Form Is Removed from Memory

When all references to a form are either out of scope or set to Nothing, the form is removed from memory and the Terminate event is fired.

Adding an ActiveX Control to the Toolbox

Adding an ActiveX control to the Toolbox is a very simple process. You simply check the desired control in the Components dialog. There are several ways to open the Components dialog:

- Project ➢ Components
- Ctrl+T
- Right-click the Toolbox and choose Components

Creating Dynamic Web Pages by Using ASP and WebClasses

VB 6 has a new project type called *IIS* (Internet Information Server). IIS projects allow you to develop an *Active Server Page* (ASP) based on applications within the VB environment.

Understanding ASP

IIS projects are a VB implementation of ASP, and therefore, it is necessary to understand the ASP paradigm in order to work with IIS projects.

In a simple Internet scenario, the browser requests an HTML file from the server, and the server simply locates the file and sends it back to the browser. The browser requests the file in the form of a URL that specifies the name of the directory and the HTML file to be sent back to the browser. Using ASP, a server can perform processing on the server before sending a response to the browser. For instance, the server can read information passed in from the browser, and based on that information, retrieve data from a database, modify the data, and send back the modified data in HTML.

An ASP page is simply a file with an `.asp` extension that sits on the server. In order to access an ASP page, the browser sends a URL that specifies the directory and ASP file to be accessed. ASP pages are not simply sent back to the browser, rather, the ASP page can contain code that is processed by the server, and it can also contain or generate HTML to be sent back to the browser. In addition, the code within the ASP page has access to information submitted by the browser in the form of HTML forms and cookies.

NOTE: *Cookies* are small pieces of information that are stored on the client's machine. By default, the cookie is erased when the ASP session ends.

There are two ways to cause a browser to send a request to the server:

- The user enters a URL into the address box on the browser and submits it.
- The user activates an element on the page that has an attribute, such as the HREF attribute that causes the browser to request the URL specified by the attribute.

It is important to understand what happens on the client as opposed to the server. Basic ASP events take place in the following sequence:

1. HTML and ASP files sit in a directory on the Web server.
2. Browser sends a URL request that specifies either an HTML or ASP file. If the user requests an HTML file then the:
   - HTML page is sent from the server to the browser.
   - browser displays the HTML page.
   - user activates an element that has an URL attribute, such as an HREF that contains a URL to an ASP page.
   - browser sends a URL request for the ASP page.
3. The server reads the ASP page and executes any code it finds.
4. The server sends both static HTML and generated HTML found in the ASP page back to the browser.
5. The browser displays the HTML received from the server.

In summary, the simple ASP paradigm allows a user to submit information to the ASP page, the page can execute code to do the necessary processing, and a response is sent back to the browser.

Understanding IIS Projects

IIS projects are made up of WebClasses. VB uses WebClasses to provide a VB front to ASP pages. When compiled, an IIS project generates an ASP page, compiles your VB code into an ActiveX DLL, and uses MSWCRUN.DLL during runtime to link your DLL to the ASP page. This allows you to write VB code within the VB environment that processes ASP requests. In addition, VB allows you to directly link HTML elements that have an attribute that contains a URL to an event procedure in your code. By doing so, VB bridges the gap between the browser and the Web server by allowing an HTML element that sits on the client to trigger a procedure sitting in a DLL on the server.

In order to develop IIS applications, you must have access to a machine that is either running IIS (NT server) or Personal Web Server (95+/NT workstation), which is a trimmed-down version of IIS.

Understanding WebClasses

A *WebClass* is the central point of WebClass development; it is what you use to write code that will be executed on the server and to link HTML elements to event procedures in your code. A WebClass can contain *WebItems,* which may either be HTML documents or custom WebItems, as described later in this section. The WebClass has a designer that consists of a visual designer and a code window. The visual designer window has a left pane that allows you to add WebItems to the project and a right pane to link elements from those HTML documents to event procedures (see Figure 4.6). The designer's code window contains the event procedures for all WebItems that are part of the WebClass.

FIGURE 4.6
WebClass designer

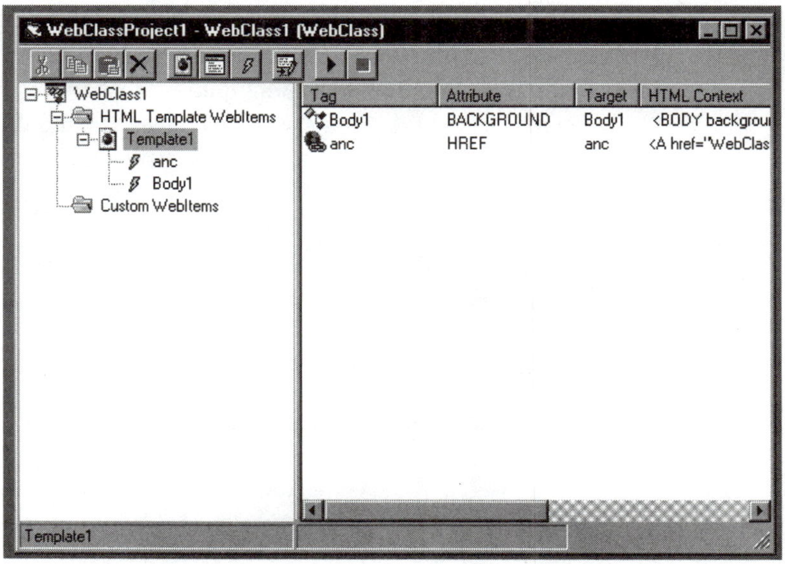

The basic flow of events that occurs in a WebClass application is as follows:

1. Browser sends a request to an ASP page linked to a WebClass.
2. WebClass (contained in a DLL on the server) is activated.
3. The Start event of the WebClass is fired.
4. Code in the Start event may perform initial (server-side) processing.
5. WebClass sends HTML back to the browser.
6. Browser displays HTML.
7. User activates an element in the HTML document that is linked to an event procedure in the WebClass, and the browser sends a URL request to the server that specifies the linked event procedure.
8. The linked event procedure is executed.
9. WebClass sends response to browser in the form of HTML.
10. Browser displays HTML.

In order to understand the events that take place in a WebClass' lifecycle it is necessary to understand how IIS manages browser requests. The HTTP protocol by itself is a *stateless protocol*, meaning that the server and the browser do not maintain any relationship between requests. Even if the browser makes numerous requests from the same HTML page, the server sees each request as new and unrelated. Through the use of cookies, IIS maintains a *session* for each user, which allows it to keep track of users and maintain state between requests. The WebClass' lifecycle mirrors that of the IIS session. It has events that correspond to the beginning and end of a session. It is created and destroyed with every request and response. However, if the WebClass' StateManagement property is set to `wcRetainInstance`, then WebClass is not destroyed after the response.

The application begins when a browser requests a URL of an ASP page that is linked to a WebClass. This ASP page is generated by VB when you run or compile the project. You can set the name of the URL by setting the WebClass' NameInUrl property.

When the WebClass is activated, the following events occur in sequence:

Initialize This event occurs when the browser requests the WebClass' ASP page and the WebClass is created. This event occurs with every request unless the StateManagement property is set to `wcRetainInstance`, in which case, the event only fires at the beginning of the session.

BeginRequest This event occurs with every browser request, regardless of the StateManagement property.

Start This event occurs the first time the ASP is accessed within a session. If the user specifies a specific WebItem and event in the URL, then the Start event does not fire.

EndRequest This event occurs when the WebClass has finished processing a request.

Terminate This event occurs when the WebClass is destroyed.

The Start event is the starting point of the application. You should use it to do initial processing and to send back the opening HTML form for the application. Do not use the Initialize and BeginRequest events for the application's starting point because these events fire with every request. Use the BeginRequest and EndRequest events for processing that needs to be done with every request, such as verifying a user's credentials.

Adding HTML Templates

You can add HTML templates (documents) to your WebClass. These templates become WebItem objects in your application. A WebItem object has events and methods that allow you to modify the document and send it back to the browser. In addition, you can create event procedures for elements of the page that can be referenced by a URL. These event procedures become events of the WebItem. The WebItem is a child of the WebClass (just like controls are objects that belong to a form); therefore, it can be referenced within the WebClass code and its procedures are added to the WebClass code window.

To add an HTML template to your WebClass, follow these steps:

1. Right-click an item in the left pane of the designer window and choose Add HTML Template.
2. In the Open dialog, choose a file.

When you add a file, VB creates a copy of that file in the project directory. If the file already exists in the project directory, then it creates a copy of it with a number appended to its name. The reason VB does this is because it modifies the file as you connect elements to events. If you want to modify the file with an external editor, make sure you modify the project copy of the file.

After you have added a template, open the designer code window and you will see the following default events and methods of the WebItem object (assuming you named the template htmWelcome):

htmWelcome_Respond This is the default event fired by the WebClass if the URL request specifies the WebItem but does not specify an event.

htmWelcome_ProcessTag Used to modify the HTML to be sent back to the browser. This is described later in the "Sending Responses to the Browser" section.

htmWelcome_UserEvent This event is raised for all custom events created during runtime. This is described later in the "Creating Dynamic Custom Events" section.

Connecting HTML Elements to Events When you add an HTML template, VB parses the file and lists all elements on the page that have an attribute that can contain a URL, in the right pane of the designer window. You now can choose which elements you want to have trigger an event for the WebItem. When you connect an element, VB adds code to the element attribute's URL that specifies the WebItem and event that should be fired.

To connect an element, either double-click the element in the right pane of the designer window or right-click the element and choose Connect to Custom Event. After you connect them, the event for the element is added to the code window:

```
WebItem_EventName
```

You can now add code to that event to process the user's action.

Adding Custom WebItems Custom WebItems are similar to the WebItems created by adding an HTML template. The difference is that custom WebItems are not directly associated with HTML templates. Custom WebItems are used to logically organize code, in the same way you use standard modules in a regular VB application. HTML elements from other WebItems can be connected to a custom WebItem. When the user activates the element, the Respond event of the custom WebItem fires.

To add a custom WebItem, right-click an item in the left pane of the designer window, and choose Add Custom WebItem.

To link an element to a custom WebItem, follow these steps:

1. Right-click the element in the right pane of the designer window, and choose Connect to Custom WebItem.
2. In the dialog, choose the WebItem to which you want to connect.

Sending Responses to the Browser After the WebClass finishes processing the request of the browser, it should send a response to the browser. There are two ways to send a response. One way is to dynamically create HTML and write back to the browser; this method is discussed later in the "Understanding ASP Objects" section. The other way is to send an HTML template back to the browser. The template is sent back using the WebItem's *WriteTemplate* method (remember that a WebItem is created for a template):

```
WebItem.WriteTemplate
```

Modifying the HTML Template Before the template is written back to the browser, the ProcessTags procedure is executed. The ProcessTags procedure looks for specially marked tags and replaces them with data that you supply. This allows you to send back customized HTML to the browser.

To mark areas of the HTML file for processing, follow these steps.

1. Set the TagPrefix property of the WebItem. The default is WC@. VB will search for this prefix when processing the file.
2. Open the HTML file in an external editor.
3. Place HTML tags around elements that you want to replace. Give the tags a unique name prefixed with the TagPrefix:

   ```
   <WC@LastName></WC@Lastname>
   ```

When you call the WriteTemplate method, VB reads the template, and for each specially prefixed tag that it finds, it raises the ProcessTag event:

```
WebItem_ProcessTag(TagName As String, TagContents As String,
SendTag As Boolean)
```

You can write conditional code in this event to determine which tag has been found by checking the TagName parameter. You can change the contents of the tag by assigning the new value to the TagContents parameter. The following sample code assumes you have module-level variables that contain user information:

```
Private htmPurchase_ProcessTag(TagName As String,
TagContents As String, SendTag As Boolean)
Select Case TagName
Case "LName"
 TagContents=strLName
```

```
Case "Fname"
 TagContents=strFName
Case "PurchaseAmount"
 TagContents=strAmount
End Select
End Sub
```

Creating Dynamic Custom Events When sending back HTML to the browser, you may want to write back new elements that raise a WebItem event; for instance, if you're sending back a dynamically created list of products and you want each product to have a hyperlink that triggers a WebItem event. This can be done using the URLFor method:

```
URLFor(WebItemobject As WebItem,[eventname])
```

This method can be used in WebClass code to generate a URL that specifies a WebItem, and optionally, a specific event.

When the user activates an element that fires a dynamically created event, the WebItem's UserEvent event is raised:

```
WebItem_UserEvent(eventname As String)
```

You can determine which event was raised by checking the eventname parameter.

Understanding ASP Objects

ASP exposes several objects that provide information submitted by the browser, allow you to respond to the browser, and allow you to create server-side resources. These objects are implicitly available from within the WebClass code; they do not have to be created.

Using the Request Object

The Request object provides information submitted by the browser. Its primary properties are listed in Table 4.17.

TABLE 4.17 Request Object's Properties

Property	Description
Form	Contains a list of name/value pairs submitted by an HTML form. An individual value can be accessed by specifying the name of the form field: `sName=Request.Form("Name")`
Cookies	Retrieves data stored in cookies. Individual cookies can be accessed by specifying the name of the cookie: `Svalue=Request.Cookies("Name")`

NOTE An HTML form is a group of input fields enclosed in FORM tags. When the Submit button is pressed, the browser posts the form to the ASP page. Code in the ASP page can access the individual fields of the form and process them.

Using the Response Object

The Response object is used to respond to the user's request. Table 4.18 lists the Response object's primary methods and properties.

TABLE 4.18 Response Object's Methods and Properties

Method/Property	Description
Write	Writes a string back to the browser to be displayed as HTML: `Response. Write String`
Redirect	Sends a different file than the one the user requested: `Response.Redirect URL`
Cookies	Writes a cookie to the browser: `Response.Cookies("Name")="Joe"`

Using the Server Object

The Server object allows you to create objects on the server using the CreateObject method:

```
Server.CreateObject (progID)
```

Using the Server object to create objects, as opposed to using VB's CreateObject method, provides better optimization by allowing IIS to manage the object.

Using the Application and Session Objects

The Application and Session objects allow you to store information in application and session-wide variables, respectively. A value is stored as follows:

```
Application("Lname")=Name
Session("Lname")=Name
```

and is read as follows:

```
Name= Application("Lname")
Name= Session("Lname")
```

The Application object has two methods used to stop multiple users from modifying an Application value simultaneously: Lock and Unlock. Use the Lock method before modifying an Application value and Unlock when you are done.

Creating a Web Page by Using the DHTML Page Designer

DHTML (Dynamic HTML) is a form of HTML that allows for elements of the HTML document to be modified even after they are rendered. This dynamic modification is performed by the browser. In fact you don't even need a Web server to run a DHTML document if the file is stored locally on your machine. Currently, not all browsers support DHTML.

Therefore, DHTML applications have a limited audience and are typically used for intranet applications.

Creating the GUI

VB provides a DHTML designer that has both a code window and a visual designer (see Figure 4.7). You can draw the user interface in the visual designer much in the same way that you would do in a standard VB form. You can:

- drag-and-drop HTML controls from the Toolbox. When a DHTML designer is added to the project, special HTML controls are added to the Toolbox.
- drag-and-drop ActiveX controls from the Toolbox.
- type text directly onto the page; text does not have to be in a control.
- change the attributes of elements using the familiar property page.
- insert tables and configure them with a custom property page (right-click the table and choose Properties).

VB does not provide a way for you to directly edit the HTML from within the VB environment; you must use an external editor instead. However, VB does integrate the external editor somewhat into the VB environment, in the following ways:

- You can launch the editor of your choice from the DHTML designer toolbar. The editor of your choice can be specified in the Options dialog by clicking Tools ➢ Options ➢ Advanced ➢ External HTML Editor.
- When VB is activated after you use an external editor, it recognizes if changes have been made, and it will prompt you to refresh the DHTML designer with the new data.

In order to use an external editor to edit your DHTML, you must save it as an external file as described later on in the "Creating Project Files" section.

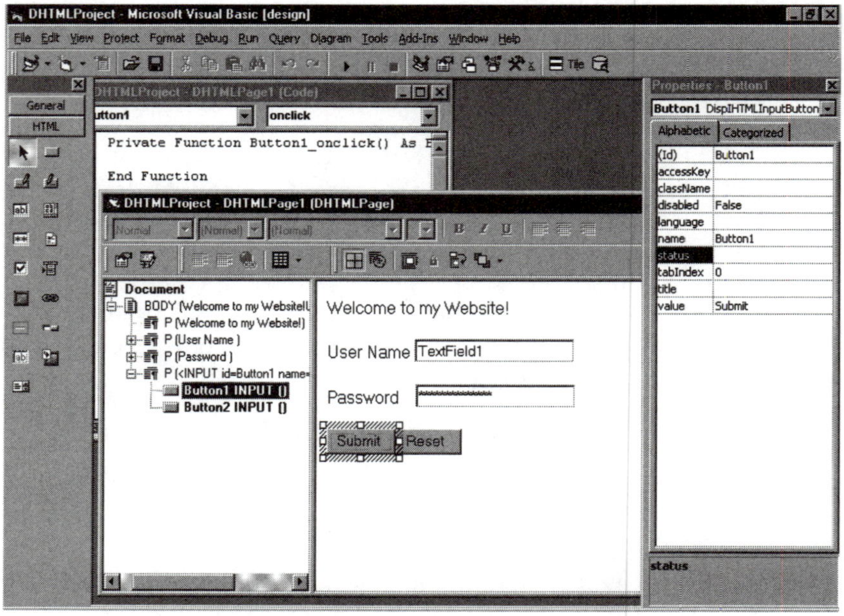

FIGURE 4.7 DHTML designer

Positioning Elements

When an element is added to the page, by default, the designer places it in the next available position in the page, and the element becomes part of the document flow. As part of the document flow, the element is arranged and rearranged with the rest of the document as the browser is resized.

DHTML has another mode of positioning, *absolute positioning*, which allows you to position an element at a specific position in the document. The absolutely positioned element is not part of the document flow; therefore, it will not be rearranged as the browser is resized.

In addition, elements that are part of the document flow and an absolutely positioned element can occupy the same position in the browser; depending on the Zorder value of the absolutely positioned element, one will hide the other.

In order to absolutely position an element, click the Absolute Position icon on the designer toolbar.

NOTE The DHTML specification actually has three positioning modes: static, absolute, and relative. The VB designer provides static (default) and absolute only. The MSDN documentation incorrectly refers to the default positioning of the designer as relative. Elements can be relatively positioned by using an external editor.

Creating Project Files

When creating DHTML pages with the DHTML designer you have the option to work with an external HTML file or to embed the HTML into the designer (`.dsr` file).

Working with an external file allows you to use an external HTML editor to modify the page. You may find it necessary to use an external editor because the HTML capabilities of VB are somewhat limited. In addition, you can use an existing HTML page created outside of VB. This allows a graphic artist to do the artwork and you to do the code development within VB.

By default, the DHTML designer does not create an external file. If you want to work with an external file, follow these steps:

1. Click the Properties icon on the designer toolbar.
2. Choose Save HTML In An External File.
3. Choose either Create New File or Use Existing File.
4. In the Save/Open dialog that opens, enter the desired external filename, and click OK.

Understanding HTML Elements and Attributes

In the world of HTML, all the items that you add to the page, both text and controls, are called *elements* and their properties are called *attributes*.

All the elements on the page have attributes that can be modified from the property page. The left pane of the DHTML designer is a treeview of all the elements of the page. The treeview, design pane, and the properties page are all synchronized, so when you select an element in one of them, it also is selected in the others.

Programming Elements

The DHTML designer exposes the DHTML object model for programming. Using the object model, all the elements on the page can be referenced and manipulated in code. In addition, many elements raise events that you can respond to from code.

In order to make an element programmable, it must have a value assigned to its ID attribute, *not* to its Name attribute. The Name attribute is used for other things such as HTML forms and style sheets. When an element is given an ID, it becomes highlighted in the treeview pane and its event routines are added to the code window.

To assign an ID to an element, highlight it in either the treeview pane or the designer pane and access the properties page. Controls added from the Toolbox are automatically assigned a default name. All IDs on the page must be unique. Table 4.19 describes the main DHTML objects.

TABLE 4.19 Main Objects of the DHTML Object Model

Object	Description
BaseWindow	Top-level object that represents the browser. Can be used for creating and navigating other windows and frames. Provides information about user configuration.
Document	Represents the page. Can be used to change attributes of the page and to access all the elements on the page.
Individual elements referenced by their ID attribute	Used to manipulate individual elements of the page.

Making Changes at Runtime

The power of DHTML over regular HTML is that all the elements of the page can be modified even after they are rendered. Elements of the page can be manipulated programmatically through the DHTML object model. You can reference individual elements by their ID attributes, as described earlier.

Dynamically Changing Attributes

Elements are modified using the standard *Object.Property* syntax; in the DHTML world it's actually *Element.Attribute*. For example, if you have a textbox with `txtName` for its ID, you can have it display a value with the following code:

```
TxtName.Value="Hello"
```

Dynamically Changing Styles

DHTML provides a rich collection of display settings, which allows you to change color, spacing, dimensions, and position. For individual elements, these display settings are exposed through the element's Style object:

```
Element.Style.backgroundColor="Blue"
```

Table 4.20 describes the primary Style properties.

TABLE 4.20 DHTML Style properties

Property	Description
BackgroundColor	Sets the background color.
Color	Sets the foreground color.
FontFamily/FontSize/FontStyle/Font-Variant/FontWeight	Sets font attributes for text displayed by the element.
PaddingLeft/PaddingRight/Padding-Top/PaddingBottom	Set the padding surrounding the element.
PosLeft/PosTop/PosHeight/PosWidth	Sets the position and dimensions of absolutely positioned elements.

The Document object exposes limited display settings as individual properties of the Document itself. The primary properties are listed in Table 4.21.

TABLE 4.21 Document Display Properties

Property	Description
BgColor	Background color.
FgColor	Forecolor.
Location	Returns and sets the current URL.
LinkColor	Forecolor of unvisited links.
VlinkColor	Forecolor of visited links.

Dynamically Changing Content

DHTML allows you to change the contents of all the elements of the page. Many elements, such as the standard controls, have a Value property that exposes the contents of the control. Text elements, such as paragraphs and headings, have the properties and methods described in Table 4.22.

Two very flexible elements are *div* and *span*. These elements are placeholders for HTML. Div creates a paragraph break after itself; therefore, you should use span within paragraphs. These elements are useful if you want to insert HTML during runtime at a specific position in the document or if you want treat multiple elements as a group. Table 4.22 describes several properties and methods of these elements that allow you to read and modify their contents.

TABLE 4.22 Properties of Text Elements

Property	Description	Example of Value Returned
		<DIV>My <b>Home</b> Page</DIV>
InnerText	Returns any text contained within the div tags, without the tags of child elements. Replaces everything contained within the element's tags. HTML tags are rendered as text.	My Home Page
InnerHTML	Returns text and tags of child elements. Replaces everything contained within the element's tags. HTML tags are processed and they affect the text displayed.	My <b>Home</b> Page
OuterText	Returns the same thing as InnerText. Replaces the entire element. Any further references to the element will raise an error. HTML tags are rendered as text.	My Home Page

TABLE 4.22 *(cont.)* Properties of Text Elements

Property	Description	Example of Value Returned
OuterHTML	Returns the entire element including the parent tags and child tags. Replaces the entire element. Any further references to the div element will raise an error. HTML tags are processed and they affect the text displayed.	<DIV>My <b>Home</b> Page</DIV>

Setting the properties listed in Table 4.22 replaces the entire contents of element. The InsertAdjacent methods in Table 4.23 allow you to insert content in or around the element as specified in the *where* argument.

TABLE 4.23 InsertAdjacent Methods

Method	Description	
InsertAdjacentHTML *where, text*	Inserts the text at the position specified in the *where* argument. HTML tags are processed and they affect the display of the text.	
InsertAdjacentText *where, text*	Inserts the text at the position specified in the *where* argument. HTML tags are not processed, rather, they are displayed as text.	
	Values of the Where Argument	
	BeforeBegin	Before the opening tag of the element.
	AfterBegin	After the opening tag of the element.
	BeforeEnd	Before the closing tag of the element.
	AfterEnd	After the closing tag of the element.

Dynamically Positioning Elements

As described earlier in the "Positioning Elements" section, elements can be positioned either statically or absolutely. Static elements cannot be dynamically positioned, but absolute elements can. An absolute element's position is based on the upper-left corner of its container. Elements positioned on the page have the page as its container, while elements positioned within a div tag have the div elements as its container. Elements are dynamically positioned through their Style property. Table 4.24 lists the properties used for dynamic positioning.

TABLE 4.24 Style Properties used for Dynamic Positioning

Property	Description
PosLeft	Sets and returns the left position of the element.
PosTop	Sets and returns the top position of the element.
PosHeight	Sets and returns the height of the element.
PosWidth	Sets and returns the width of the element.

Using Data Binding to Display and Manipulate Data from a Data Source

This section assumes you are familiar with basic concept of binding controls to a data control. For information about using the ADO Data control see Unit 6, "Creating Data Services." This section discusses some advanced new topics.

VB 6 has two new and very useful features:

- The ability to bind controls to a data source during runtime. Simply set the appropriate properties in code, such as DataSource and DataField. Currently, only ADO data sources such as the ADO Data control and the ADO recordset support runtime binding.
- The ability to bind a control to an ADO recordset. Add to this the fact that ADO recordsets can be disconnected from a data source and you can now build scalable solutions using data-bound controls. This is a

great advantage over previous versions of VB in which binding controls to a data control meant maintaining a live connection between the front end and the database.

Some controls may allow you to bind multiple properties to a data source. See Unit 5, "Creating and Managing COM Components," for information on creating controls that provide multiple data-bound properties. A control can only have one field designated as the data field. Therefore, a control that allows for multiple data-bound properties exposes a *DataBindings collection*. Each bindable property has a corresponding *DataBinding object* that has properties that provide the necessary information to bind to a data source (see Table 4.25). DataBindings can be set at runtime, and depending on the control, also at design time.

To set DataBindings at design time, follow these steps:

1. Open the control's property window.
2. Click the ellipsis for the DataBindings property.
3. The DataBindings dialog is displayed. It has a list of all the bindable properties, DataSource, DataField, DataMembers, and DataFormat list boxes.
4. Select the desired property.
5. Choose a data source, data field, and optionally, a data member and data format from the list boxes. Click OK.

To bind a property to a data source during runtime you must use a data source that supports runtime binding such as the ADO Data control. You can reference the DataBindings collection through the DataBindings property of the control by following these steps.

1. Retrieve an individual DataBinding object by passing the name of a property as the argument of the Item method. (Item is the default property for collections, so it doesn't have to be spelled out):

   ```
   Control1.DataBindings("LastName")
   ```

2. Set the DataSource and DataField properties:

   ```
   With Control1.DataBindings("LastName")
    Set.DataSource =ADOData1
    .DataField="AU_Lname"
   End With
   ```

```
With Control1.DataBindings("BookTitle")
 Set .DataSource =ADOData2
 .DataField="Title"
End With
```

TABLE 4.25 DataBinding Object's Properties

Property	Description
DataField	The field in the recordset to which the property is bound.
DataSource	The data source to which the property is bound.
DataMember	Some data sources have several data sets to choose from. These data sets are exposed as data members. For example, the Data Environment can expose multiple Command objects.
DataFormat	The stdDataFormat object to which the property is bound.

Instantiating and Invoking a COM Component

Working with COM components involves the following tasks:

- optionally referencing the components type library
- declaring a variable to contain an instance of the component
- instantiating an instance of the component, otherwise known as an object
- setting properties of the component as needed
- calling methods of the component as needed

Referencing COM Components

Before VB accesses a COM object it reads the object's type library in order to see the interface (the methods and properties) exposed by the object. This procedure is known as *binding*. VB can perform binding during design time (*early binding*) or runtime (*late binding*).

Early binding provides the following benefits:

- more efficient code compilation based on information gathered from the type library
- ability for you to work with any events the object might raise
- design time and compile time syntax checking on property and method calls to the object; this provides some protection from runtime errors
- auto listing of method parameters and syntax for the object during design time
- ability for you to view the methods and properties of the object using VB's Object Browser

When VB performs late binding it is unable to:

- directly access properties and methods of the object. COM must perform extra tasks to hook up VB's property/method request with the actual property/method.
- validate syntax referring to the object and its properties and methods. This increases the possibility of runtime errors.

However, late binding does provide the following luxuries:

- You do not have to maintain a reference to the component, which can be complicated, as described in Unit 7, "Testing the Solution."
- Even after the application is compiled, you can change which object is instantiated by reading the progID passed to the CreateObject function from an external source. Of course, you must make sure that the new object provides the properties and methods that the application calls.

Performing Late Binding

In order to perform late binding in your application, you should:

1. Declare a variable as Object.

2. Create an instance of the desired component with the `CreateObject` function:

   ```
   Set MyObject=CreateObject (progID)
   ```

The *progID* (programmatic ID) is a two-part string that identifies the component *Component.Class*. See the component's documentation for the progID.

Performing Early Binding

To perform early binding in your application, follow these steps:

1. Open the References dialog by clicking Project ➢ References.
2. Find and check the component you want to reference, and click OK.
3. Declare a variable as the progID:

   ```
   Dim MyObject as MyComponent.MyClass
   ```

4. Instantiate an instance of the component using the New keyword or using the `CreateObject` function:

   ```
   Set MyObject=New MyComponent.MyClass
   ```

   or

   ```
   Set MyObject=CreateObject ("MyComponent.MyClass")
   ```

A more compact but less efficient way of declaring and instantiating an object is as follows:

```
Dim MyObject as New MyComponent.MyClass
```

The object is not instantiated right away, rather, it is instantiated the first time the object is referenced in code. Some disadvantages of this method are:

- It is less efficient because it requires VB to check whether the object has already been created, every time it is referenced.
- It does not allow you to check whether the object has already been instantiated using the Is Nothing statement. It always returns False, but a variable that has been declared without the New keyword will return True before it has been instantiated.

Handling Events from a COM Component

Some COM components raise events that you can handle from within your code. If you simply declare a variable and instantiate it, these events will not be available to you. In order to have access to the events, you must declare the variable using the WithEvents keyword:

```
Dim WithEvents MyObject as MyComponent.MyClass
```

In order to use the WithEvents keyword:

- You must use early binding; WithEvents cannot be used with variables declared as Object.
- You cannot use the New keyword in the declaration.

Creating Call-Back Procedures between COM Components and VB Client Applications

Usually when a client application needs a return value from a server, it requests it by calling the designated function. This method, known as *synchronous processing*, requires the client application to explicitly request the information and does not allow the client to proceed until the value returns from the server. In certain situations, the client may have to be notified when an event occurs and/or be able to continue processing while the server carries out its task. There are three ways to achieve this:

- Events. "See "Compiling a Project with Class Modules into a COM Component," in Unit 5, "Creating and Managing COM Component."
- Call-back functions using the AddressOf keyword. This is commonly used with API functions and is not discussed in this book.
- Call-back objects and procedures.

Creating a Call-Back Object

The concept of a call-back object is very simple. The client passes an object (referred to as the *call-back object*) to the server through a procedure parameter of the server, and the server calls a method (referred to as the *call-back procedure*) of the call-back object when it wants to notify the client. In addition, the server component can pass information to the client through parameters of the call-back procedure.

NOTE In order to successfully implement a call-back object, the client and server applications must agree on the syntax of the call-back method. In order to facilitate this agreement, you may consider defining an abstract interface for the call-back object and using the Implements keyword to force both the client and server to conform to the same interface.

To implement a call-back object, follow these steps:

- For the server:
  1. Declare a variable to contain the call-back object.
  2. Call the call-back object's call-back method as necessary, and pass to it any required information.
- For the client:
  3. Create a class that will serve as the call-back object.
  4. Add the appropriate method to serve as the call-back method.
  5. Add code to the call-back method to process call-backs from the server.

Implementing Online User Assistance in a Distributed Application

The following sections discuss how to implement help for distributed applications.

Setting Appropriate Properties to Enable User Assistance

This section discusses linking a help file to your application. Help properties include HelpFile, HelpContextID, and WhatsThisHelp. Linking a help file is a very simple process and does not require any coding. VB allows you to link both a WinHelp file (`.hlp`) and an HTML Help file (`.chm`).

By linking a help file to your application, you allow your users to:

- set the focus on an item that they need help with and press F1 to be presented with a help file.
- click a help button in the control box of a form and then click the item they need help with, to be presented with a help window.

Help files are organized by topic, with each topic having a unique number (long) as an ID. You use these IDs to link forms and controls to specific help topics.

Designating the Help File

The first step is to set the help file for the project. There may only be one help file per project. There are two ways to set the help file:

1. Open the Project Properties dialog by clicking Project ➢ Properties.
2. Enter the file into the Help File Name field.

The help file can also be set in code:

```
App.HelpFile=FileName
```

The next step is to link forms and controls to specific help topics. There are two types of help: context help and WhatsThisHelp.

Setting Context Help

Context help allows users to set their focus on a form or control and press F1 to be presented with a help file. Forms and (most) controls have a HelpContextID property in which you specify the help topic ID. When a user presses F1, VB calls the help topic associated with the specified ID. But what happens if the control does not have a HelpContextID? Then VB looks for the lowest-level HelpContextID. In other words, if the control that has the focus does not have a HelpContextID, then the VB looks for the HelpContextID of the control's container. If the container is a Frame control that does not have a HelpContextID, then VB looks for the HelpContextID of the form. If the form does not have one, then the help topic specified in the Project Properties dialog is presented.

Setting WhatsThisHelp

Instead of presenting the user with an entire help file, you may want to present a little ToolTip instead. When a form is set to use WhatsThisHelp, a help button is added to the form's control box, allowing the user to click the help button and then the control that they want help with. If the control has a WhatsThisHelpID specified, then the associated help information is displayed in a ToolTip window.

WhatsThisHelp and context help are mutually exclusive. If a form is set to have WhatsThisHelp then context help is disabled.

A form has several properties that affect the WhatsThisHelp functionality. These properties are listed in Table 4.26.

TABLE 4.26 WhatsThisHelp Properties

Property	Description
WhatsThisHelp	Boolean. Enables WhatsThisHelp for the form.
WhatsThisButton	Boolean. Causes the form to display a help button in the control box. When this property is set to True, the WhatsThisHelp property is automatically set to True.
BorderStyle MaxButton MinButton	A WhatsThisButton cannot coexist with min/max buttons. Therefore, either the BorderStyle property must be set to a style that does not have min/max buttons (the ToolWindow style is also invalid) or the min/max button properties must be set to False.

Creating HTML Help

HTML help is now the latest form of help files being used by Microsoft (MSDN 98) and other software vendors. HTML help files can be created with HTML Help Workshop, which can be found on the Visual Basic CD. For full coverage of HTML Help Workshop program, review the documentation that is provided with the product. This section presents a brief overview of the product.

Creating HTML Help Elements

HTML help allows you to create several elements that correspond to different elements of the HTML help viewer:

Help Topics These are the actual help pages. They are written using HTML.

Help Contents Corresponds to the Contents tab. This is a treeview table of contents that the user can use to navigate the help topics. HTML help provides a dialog where you can enter the table of contents listing and link it to a specific help topic. In addition, it provides a form that allows you to organize the listings into different levels in the treeview.

Help Index Corresponds to the Index tab. This creates a list box of keywords from which the user selects a keyword to display the associated help topic. HTML help provides a dialog that allows you to enter keywords and link them to specific help topics. In addition, it provides a form that allows you to indent keywords to identify them as subtopics and it allows you to sort the keywords alphabetically.

Designing HTML Help

You can create a HTML help project (`.hhp`) that keeps track of all the files associated with your help file. From the File ➢ New menu, you can choose to create the different elements just described. The Project Properties dialog allows you to specify the associated table of contents and index.

You can set an ID for a help topic that allows you to link VB controls to the topic as described above. To set an ID, follow these steps:

1. Open the HTMLHelp API dialog by clicking the HTMLHelp API icon on the toolbar.
2. On the Alias Tab, click Add.
3. In the HTMLHelp API Number field, enter a number to be used as the ID.
4. In the HTML File field, choose the help topic to associate with the ID. Click OK.
5. Repeat steps 2 through 4 as necessary.
6. Click OK.

Compiling HTML Help

Compiling an HTML help file is as simple as compiling a VB application—simply choose File ➢ Compile. The compiler compiles all the project files into a compiled help file (`.chm`).

Implementing Messages from a Server Component to a User Interface

As described in the "Handling Server Side Errors" section later in this chapter, server components can raise errors back to the client. The server component can supply the name of a help file and help context ID to the client. The specified help topic is displayed when the client developer clicks the help button on the error message dialog. In addition, the developer can read the help properties of the Err object.

The HelpFile and HelpContextID can either be set as individual properties of the Err object or as arguments of the Err object's Raise method:

```
Err.Raise number, source, description, helpfile, helpcontext
```

Implementing Error Handling in Distributed Applications

Effectively handling runtime errors is critical to an application's success. Unhandled runtime errors will cause the application to crash. When handling an error, the best course of action is to correct the problem and continue on. Sometimes it is necessary to notify the user that an error occurred and the current task could not be completed. Or you may want to prompt the user for information that would correct the problem, such as the location of a missing file. In a distributed application where a component may be running on a server, you cannot simply have a message box pop up for the user. This section discusses how to handle errors on both the client and server sides.

Identifying and Trapping Runtime Errors

Handling runtime errors requires you to trap the error when it occurs and to handle it appropriately. There are two basic ways to trap runtime errors: with an error handling routine or with inline error handlers. Both of them use the `On Error` statement.

Using the *On Error* Statement

By default, when a runtime error occurs, VB halts program execution and displays a message box with the error message and an OK button. When the user clicks OK, the message box and program disappear from the scene. The On Error statement instructs VB what to do when an error occurs. Table 4.27 describes the various options for this statement.

TABLE 4.27 On Error Statement Options

Option	Description
On Error Goto 0	Default behavior. Program execution is halted.
On Error Goto *line label*	When error occurs, program execution continues at the line specified by the line label.
On Error Resume Next	Error is ignored and execution continues as normal. Error information is retained by the Err object.

Using the Err Object

The Err object contains properties that provide information about the most recent error. Use the Err object in error handling to determine what course of action to take. Table 4.28 describes the properties of the Err object.

TABLE 4.28 Err Object Properties

Property	Description
Description	A string that describes the error.
Number	A number that uniquely identifies the error.
HelpFile	Filename of the associated help file.
HelpContextID	ID of the associated help topic.
Source	String identifying the source of the error. This may be either the name of the current project or the progID of the component that raised the error.

Using Error Handling Routines

When using the On Error Goto *line label* you instruct VB to continue at the line labeled *line label*. A line label consists of a label followed by a colon:

```
ErrHandler:
'error handling code goes here
```

WARNING

Labeled lines will execute with the rest of the code even if they were not explicitly directed to do so. Therefore, you should place them at the end of the procedure after an Exit Sub statement.

Place the On Error statement at the point where you want to begin checking for an error. This will usually be at a place that you feel is error prone, such as the place where the code begins working with an external file where the file may be missing or locked. The On Error statement should direct execution to a labeled line that begins an error handling routine.

You should check the Number property of the Err object in your error handling routine to determine which error occurred and take the appropriate action, which may be one of the following:

- If the problem is corrected then you can either resume execution at the line that raised the error by using the Resume statement or at the following line by using the *Resume Next* statement.
- If the error is not corrected, then you may notify the user that the current task failed and exit the procedure by using Exit Sub.

Handling Inline Errors

If you think an error may occur on a specific line, you can write line error handling code to handle the error. To do so, you should:

1. Instruct VB to ignore the error by using the On Error Resume Next statement.
2. On the line following the error-prone code, check if `Err.Number` is not zero (some errors are negative numbers).
3. If an error is raised, determine what error occurred by examining the Err object and taking appropriate action to correct the problem.

Handling Server-Side Errors

When a server component encounters an error while processing a client's request there are two approaches it may take to notify the client: a soft approach and a hard one.

The soft approach is to make the error-prone procedure a method and pass a success/fail value as a return value.

The hard approach is to raise an error in the server's procedure, resulting in a runtime error in the client. You can raise an error in the server using the Err object's Raise method:

```
Err.Raise number, source, description, helpfile, helpcontext
```

Set the Number and Description properties to identify the error. When setting the error number in the server, add the `vbObjectError` constant to the number to ensure that the error number is in the appropriate range of error numbers set aside for VB component errors. You may specify help file information in the last two parameters, as described previously in "Implementing Messages from a Server Component to a User Interface."

Using an Active Document within a Web Browser

This subject is covered in detail in "Creating an Active Document" in Unit 5, "Creating and Managing COM Components."

STUDY QUESTIONS

Implementing Navigational Design

1. How do you create a submenu?

____

____

2. What does the WindowList property of a menu do?

____

3. When you create Menu arrays, what are two restrictions you should keep in mind?

____

____

4. True or False. In code, individual menu items are treated as individual objects.

5. __________ is the syntax for adding a new menu at runtime to a Menu array called `mnu` that already contains two menu objects (option base 0).

6. True or False. Only menus that were added at runtime can be unloaded at runtime.

7. What type of menu can be used as a pop-up menu? What part of the menu is displayed?

____

STUDY QUESTIONS

Creating Data Input Forms and Dialog Boxes

8. What is the ImageList control used for?

____

9. How are images added to ImageList at runtime?

____

10. How is the LoadPicture method used with the ImageList control?

____

11. How is a TreeView control populated?

____

12. How do you set a Node object's position in the TreeView hierarchy?

____

13. How do you navigate the TreeView?

____

____

14. When adding a new Node to the Nodes collection, how do you get a reference to the newly added Node?

____

STUDY QUESTIONS

15. __________ and __________ are the two main views of the ListView control.

16. If you have a ListView in Report view that has a ListItem with four ListSubItems, how many ColumnHeaders must there be?

____

17. How do you sort the ListView control by a specific column?

____

18. How do you handle the Click event of a specific button on a toolbar?

____

____

19. How do you create dropdown buttons on a toolbar?

____

20. What are the two styles for the StatusBar control? What effect do they have on the Panels collection?

____

____

21. If you create a new instance of Form1, what is its name and how should it be retrieved from the Forms collection?

____

STUDY QUESTIONS

22. True or False. MDI child forms are added to the Forms collection.

____

23. How would you determine which type of control is retrieved from the Controls collection?

____

24. True or False. You create a control array by setting the Index property of the control to a numeric value.

25. At runtime, how are controls added to and removed from a control array called `cmd` that contains one command button?

____

____

```
Load cmd(1)
Unload cmd(1)
```

26. Where is a new addition to a control array positioned on the form at runtime?

____

27. How are new controls added to the Controls collection?

____

28. How are events handled for new unreferenced controls?

____

STUDY QUESTIONS

29. What is the EventInfo object? What is its property and collection?

____

____

Writing Code that Validates User Input

30. How would you restrict input in a text box to numbers?

____

____

____

31. What does the CausesValidation property do?

____

Writing Code that Processes Data Entered on a Form

32. If Form1 is currently not loaded and Form2 calls a procedure on Form1, which event of Form1 is fired? ____________________

33. True or False. The GotFocus event of a form is a good place to put graphical initialization code for controls on the form.

34. When does the Terminate event of a form fire?

____

STUDY QUESTIONS

35. You have an owner form and an owned form, and the owner form is being closed by the user. Which events occur in the owner and owned forms and in what order?

36. In an MDI application, what happens if the Task Manager is closing the MDI form and one of the children sets the Cancel parameter of the Unload event to True?

37. What parameter does the QueryUnload event have that the Unload event doesn't have? What is it used for?

Adding an ActiveX Control to the Toolbox

38. Name three ways to open the Components dialog.

STUDY QUESTIONS

Creating Dynamic Web Pages by Using ASP and WebClasses

39. In a WebClass, you should place initialization code that must run with every request in the __________ event.

40. Where in a WebClass should you place initialization code that must run at the beginning of a session?

____

41. What is the difference between HTML templates and Custom WebItems?

____

____

42. What happens when an HTML element is connected?

____

43. Which HTML elements are listed in the right pane of the WebClass designer window?

____

44. WriteTemplate is a method of which object? What does it do?

____

45. When does the ProcessTag event occur? What is it used for?

____

____

STUDY QUESTIONS

46. What does the `URLFor` function do?

____

47. How are dynamically created events handled in a WebItem?

____

48. With what does an ASP page read the contents of an HTML form?

____

49. How can you send HTML to a browser using one of the ASP objects?

____

50. In an ASP page, what is a benefit of creating objects with the Server object as opposed to creating them with just CreateObject?

____

51. How are values stored in the Session object?

____

Creating a Web Page by Using the DHTML Page Designer

52. What must you do in order to edit the HTML of a DHTML designer?

____

STUDY QUESTIONS

53. What are the two positioning modes offered by the DHTML designer, and what do they do?

____

____

54. Which HTML attribute is used to reference an element in code? ________________

55. The __________ is the top-level object in the DHTML object model.

56. How is the background color of an element changed at runtime?

____

57. What is the difference between InnerHTML and InnerText?

____

58. What happens to an element if you set its OuterHTML property?

____

59. If you have a div tag called `dvWelcome` that displays 'Welcome' and you want it to display 'Welcome John', how would you change it using the `InsertAdjacentText` method?

____

60. What setting allows an element to be dynamically positioned?

____

STUDY QUESTIONS

61. How do you dynamically move an element to the left?

____

Using Data Binding to Display and Manipulate Data from a Data Source

62. At runtime, how do you set the DataSources of a control that exposes multiple data-bound fields?

____

____

63. Which data sources can you bind to at runtime?

____

Instantiating and Invoking a COM Component

64. How does early binding enhance the efficiency of a program?

____

65. Why can't you handle events from a late-bound component?

____

66. How do you create early-bound components?

____

STUDY QUESTIONS

67. What restriction is there regarding use of the New keyword when working with objects that have events?

____

Creating Call-Back Procedures between COM Components and VB Client Applications

68. When working with call-back objects, does the client or the server instantiate an instance of the call-back object, and who calls the call-back procedure?

____

Implementing Online User Assistance in a Distributed Application

69. How do you set the help file for an application?

____

70. A text box that does not have a HelpContextID is placed on a frame that has a HelpContextID. The form also has a HelpContextID. When the focus is on the control and the user presses F1, the __________ help topic is displayed.

71. In order to for a control to display a WhatsThisHelp topic, which properties have to be set?

____

72. _______________, _______________, and _______________ can be created with HTML Help Workshop.

STUDY QUESTIONS

73. Using HTML Help Workshop, you can associate an ID with which help element? _________

74. What type of file does an HTML Help Workshop project compile into? _________

75. What are two ways for a server component to notify a client application that an error has occurred?

____

____

76. How do you turn off an error handler?

____

77. How is help file information passed from a server component to a client application?

____

78. How do you implement inline error handling?

____

SAMPLE TEST

4-1 Submenus are created by:

A. setting the subMenu property.

B. setting the childMenu property.

C. using the Menu control from the Toolbox.

D. indenting the menu in the Menu Editor.

4-2 Which of the following is a valid way of setting the `Picture` argument of the ListImages' Add method?

A. `ListImages.Add picture:= FileName`

B. `ListImages.Add picture:= LoadPicture(FileName)`

C. Images can only be added at design time.

4-3 Only menus that are added at runtime can be unloaded at runtime.

A. True

B. False

C. Menus cannot be added or removed at runtime.

4-4 There is one Click event for all menus on a form, and you can determine which menu was clicked by checking the Index parameter.

A. True

B. False

SAMPLE TEST

4-5 How do you display a pop-up menu?

A. Call the form's popupMenu method on a menu created with the Menu Editor.

B. Call the form's popupMenu method, and pass the menu's properties as arguments.

C. Use the Windows API.

D. Add the PopupMenu custom control to the form.

4-6 In order to organize all the icons used in a TreeView and Toolbar you should:

A. set the TreeView and Toolbar's ImageList property to an ImageList control.

B. add the ImageList to the ActiveXControls collection.

C. add the TreeView and Toolbar to the ImageList's Controls collection.

4-7 Suppose you have a TreeView control that has a Node with a Key value of `ndDirectory`. How would you add a child node with a Key value of `ndFile`?

A. `TreeView1.Nodes ("ndDirectory").Child="ndFile"`

B. `TreeView1.Nodes.Add "ndDirectory", tvwChild, "ndFile"`

C. `TreeView1.Nodes.("ndDirectory").Children.Add, tvwChild, "ndFile"`

4-8 If you have a ListView control with a ListItem that has three ListSubItems then there will be ____________ColumnHeader object(s).

A. four

B. three

C. one

SAMPLE TEST

4-9 A control can only be added to the Controls collection if it is in the Toolbox.

A. True

B. False

4-10 Each button on a toolbar has its own Click event.

A. True

B. False

4-11 If a Panel of a StatusBars collection has its Style property set to `sbrNum` and its Text property set to `Loading`, what will be displayed in the Panel?

A. Loading

B. NUM

4-12 When is the SimpleText property of the StatusBar used?

A. When the Panels collection is empty.

B. When the Style property is set to Simple.

C. There is no SimpleText property.

D. When there is only one Panel in the Panels collection.

4-13 Which controls can be unloaded at runtime?

A. all controls

B. no controls

C. controls added at runtime to the Controls collection and control arrays

D. only controls added to the Controls collection at runtime

SAMPLE TEST

4-14 An application has an MDI form with six children forms and one regular form. If two of the child forms and the regular form are loaded, how many forms are there in the Forms collection?

A. six

B. seven

C. four

D. two

4-15 How do you open multiple instances of a form called Form1?

A. `Form1.Clone NewForm`

B. `Forms.Add Form1, NewForm`

C. `Dim NewForm as New Form1`

4-16 How would you add controls to a control array called cmd at runtime?

A. `Load cmd(`*`number`*`)`

B. `cmd.Add number`

C. `Set NewControl= cmd.Add` *`number`*

4-17 How are controls added to the Controls collection at runtime?

A. `Controls.Add ProgID,` *`Name`*

B. `Load Controls` *`ProgID`*

SAMPLE TEST

4-18 When does a text box's Validation event fire?

A. when the CausesValidation property is set to True and the user leaves the text box

B. when the CausesValidation property is set to True and the user leaves the text box after having entered invalid data

C. whenever the user leaves the text box

D. whenever the user enters anything into the text box

4-19 Why isn't the Terminate event a good place to prompt the user to save changes?

A. The Terminate event only fires if all the instances of a form have been unloaded.

B. The Terminate event only fires once in an application.

C. The Terminate event only fires if the form is explicitly set to Nothing.

4-20 What kind of HTML elements can be connected in a WebClass?

A. hyperlinks

B. all elements

C. those with attributes that can contain a URL

D. ActiveX elements

4-21 If you have an owner form and the Windows operating system is being shut down, what happens if the owned form cancels the unload in the Unload event?

A. Neither the owner form or the owned form are unloaded.

B. Only the owner form is unloaded.

C. You can't cancel an unload caused by Windows shutting down.

SAMPLE TEST

4-22 What is the EventParameters collection?

A. A property of the Controls collection that contains all of the events and parameters of the controls in the collection.

B. An optional argument of the `Controls.Add` method that allows you to create new events for newly added controls.

C. A property of the EventInfo object that is a parameter of the ObjectEvent event procedure.

4-23 If you have an MDI form with three children loaded and the second child form cancels an Unload in the QueryUnload event, how many forms are left in the Forms collection?

A. four

B. three

C. one

4-24 What does a connected element do in a WebClass?

A. It connects the WebClass to the ASP page.

B. It fires the event that it is connected to.

C. It sets the PrefixTag of the element.

4-25 What does the PrefixTag property of a WebItem do?

A. It marks the tags for which the WebClass should raise the ProcessTags event.

B. It marks tags that can be connected.

C. It must be used for elements that generate dynamic events.

SAMPLE TEST

4-26 The ProcessTags event:

A. automatically replaces all specially marked tags.

B. has parameters that provide information about specially marked tags, but you have to write code that replaces them.

C. triggers the WriteTemplate method.

4-27 To process HTML forms, use the:

A. `Request.Form` collection

B. `Response.Form` collection

C. `Page.Form` collection

D. `Form.Fields` collection

4-28 What do you need in order to develop a DHTML application?

A. IIS

B. IIS or Personal Web Server

C. none of the above

4-29 In DHTML, elements are referenced in code by their:

A. name.

B. ID.

C. tag.

D. attribute.

SAMPLE TEST

4-30 Which of the following statements would cause a div tag to display 'Hello' in bold?

A. `InsertAdjacentText "AfterBegin", "Hello"`

B. InnerText=<b>Hello</b>

C. OuterHTML=<b>Hello</b>

D. InnerHTML=<b>Hello</b>

4-31 How can you make a paragraph element called pBounce move dynamically down the page?

A. by increasing `pBounce.Style.posTop`

B. by increasing `pBounce.posTop`

C. by increasing `pBounce.Style.offsetTop`

4-32 In order for an object to raise events it must be declared:

A. as the component type using the WithEvents keyword.

B. using the WithEvents and New keywords.

C. as the component type.

D. using the WithEvents keyword.

4-33 In order for an object to be early-bound you must:

A. include the components header file.

B. select the component in the References dialog.

C. use the New keyword.

SAMPLE TEST

4-34 A late-bound object cannot raise events.

A. True

B. False

4-35 Which position mode allows you to dynamically move DHTML elements?

A. absolute

B. dynamic

C. nonstatic

D. all modes

4-36 When working with call-back objects, who creates an instance of the call-back object?

A. server

B. client

4-37 How many help files can there be for an application?

A. two, one for context help and one for WhatsThisHelp

B. one

C. unlimited

4-38 What HTML Help items can be created with HTML Help Workshop?

A. Topics, Contents, Index

B. Topics, Contents

C. Topics, Index

SAMPLE TEST

4-39 Which of the following must be true of a form in order for it to display a WhatsThisHelp button?

A. The form must be a fixed dialog.

B. The form can't be an MDI child.

C. The form can't have Min/Max buttons.

4-40 What kind of file does HTML Help Workshop produce?

A. `.chm`

B. `.hlp`

C. `.hhw`

D. `.hhp`

4-41 If you have a text box on a form and neither the text box nor the form have HelpContextIDs set, which help topic, if any, is displayed?

A. No help topic is displayed.

B. The application's help topic is displayed.

C. An error occurs.

4-42 How is help file information passed from a server component to a client application?

A. as Err object properties

B. as Windows API

C. from the Project Properties dialog

D. the client must check the server component's HelpFile property

SAMPLE TEST

4-43 You have a control called `Control1` that has four data-bound properties. One of those properties is named `ID`. How would you bind the `ID` property to the `CustID` field of an ADO Data control name `Data1`?

A. DataBindings.Add "ID", Data1, "CustID"

B. Set Control1.DataSource=Data1

```
Control1.DataField("ID")= "CustID"
```

C. Set Control1.DataBindings ("ID").DataSource=Data1

```
Control1.DataBindings ("ID").DataField= "CustID"
```

4-44 What does Resume Next do?

A. Execute the next line of code regardless of errors.

B. Execute the line following the line that raised the error.

UNIT 5

Creating and Managing COM Components

Test Objectives:

- **Create a COM component that implements business rules or logic. Components include DLLs, ActiveX controls, and active documents.**
- **Create ActiveX controls.**
  - Create an ActiveX control that exposes properties.
  - Use control events to save and load persistent properties.
  - Test and debug an ActiveX control.
  - Create and enable property pages for an ActiveX control.
  - Enable the data-binding capabilities of an ActiveX control.
  - Create an ActiveX control that is a data source.
- **Create an active document.**
  - Use code within an active document to interact with a container application.
  - Navigate to other active documents.
- **Design and create components that will be used with MTS.**
- **Debug Visual Basic code that uses objects from a COM component.**
- **Choose the appropriate threading model for a COM component.**
- **Create a package by using the MTS Explorer.**
  - Use the Package and Deployment Wizard to create a package.
  - Import existing packages.
  - Assign names to packages.
  - Assign security to packages.
- **Add components to an MTS package.**
  - Set transactional properties of components.
  - Set security properties of components.

- **Use role-based security to limit use of an MTS package to specific users.**
  - Create roles.
  - Assign roles to components or component interfaces.
  - Add users to roles.
- **Compile a project with class modules into a COM component.**
  - Implement an object model within a COM component.
  - Set properties to control the instancing of a class within a COM component.
- **Use Visual Component Manager to manage components.**
- **Register and unregister a COM component.**

NOTE

Exam objectives are subject to change at any time without prior notice and at Microsoft's sole discretion. Please visit Microsoft's Training & Certification Web site (`www.microsoft.com/Train_Cert`) for the most current exam objectives listing.

Microsoft's COM (Component Object Model) specification allows for the creation of components that can easily communicate with COM-compliant applications. In a distributed application, the middle tier typically hosts COM components that are accessed by the front tier to execute business functions and enforce business rules. These components are not designed for direct user interaction, and therefore, don't have a user interface. This unit discusses creating these code-only components and how they should be designed for the middle tier. We will also look at creating COM components that are used on the front tier, such as ActiveX controls and ActiveX documents.

Creating a COM Component that Implements Business Logic

Visual Basic allows you to create several types of components using ActiveX technology that is based on COM. COM components expose a public interface that is made up of properties, methods, functions, and events through which COM-compliant applications can communicate. COM components provide their functionality as objects to client applications that instantiate them. Therefore, when discussing COM objects, the COM object is seen as the server, and the application that instantiates it is seen as the client.

There are four types of ActiveX components that VB allows you to create:

ActiveX DLL ActiveX DLLs are used to create code components. They are made up of class modules that contain the public procedures that make up the public interface. They may also contain private procedures and variables for internal processing. They can safely display modal forms and dialogs. Some clients will raise a runtime error if an ActiveX DLL attempts to display nonmodal forms (check the NonModalAllowed property of the App object before displaying a nonmodal form). ActiveX DLLs run in the process of the client application. This means they live and die with the client, cannot run asynchronously, and provide better performance because communication between the client and the object are within the same process space. They are usually the best choice for creating middle-tier business components.

ActiveX EXE An ActiveX EXE can provide all the functionality of a standard EXE and more. It can run both as a stand-alone application and as a server component. When used as a server component, it exposes a public interface through class modules that can be manipulated by a client application. A well-known suite of ActiveX EXEs is the Microsoft Office applications. As server components, they run out-of-process, and therefore, have slower performance. However, since they run out-of-process, they can execute tasks asynchronously.

NOTE

Note that procedure calls to out-of-process components are not automatically asynchronous; the client application must wait until the procedure is complete before continuing execution. In order for a task to be asynchronous, it must be triggered by a source other than the client application. A common scenario is when the client application turns on a timer in the server and the timer's Timer event starts the execution of the task.

ActiveX Control An ActiveX control is a special type of ActiveX DLL that provides a user interface and can be embedded in an ActiveX container such as a VB form or Web page.

ActiveX document An ActiveX document is a form-based application that can be hosted in an ActiveX document container such as Microsoft Internet Explorer or Microsoft Office Binder.

Developing with Class Modules

This book assumes that you are familiar with the basics of creating classes and their procedures and events. This section highlights important points related to class modules. The information in this section applies to creating all types of components.

Using Property Procedures and Variables

If you want your object to retain some state that clients can get and set, you must use property procedures and variables. Variables alone are not enough because they cannot be part of a public interface. Property procedures on their own are not enough because they do not maintain state; they only execute the code within them. Therefore, you must use a variable to internally maintain state and expose the value of the variable through property procedures. There are three types of property procedures:

Get This is used to return the value of the property that is maintained in a variable to the user:

```
Public Property Get ID() as String
 ID=strID 'strID is a module variable
End Property
```

The user would read this property as follows:

```
s=Object.ID
```

Let This is used to set the value of a property that will be stored in a variable. The procedure takes the value to be used as a parameter:

```
Public Property Let ID(Value as String)
 strID=Value 'strID is a module variable
End Property
```

The user would set this property as follows:

```
Object.ID=s
```

Set This is similar to let, the only difference is that the user sets the value of the property using the Set keyword. It is usually used when a property contains an object:

```
Set Object.Property = Object
```

In order to implement a read-only property, you supply a property get and not a let or set.

Property get, let, and set procedures work together to provide read-write functionality to a property. The parameters of get and the let/set pair have to match. Here are the rules:

- Let and set always have one more parameter than get because they take the new value of the property as a parameter.
- Get has a return value, while let and set don't.
- When let or set has multiple parameters, the property is set by the user with the last parameter on the right side of the equal (=) sign, and the other parameters are enclosed in parentheses on the left side of the equal sign:

```
Public Property Let Size(Dimension as integer, Scale as
 integer, Value as long)
End Property
' the property is set as follows
Object.Size(Dimension:=3,Scale:=2)=54345
```

- When a get has multiple parameters, the property is read with all the parameters in parentheses on the right side of the procedure name:

```
Public Property Get Size(Dimension as integer, Scale as
 integer) as long
End Property
' the property is get as follows
Num=Object.Size(Dimension:=3,Scale:=2)
```

- The parameter names and types must match.
- The return value of get must be the same type as the last parameter of let and set. They both refer to the value of the property.

Raising Events

Within the class module, events are not procedures, rather, they are declared in the Declarations section. The declaration can have parameters. Events are manifested in clients as event procedures, in which a client writes code to handle the event. When you want your object to raise an event, use the Raise-Event statement followed by the event name and any parameters enclosed in parentheses.

```
'event declaration
General Declarations
Public Event Connected (Cancel as Boolean)

'Object procedure that raises the event
Public Sub() Connect
 Dim bCancel as boolean
 'code to establish connection
 RaiseEvent Connected(bCancel)
 If bCancel = True then
 'break connection
 End if
End Sub
```

Defining Procedure Scopes

A procedure within a class module can have three scopes: private, public, and friend. *Public procedures* are part of the public interface of the class. *Private procedures* are only visible within the class itself. *Friend procedures* are visible throughout all classes in a component, but are not part of the public interface.

Compiling a Project with Class Modules into a COM Component

One component can expose multiple objects by including multiple class modules within its ActiveX project. To make it easy to work with your component, you should arrange its objects into a logical model, or *object model.* An object model should be arranged to allow direct access to the main objects of a component. Secondary objects that work in conjunction with the main objects should be accessed only through the main objects. This arrangement is called a *parent-child model.* In some cases, a parent object may contain many instances of a child object; for instance, in an object model that mimics the structure of an invoice. An invoice can contain many line items, but line items cannot be accessed directly; rather, you must first create an invoice object and access the line item objects through the invoice object. The following sections discuss how to organize the classes in a project into a working object model.

Implementing an Object Model within a COM Component

As was just explained, a component can expose multiple objects in a hierarchical arrangement to form an object model. Forming an object model where one object contains another in a one-to-one relationship is done as follows:

1. Set the child class' Instancing property to PublicNotCreatable.
2. In the parent class, declare and set a variable to contain an instance of the child class.
3. Implement property procedures in the parent class that set and retrieve the child class.

The following is the easiest way to create a one-to-many relationship between a parent and child object. Note that a better approach is described later.

1. Set the child class' Instancing property to PublicNotCreatable.
2. In the parent class, declare and set a collection variable that will contain instances of the child class.
3. Implement property procedures in the parent class that sets and retrieves instances of the child class.

The problem with this method is that a client can add any type of object to the collection. The only protection you have is to raise a runtime error. It would be more robust if a compile time error was raised. Also, because the collection is not publicly accessible, the client can't use the collection's Item and Count properties. You can resolve these issues by creating three classes: the parent class, a collection wrapper class, and the child class. For example, suppose you have a Customer object that has a one-to-many relationship with an Order class. You would create the following classes and procedures:

- A class called Orders that functions as a wrapper around a collection variable. The class has the following:
  - A collection variable called colOrders that contains all instances of the child class.
  - An Add method with a parameter called NewOrder that is of the child class' type:

```
Public Sub Add(NewOrder as Order)
```

(If the developer tries to add an object of a different type, then a compiler error is raised.)

- Item and Count properties that read the Item and Count properties of the collection variable colOrders:

```
Public Function Count()
 Count=colOrders.Count
End Function
```

- A parent class called Customer that contains a property called Orders that returns a reference to the Orders object. The parent class by itself cannot be used to add or access child objects. Child objects are referenced through the parent's Orders procedure, which in turn, returns a reference to the Orders class:

```
ObjCustomer.objOrders.Add NewOrder
ObjCustomer.objOrders.Item(1).Property= Value
Num=ObjCustomer.objOrders.Count
```

- A child class called Order that has properties and methods appropriate for an Order object.

As you can see, using this method provides a robust object model similar to those exposed by many COM components.

Setting Properties to Control Instancing

The Instancing property of a class controls when and how a client application can instantiate an instance of a class. These settings are used to help form parent-child relationships between classes as described previously. In addition, the MultiUse and SingleUse settings determine how components are loaded into memory as described in "Choosing the Appropriate Threading Model for a COM Component," later in this unit. Some types of VB projects do not allow for all types of instancing. Table 5.1 describes the valid settings and the types of projects to which they apply.

TABLE 5.1: Valid Settings for a Class' Instancing Property

Setting	Description	When to Use	Project
Private	Can only be instantiated and referenced within the project.	For classes that do internal processing and are not touched by a client.	ActiveX EXE ActiveX DLL ActiveX control Standard EXE
SingleUse	Can be instantiated and referenced by a client. For every object created, a new copy of the component is loaded into memory, thereby starting a new process.	For classes that need to be instantiated by a client. Used to simulate multi threaded functionality in a single threaded component. See "Choosing the Appropriate Threading Model for COM Components" later on for more information. SingleUse objects consume a lot of memory so use only when required.	ActiveX EXE
MultiUse	Can be instantiated and referenced by a client. One copy of the component can supply multiple instances of the class.	For classes that need to be instantiated by a client.	ActiveX EXE ActiveX DLL
PublicNotCreatable	Cannot be instantiated by a client. It can be referenced once it is created by the component and passed to the client. The client can declare variables of the class type.	To be used with object models in which the class is a child class. The parent class is used to create the child class.	ActiveX EXE ActiveX DLL ActiveX control
GlobalSingleUse	Same as SingleUse except that the client does not have to explicitly instantiate the object. Rather, its procedures are called as if they were global functions built into VB.	Commonly used for utility classes that add functionality to VB.	ActiveX EXE

TABLE 5.1: Valid Settings for a Class' Instancing Property *(continued)*

Setting	Description	When to Use	Project
GlobalMultiUse	Same as MultiUse with the functionality described for GlobalSingleUse.	Same as GlobalSingleUse.	ActiveX EXE ActiveX DLL

Creating ActiveX Controls

Working with ActiveX controls is significantly more complex than working with any of the other VB project types. In order to successfully create a control you must:

- understand a control's lifecycle.
- persist design time properties.
- examine the control's container.

In addition we will look at the more advanced topics of creating:

- custom property pages.
- a control that can be both a data source and consumer.

Understanding ActiveX Controls

As explained earlier, ActiveX components act as server components to client applications. Controls have an added complexity because they can exist in a client application in both design mode and run mode. In order to differentiate between when the control is in design mode of a client and when it is in the middle of being developed in the design mode of a control project, we will use the following categories:

Design mode The control is in design mode when it is being developed inside the VB development environment by the *control developer*.

Client design mode A control is in client design mode when a *client developer* takes the control from the Toolbox and places it on a form. Technically, when the control is in client design mode, it is actually running and executing the code within its property procedures. This fact is very important when it comes to persisting properties, as you will see later.

Run mode A control is in run mode when either a client developer puts the application that contains an instance of the control into run mode, or when a compiled version of the client application is in run mode.

To create a control, VB supplies you with a control designer and a corresponding object called a UserControl. It has a visual designer like the standard form upon which you place controls from the Toolbox. Controls placed on a UserControl are known as *constituent controls*. UserControl also has a code window in which you can add properties, procedures, and events.

An ActiveX control can be either part of a project or a stand-alone component compiled into an `.ocx` file that can be added to the VB Toolbox or embedded into a Web page.

Understanding a Control's Lifecycle

This section discusses a control's lifecycle when it is used by a client. Knowledge of a control's lifecycle is required in order to properly handle control initialization and property persistence. A control's lifecycle is very volatile—throughout client development it is constantly being created and destroyed. There are several events that fire during the creation and destruction process. Table 5.2 describes the lifecycle and its associated events. The usage of these events is discussed in the next section, "Creating and Persisting Properties."

TABLE 5.2: A Control's Lifecycle in a Client Application

Cause	Creation/Destruction	Events
Control is taken from the Toolbox and placed on a form.	Creation	Initialize InitProperties
Client developer closes form.	Destruction	WriteProperties Terminate
Client developer opens form.	Creation	Initialize ReadProperties
Project is put into run mode.	Destruction when design mode ends.	WriteProperties Terminate
	Creation when run mode begins.	Initialize ReadProperties

TABLE 5.2: A Control's Lifecycle in a Client Application *(continued)*

Cause	Creation/Destruction	Events
Project is put back into design mode.	Destruction when run mode ends.	WriteProperties Terminate
	Creation when design mode begins	Initialize ReadProperties
Form is saved.	Status quo	WriteProperties
Project is closed, thereby closing the form.	Destruction	WriteProperties Terminate
Project is opened for a new design session, and form is shown for the first time.	Creation	Initialize ReadProperties (For some reason, WriteProperties is also fired at this point.)

Creating and Persisting Properties

There are two sets of properties for a UserControl: properties available to the control developer and properties available to the client developer. This section discusses client properties. There are several standard properties (and events) that come free with the UserControl, including:

- Name
- Height
- Width
- Visible

These properties are provided by the Extender object. All UserControls contain an implicit reference to the Extender object. You can examine the values the client sets for these properties by referencing the Extender object as follows:

```
UserControl1.Caption=Extender.Name
```

However, you should never attempt to change the Extender properties; they are intended for the client developer's use and any changes you make may result in unexpected behavior.

In order to provide custom properties for your control you must add property let/get/set procedures the same way you add them to class modules (described earlier in "Using Property Procedures and Variables"). Of course, you must add code to these property procedures in order to implement the desired results.

Whenever a control is instantiated in a client environment it is in run mode, even if the client is using the control in design mode. When properties of the control are changed, the associated property let procedure runs and stores the new value in memory maintained by the runtime instance of the control. Therefore, when the control is destroyed, all of its property settings are lost. For properties set during client runtime this is fine because you don't want the runtime state to carry over into design time. However, you do want properties set in design time to carry over to when the control is re-created. For instance, let's say the default name of your control is 'Widget1'. When a client developer sets the Name property to 'wdg1', the Name property procedure runs, and the control stores 'wdg1' in a variable. When the developer closes the form, the control and all its state, including its variables, are destroyed. Therefore, when the developer reopens the form and a new instance of the control is created, it will have the default name of 'Widget1'. In order to maintain state across the destruction and creation of a control, you must manually save the properties when the control is destroyed and set them when the control is created.

The UserControl has two events that tell you when to persist and read properties. These events also pass you an object called a PropertyBag in which you store the properties. The PropertyBag has two methods:

WriteProperty This method writes a property to the PropertyBag:

```
PropBag.WriteProperty PropertyName as string, Value,
 [Default]
```

ReadProperty This method reads a property from a PropertyBag:

```
Property=PropBag.ReadProperty (PropertyName)
```

The two events of the UserControl that notify you that it is time to either persist or read properties are:

WriteProperties This event fires whenever the control is about to be destroyed and the properties should be persisted. In this event you should call the PropertyBag's WriteProperty method:

```
Private Sub UserControl_WriteProperties(PropBag As _
 PropertyBag)
 With PropBag
  .WriteProperty "Caption",Caption
  .WriteProperty "Value", Value
 End With
End Sub
```

ReadProperties This event fires whenever a control is being re-created. In this event you should write code that reads properties from the PropertyBag into properties:

```
Private Sub UserControl_ReadProperties(PropBag As
 PropertyBag)
 With PropBag
  Caption= .ReadProperty("Caption")
  Value= .ReadProperty("Value")
 End With
End Sub
```

Using these events and methods you can properly persist and set properties throughout the life of your control.

In order to ensure that the control behaves properly when a property is changed you should call the PropertyChanged method:

```
PropertyChanged PropertyName
```

This will ensure that the:

- control's properties window is properly synchronized.
- WriteProperties event is raised when the control is destroyed.
- changes to data-bound properties update the data source.

Examining the Control's Container

The UserControl exposes an AmbientProperties object that provides information about a control's container. There are several reasons why you might need information about the control's container:

- To synchronize the control with its container; for example, if you wanted to match the control's BackColor to the form's BackColor.
- To determine if the control's container supports certain behaviors. For example, you can check whether the container will handle access keys of its contained controls.
- To determine what mode the container is in.

All of the AmbientProperties are read-only. From code you refer to the AmbientProperties object through the Ambient property of the control. Table 5.3 explains the primary AmbientProperties properties.

TABLE 5.3: Primary AmbientProperties Properties

Property	Description
BackColor, ForeColor	Colors of the control's container.
DisplayName	Value of the Name property of the current instance of the control. Should be used when displaying error messages.
Font	Returns a Font object identical to the container's font.
SupportsMnemonics	Indicates whether the container handles access keys for contained controls. Most containers do.
TextAlign	Indicates how the container wants to align text. Takes one the following values: • 0 General—text to the left; numbers to the right • 1 Left • 2 Center • 3 Right • 4 FillJustify
UserMode	Boolean. Indicates whether the control is in run mode (True) or in client design mode (False).

Testing and Debugging an ActiveX Control

This topic is fully covered in Unit 7, "Testing the Solution."

Creating and Enabling Property Pages for an ActiveX Control

VB automatically provides the standard properties window for controls you create using the UserControl designer. You do have the ability to modify the properties window in the following ways:

- Suppress the display of a property.
- Specify the default property to be displayed when the properties window is first displayed.

- Categorize properties to be displayed on the Categorized tab of the properties window.
- Provide a dropdown list of enumerations for a property.
- Connect a property to a standard dialog such as Font or Color.

If your control is complex, a user may find it easier to set its properties using a dialog-style form such as those you find with complex controls like grids and the Windows Common Controls (right-click the control and choose Properties). You can create property dialogs for your controls using the property page designer. This section first discusses modifying the standard properties window and then creating custom property pages.

Modifying the Properties Window

Most of the modifications to the standard properties window that is provided to the user of your control are made in the Advanced section of the Procedure Attributes dialog (click Tools ➢ Procedure Attributes ➢ Advanced) (see Figure 5.1). The standard Procedure Attributes dialog has a combo box that contains all of the procedures in the active module. Choose the desired procedure from the combo box before you set its attributes.

FIGURE 5.1

Procedure attributes dialog

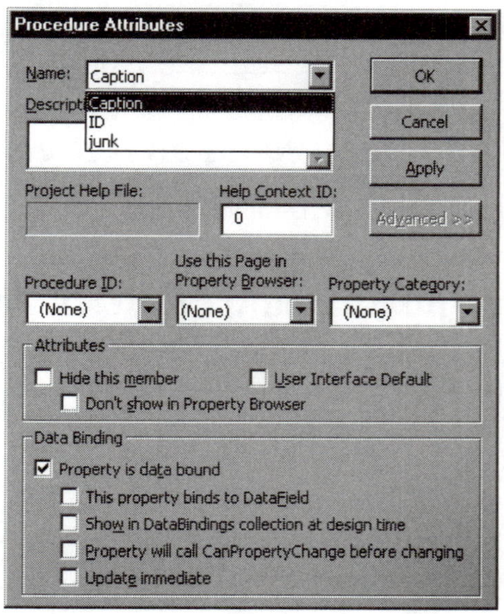

Suppressing the Display of a Property You can suppress a property from being displayed in the properties window. You may want to do this for a runtime-only property. To do so, follow these steps:

1. Open the Procedure Attrributes dialog.
2. Click the Don't Show in Property Browser option.

> **NOTE** The Hide This Member option hides the member from the Object Browser, too.

Setting the Default Display Property To make a property the default property that is highlighted when the properties window is displayed for the first time, follow these steps:

1. Open the Procedure Attrributes dialog.
2. Check the User Interface Default option.

> **NOTE** For events, this option indicates that the event is displayed when the user double-clicks the control.

> **NOTE** To designate a default code property (when a value is assigned to the control without any property specified) choose (Default) in the Procedure ID list.

Categorizing Properties From VB 5 on, the standard properties window has a Categorized tab that displays properties by category instead of in alphabetical order. By default, all of the control's Extender properties are grouped into appropriate categories while the custom properties you create are grouped into the Misc. category. You can either place your custom properties into predefined categories or make new categories, by following these steps:

1. Open the Procedure Attributes dialog.
2. In the Property Category combo box, either choose a category or type in a new category.

NOTE When you type in a new category, the Procedure Attributes dialog doesn't remember it for use with other properties. You must re-enter it for each property that you want to put in that category.

Providing Enumerations for Property Values If a property has a defined set of values, you can assign an enumeration to the property by following these steps:

1. Create an enumeration of the valid property values with the following syntax:

```
'General Declarations
Enum wdgSize
 wdgSmall
 wdgMedium
 wdgLarge
End Enum
```

2. Set the data type for the property let/get to the enumeration by using the following syntax:

```
Property Let Size(Value as wdgSize)

End Property

Property Get Size()as wdgSize

End Property
```

By doing this, both the control's properties window and code window will display a dropdown of the enumerations when the user attempts to set the property.

Connecting to a Standard Dialog You can use prebuilt dialogs for properties that are of the color, font, picture, or data format type. When the user accesses the properties window, the property displays as a button with ellipses, which when clicked, shows the appropriate dialog. To set this up, follow these steps:

1. Open the Procedure Attributes dialog.
2. In the Use This Page In The Browser list, choose the appropriate dialog.

Creating Custom Property Pages

If setting your control's properties is a complex task, then you may want to provide your users with a dialog-style property page. VB provides a designer that creates property pages that have a (`.pag`) extension. Like a standard VB form, it has a visual designer upon which you can place controls from the Toolbox and a code window that has events for its associated *PropertyPage* object and for the constituent controls that are placed on the property page. You can create a property page that allows the client developer to set multiple properties of a control. The property page is linked to the control and a client developer accesses it by right-clicking the control. You can also create a property page for a single complex property. Such a property page is linked to the property and is accessed by clicking the ellipses displayed for the property in the control's properties window. The steps for creating property pages are:

1. Add a property page to the project by clicking Project ➢ Add Property Page.
2. Design the interface by placing controls on the page.
3. Add functionality by writing code in the property page's code window.
4. Connect a control to the property page.

Designing the Interface The interface of the property page should have all the necessary elements (such as text boxes, lists, and check boxes) to allow the user to set the desired properties. You must programmatically read the values of these controls and set the control's properties when the user clicks OK. You do not have to supply OK, Cancel, and Apply buttons; the property page provides them for free.

Writing Code for the Property Page After designing the interface, you have to add functionality to the property page. It does not set control properties by itself. It is also possible to connect multiple controls to a property page; therefore, you may have to determine which controls are currently selected by the user. The property page has a PropertyPage object that has event procedures in which you perform these tasks. Here are the basic coding tasks and their associated events:

Determine which control(s) the user has selected The *SelectionChanged* event is fired when the user first displays the property page or changes the selection of controls. Use the PropertyPage object's *SelectedControls* collection to determine which control(s) the user has selected.

Initialize the property page appropriately for the selected control(s) The property page should be initialized to display the current property values. If the user has selected multiple instances of the same control, the property page should only display a property value that is the same for all the controls. If the property page is connected to multiple controls then you should check whether the user selected more than one type of control. If the user has done so, then the property page should only allow the user to change properties that are common to all the controls.

Notify the property page that a property has changed Doing so achieves two things: it tells the property page to raise the *ApplyChanges* event when the user clicks OK, and enables the Apply button which is disabled until the property page is notified that the user has changed a property. To notify the property page, set the PropertyPage's *Changed* property to True. You should do this in the event procedures of the controls that the user uses to set a property.

Manually set properties when the user clicks OK or Apply When the user clicks OK or Apply, the ApplyChanges event fires. In this event, you should use the SelectedControls collection to set the properties that the user has changed.

Connect a control to the property page In order to associate a control with a property page, click *PropertyPages* in the control's properties window. A list of the available property pages will display. Choose the appropriate property page.

Connect a single property to a property page As described at the beginning of this section, if you have a complex property that deserves its own dialog, you can also link it to a property page. To do so, in the Procedure Attributes dialog, choose the property page from the Use This Page In The Browser list. Note that this list displays all the property pages in the project, including predefined property pages (as mentioned in "Connecting to a Standard Dialog"). When the client developer clicks the ellipses on the control's properties window to display the property page, the *EditProperty* event is fired. Use this event to initialize the property page with the current property value. If the property page is connected to multiple properties you can determine which property was clicked by examining the *PropertyName* parameter of the event.

Enabling the Data-Binding Capabilities of an ActiveX Control

VB allows you to create ActiveX controls that can be bound to a data source, similar to many standard controls that have DataSource and DataField properties. In addition, you can make multiple fields data-bound, which the client developer sets using the DataBindings collection. Adding data-aware functionality requires very little additional code; most of the functionality is added by choosing the appropriate settings in the Data Bindings section of Procedure Attributes dialog.

To make a field data-bound, follow these steps:

1. Set the control's DataBindingBehavior to `vbSimpleBound`.
2. Open the Procedure Attributes dialog.
3. Choose the property procedure from the list of procedures.
4. Check the Property Is Data Bound option.
5. Check the This Property Binds To Datafield option. This option binds the property to the database field that the client developer specifies as DataField.

The control's properties window will automatically display the DataSource and DataField properties. To enable the control to properly get and set data, there are three things you have to code:

Display the data If you want the data-bound property to be displayed in a constituent control, then you must manually display it by writing code in the property let procedure. The property let procedure runs whenever the underlying data changes.

Notify the control to update the data source When a user changes the data by using your control, you must notify the control to update the data source. To notify the control, pass the name of the property that changed to the control's *PropertyChanged* method. For example, if a text box displays the Text property that is data-bound, then in the Change event of the text box you should write the following code:

```
Private Sub TextBox1_Change()
 PropertyChanged "Text"
End Sub
```

The data source is updated when the user moves off the current record.

Check if property is read-only Before notifying the control that the data source should be updated, you should first find out if the data source is read-only. The control's *CanPropertyChange* method takes the name of a property and returns a Boolean value indicating whether the field can be updated.

If you want multiple properties to be data-bound, then set the control's DataBindingBehavior property to `vbComplexBound`. Set one property as the data field, as described previously. For each additional property, choose the property in the Procedure Attributes dialog and check Property Is Data Bound. This allows the user to bind the property to a database field during runtime using the *DataBindings* collection. To allow the user to bind the property during design time from the properties window, check Show In DataBindings Collection At Design Time.

Creating an ActiveX Control that Is a Data Source

VB allows you to create components such as controls and class modules that can act as data sources to which other components can be bound. This section focuses on creating an ActiveX control data source; the process is similar for class modules. A data source is created using a three-step process:

Set the DataSourceBehavior property The first step is to set the DataSourceBehavior property of the control to `vbDataSource`. This will enable the control to be used as a data source. It will also add the GetDataMember event to the code window.

Implement data connection properties Depending on the nature of your control, you may want to provide properties that indicate information about the data source, such as ConnectionString and RecordSource. You must manually implement such properties using property let/get statements.

Return a recordset to the client When the client sets the DataSource of a control to point to your component, the *GetDataMember* event is fired, and you are expected to return a recordset. In this event you should create a recordset. If the control has properties that indicate information about the data source, then you should configure the recordset accordingly. The GetDataMember event has two parameters:

```
Private Sub UserControl_GetDataMember(DataMember As
 String, Data As Object)

End Sub
```

The Data parameter is what you use to return the recordset:

```
Set Data=rs
```

The DataMember parameter indicates the name of the data member the user has chosen using the DataMember property (explained next).

Add data members In addition to providing a property such as RecordSource that allows a user to indicate the name of a database table or an SQL statement, you can expose predefined data members for the user to choose from. This is a two-step process:

1. In the Initialize event of the control, add items to the DataMembers collection. The DataMember property in the properties window of a control bound to this data source control will display a list of the available data members. If you do not add items to the collection, the client developer will still be able to choose a data member by manually entering its name. The syntax is:

   ```
   Datamembers.Add String
   ```

2. The string argument should be a unique for each item in the collection. For example:

   ```
   With DataMembers
    .Add "Customers"
    .Add "Employees"
    .Add "Orders"
   End With
   ```

3. In the GetDataMember event (described later), examine the DataMember parameter to determine which data set to return to the client. For example:

   ```
   Private Sub UserControl_GetDataMember(DataMember As
    String, Data As Object)
   Dim rs as New ADODB.Recordset
   Dim strSource as String
   Select Case DataMember
   Case "Customers"
     strSource="SELECT * FROM Customers"
   ```

```
Case "Employees"
 strSource="SELECT * FROM Employees"
Case "Orders"
 strSource="SELECT * FROM Orders"
End Select
rs.Open strSource
Set Data=rs
End Sub
```

Creating an ActiveX Document

An *ActiveX document* is an application that can run inside an ActiveX container such as Internet Explorer (IE), MS Binder, or the VB environment (used with add-ins). This section will focus on creating Internet-aware ActiveX documents that are hosted in IE. ActiveX documents allow you to leverage your VB skills to develop applications that can be distributed and run over the Internet.

Developing ActiveX Documents

Visual Basic has two ActiveX document project types: ActiveX document DLL and ActiveX document EXE (see the discussion of DLL vs. EXE at the beginning of this unit in "Creating a COM Component that Implements Business Logic"). When you choose to develop an ActiveX document project, you are provided with an ActiveX document designer that has an associated UserDocument object. The designer has a formlike window upon which you can place controls from the Toolbox and add menus. It also has a code window that contains the events of the UserDocument object and the procedures of constituent controls. The ActiveX document is saved as a `.dob` file and for binary information, as a `.dox` file. When compiled, the visual design and code are compiled into either an EXE or a DLL, depending on the project type. VB also generates a `.vbd` file that contains the Registry information needed by an ActiveX container to host the document. To run the ActiveX document from Internet Explorer, simply navigate to the `.vbd` file. To run the document during design time, VB generates a temporary `.vbd` file.

In order to create an ActiveX document you must:

- design the user interface.

- write code to add functionality.
- interact with the container.

Designing the User Interface

Designing the user interface is similar to designing standard forms; however, there are two special issues that you must deal with:

Document visibility Because an ActiveX document is hosted in a container application, the visibility of the document depends on the size of the container and where the user scrolls. You may want to control which part of the document is visible for several reasons:

- When it shows for the first time you may want to ensure that a specific section is visible.
- When the user scrolls, you may want to keep certain user interface elements visible.
- You may want to programmatically scroll to a certain position.

Table 5.4 describes the properties and events of UserDocument that allow you to control the document's visibility.

TABLE 5.4: UserDocument Properties, Method, and Events Used to Control a Document's Visibility

	Description	Used For
Property		
ViewportHeight (Read-only) ViewportWidth (Read-only)	The height and width of the container application. These values change as the user resizes the container.	Determining how much of the document is displayed.
ViewportLeft (Read-only) ViewportTop (Read-only)	The xy coordinates of the document that are at the top left corner of the container.	Determining which portion of the document is being displayed.
ScrollBars	Boolean. Sets whether scrollbars are displayed when the size of the container is less than the MinHeight and MinWidth properties.	Setting whether the document can be scrolled.

TABLE 5.4: UserDocument Properties, Method, and Events Used to Control a Document's Visibility *(continued)*

	Description	Used For
Property		
MinHeight MinWidth	See ScrollBars.	
Method		
SetViewPort x,y	Causes the document to scroll to the specified xy coordinates.	Scrolling the document in order to display a specific portion of the document.
Event		
Resize	Fires when the container is resized.	Managing the visible portion of the document.
Scroll	Fires when the user scrolls the document.	Managing the visible portion of the document.

Menu design Since the document will be hosted by a container application, the document's menus will be displayed on the container's menu bar. In order to have well-behaved menus, there are several things you have to keep in mind:

- Give your menus distinct names in order to distinguish them from the container's menus.
- Set the NegotiatePosition property (available in the Menu Editor) to where you want your menus to be displayed.
- Merge your help menu with the container's help menu by naming the menu 'Help' and setting NegotiatePosition to 'Right'.

Writing Code to Add Functionality

Like all other VB projects, you can write code in the code window and implement custom procedures in an active document. What you have to pay special attention to is managing data when the document is destroyed and created. The concept of data persistence and how it's done using the PropertyBag is explained earlier in the "Creating and Persisting Properties" section of this unit. The lifecycle of a document can be very abruptly terminated, especially when hosted in a Web browser. When the user closes the container or navigates to a different document, then the current document is destroyed. In order to manage cleanup code and data persistence, you must be familiar with the following key events of a document's lifecycle:

Initialize This event fires whenever the document is created. Since the document is not yet *sited* in the container, the UserDocument's properties are not available.

InitProperties This event fires when the document is created and if no data are persisted to the `.vbd` file via the PropertyBag.

ReadProperties This event fires when the document is created and if data are persisted to the `.vbd` file via the PropertyBag. It is the same as the ActiveX control's ReadProperties event.

Show This event fires when the document is created and fully sited on the container. The UserDocument's properties are now available.

EnterFocus This event fires when the focus moves from outside the document to the document or any of its constituent controls.

ExitFocus This event fires when the focus leaves the document or any of its constituent controls to outside the document.

WriteProperties This event fires before the document is destroyed and is used for persisting data. It is the same as the ActiveX control's WriteProperties event.

Terminate This event fires when the document is about to be destroyed. Use this event for cleanup code.

Using Code to Interact with a Container Application

Before you interact with a document's container you should first determine which container is hosting the document. Not all containers provide the same functionality. Use the `TypeName` function on the document's Parent property to determine the host container, as follows:

```
If TypeName(UserDocument.Parent)= "IwebBrowserApp"
```

Table 5.5 lists the return values for common containers.

TABLE 5.5 TypeName of Common ActiveX Document Containers

Container	Identifier
Internet Explorer	IwebBrowserApp
MS Binder	Section
Window (e.g., VB environment)	Window

Navigating to Other ActiveX Documents

Each container exposes its own object model through which you can interact with the container. You can access the container's object model through the UserDocument's Parent property. Internet Explorer exposes several methods that you can use to navigate to other ActiveX documents (`.vbd` files) and files (see Table 5.6).

TABLE 5.6 Internet Explorer's Navigation Methods

Method	Description
Navigate filepath	Navigates to the specified file.
GoBack	Acts the same as a user pressing the Back button.
GoForward	Acts the same as a user pressing the Forward button.

Designing and Creating Components that Will Be Used with MTS

In a distributed application there are many shared resources such as service components, database connections, and processor threads. In addition, there are general system services such as security, transactions, and remote activation. The management of these services and resources is known as the *application infrastructure*. The development of an application infrastructure is difficult and costly. Microsoft Transaction Server 2 (MTS), which is part of the Windows NT 4 Option Pack, provides a robust and scalable application infrastructure.

MTS provides its services to COM DLL components. When a component is registered to run under MTS, it automatically benefits from some of the services provided by MTS. However, a component must be specially designed to take full advantage of MTS. Such components can be created with ActiveX DLL class modules (apartment threaded). The MTS type library (`mtxas.dll`) exposes objects with which you can interact programmatically. In addition, ActiveX DLL class modules have a property related to MTS called MTSTransaction-Mode, which is explained later in "Understanding Transactions."

Reviewing MTS Services

The following is a brief description of the services provided by MTS. Later in the chapter, we will look at the implementation details of these services.

Concurrency management In a multiuser environment, multiple clients may request an instance of a single component which can lead to blocked requests. Another thing to think about is component location, since a client may use components that reside on different servers. The synchronization of multiple threads on multiple computers is difficult to work with. MTS provides a *simple concurrency model* that allows developers to develop as if one client is accessing components on one server. MTS manages the multiuser and component location issues behind the scenes. The simple concurrency model is based on the concept of an activity. An *activity* is a logical thread of execution that can involve multiple objects. All the objects within an activity are isolated from objects in other activities. MTS starts an activity when a *base client* requests an object. The base client can then add objects to the activity, as explained later in the section.

Resource management MTS helps conserve memory and enhance performance by managing and dispensing shared resources. MTS keeps components running after they are released by a client in order to have them readily available for the next client request. In some cases, MTS uses *just-in-time activation* to deactivate and reactivate component instances between client method calls, which conserves memory and allows for a greater number of clients to access the component simultaneously. (In "Designing Objects for MTS," later in this section, you will learn how to design components that take advantage of just-in-time activation.) Since database connections are expensive to open, the ODBC resource dispenser provided by the ODBC 3 driver manager pools discarded connections and dispenses them to new clients. The ODBC driver manager is installed with MTS.

Security MTS allows you to apply Windows NT security to components. A great benefit of this is that it is logically easier to map users to a component that represents business functions than it is to map users to a database table. MTS provides an interface from which you can easily perform security administration.

Transactions In a distributed application, a business function may involve updating several data sources. In many scenarios it is necessary for all of the updates to either succeed or fail as a unit. Such functions are known as *transactions*. An MTS transaction allows multiple components to enlist in a transaction and upon the failure of one of the components, MTS can abort the entire transaction.

Remote activation A distributed application in which clients access components on remote servers maintaining client and server remote activation settings is a huge headache. When a component is added to an MTS package, MTS automatically configures the server to allow for remote activation of the component. In addition, when exporting a package, MTS generates a small EXE that painlessly configures the client.

Understanding the MTS Environment

You can run MTS from Start ➢ Programs ➢ Windows NT Option Pack ➢ MTS ➢ MTS Explorer. MTS Explorer is a snap-in to the Microsoft Management Console, from which system services such as Internet Information Server are managed. The console, similar to Windows Explorer, consists of a treeview in the left pane and details in the right pane (see Figure 5.2). In the left pane, the MTS folder expands to display a Computers folder that contains all of the computers that are currently being administered from the console. By default, it contains a My Computer node for the local machine. The My Computer folder contains a folder called Packages Installed. In MTS, DLL components are organized into groups called *packages*. A package defines several bounds:

Unit of distribution MTS facilitates the distribution of components to other machines, and a package is the smallest unit of distribution.

Process boundary All components within a package run in the same process. If one of the components crashes, it affects all the components in the package, but not components in other packages. This is otherwise known as *fault isolation*.

Resource pooling MTS performs resource pooling within a package; therefore, if you have several components that share a common resource, you can enhance performance by grouping them together in a package.

Trusted security domain MTS does not check security when a component accesses another component within the same package.

FIGURE 5.2
The MTS Explorer

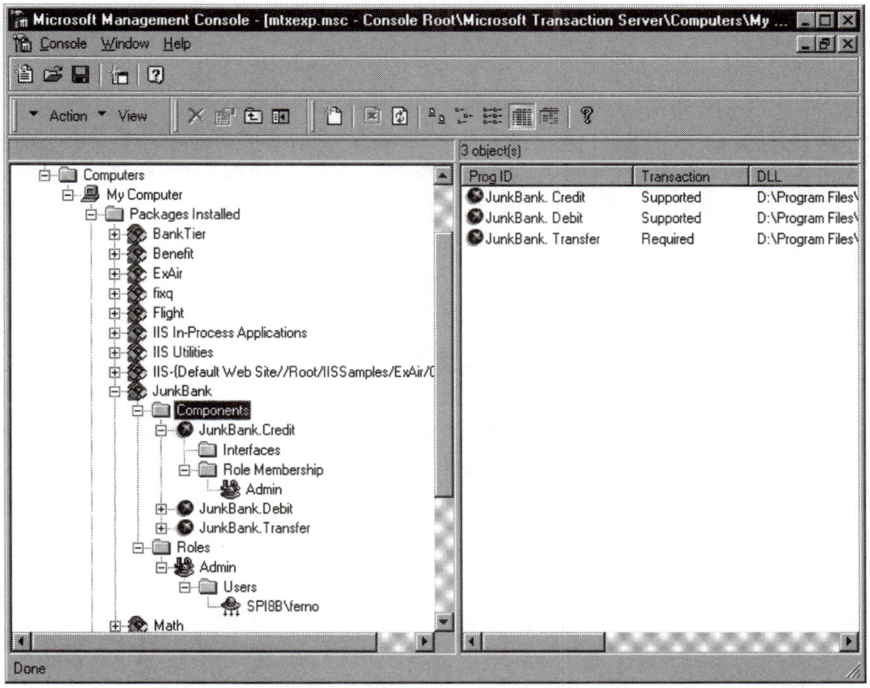

Working with the MTS Explorer

As described previously, the left pane of the MTS Explorer provides a hierarchical view of a computer and its installed packages. This section explains the primary tasks and settings that can be performed at the main levels of the hierarchy.

Using the Computers Folder In addition to managing the local machine, the My Computers folder can be used to administer remote machines. To do so, right-click the Computers folder and choose New ➢ Computer. In the dialog that follows, enter or browse to the remote computer.

Working with Individual Computers An individual computer folder allows you to perform the following computer-wide tasks and properties:

Start/Stop MS DTC In order for a computer to execute transactions, the Distributed Transaction Coordinator (DTC) must be turned on. To shut down or start the DTC, right-click the computer icon and choose Start/Stop MS DTC.

Shut Down Server Processes To shut down all of the components running on the computer, right-click the computer icon and choose Shut Down Server Processes.

Refresh All Components When you add a component to a package, MTS writes special Registry settings that redirect local and remote requests for the component to MTS, and MTS manages the creation and life of the component. When you recompile a component, VB reregisters the component, thereby undoing the MTS settings. The Refresh All Components command rewrites the special MTS settings. To make life easier, you can enable the MTS add-in in the VB environment to ensure that MTS components remain correctly registered.

Transaction Timeout Transaction Timeout is a computer-wide setting that indicates the maximum time a transaction can be active. If a transaction exceeds the limit without coming to completion, MTS aborts the transaction. The default limit is 60 seconds. To adjust it, right-click the computer icon, choose Properties, and enter the new amount in the Transaction Timeout field on the Options tab of the property page.

Remote Server Name When exporting a package, MTS generates an EXE that configures a client machine to remotely access the package's components. By default, it directs the client to the server from which the package was exported. In some cases, this may not be the production server. To indicate the server to which clients should be directed, follow these steps:

1. Right-click the computer icon and choose Properties.
2. On the Options tab of the property page, enter the name of the server in the Remote Server field.

Using the Packages Installed Folder The Packages Installed folder contains all the packages installed on the computer. You can install a new package using the Package Wizard by following these steps:

1. Right-click the Packages Installed folder.
2. Choose New ➢ Package. The Package Wizard displays.
3. Choose to either create a new package or install a prebuilt package from a `.pak` file generated by an exported package from MTS.
4. If you've chosen to install a prebuilt package, then enter or browse to the `.pak` file and click OK and Next.

5. In the Set Identity dialog choose either Interactive User or specify a Windows NT account.

6. If you've chosen to install a prebuilt package, then there are additional dialogs available for indicating where components should be saved to and for configuring security settings.

Working with Individual Packages An individual package folder allows you to perform the following package-wide tasks and properties:

Shut Down This command allows you to shut down all components that belong to the package. As part of MTS' resource management functions, it may keep a component running for a while (the exact amount of time is determined by the Server Process Shutdown property) after a client releases it, in order to have the component readily available when it is requested again. While MTS keeps a component alive it cannot be modified; therefore, if you want to recompile, you may have to shut down the package.

Export This command allows you to create a package that can be exported to other machines running MTS. To do so, follow these steps:

1. Right-click the package and choose Export.
2. Enter the directory to which MTS should save the package.
3. Choose whether you want to save the Security Roles associated with each component. When deploying to a production server you will probably choose not to because the development server typically does not have the same NT accounts as the production server.
4. MTS places the following items in the specified directory:
   - the package's DLLs
   - a `.pak` file generated by MTS that is used by another machine's MTS to install the package
   - a directory called `Clients` that contains an EXE used to configure clients to allow them to access the package's components through remote activation

Enable authorization checking This option, available on the Security tab of the package's property page, indicates whether MTS should enforce the security settings of the components in the package. This setting overrides the Enable Authorization Checking setting of the individual components in the package.

Authentication Level This setting, available on the Security tab of the package's property page, determines how often a client's credentials are checked. They can be checked during the connection, with every single communication, or with the transmission of every packet (there are also varying degrees of security for packets).

Server Process Shutdown This option, available on the Advanced tab of the package's property page, indicates how MTS should manage the components of the package after it is released by its clients. You may choose the Leave It Running While Idle option or set the number of minutes it should continue to run after becoming idle.

Identity This setting, available on the Identity tab of the package's property sheet, indicates the Windows NT account assumed by the components of the package when accessing computer and network resources. The valid options for this setting are:

- Interactive User—This is the user currently logged on to the server. This option should only be chosen on the development server. It allows the components to display a GUI, which may be useful for debugging. However, on a production server it rarely makes sense to have a component run under the account of whoever is logged on to the server.
- This User—Allows you to specify a dedicated NT account under which the components will always run.

Permission–Disable Changes, Disable Deletion These two settings are available on the Advanced tab of a package's property page, and they allow you to protect a package from accidental deletion or modification.

Using the Components Folder Each package has a Components folder that contains all of the components in the package. You can add components that have an associated type library to a package by following these steps:

1. Right-click the Components folder and choose New ➢ Component.
2. Choose Install A New Component(s) (for an unregistered component) or Import Component(s) That Are Already Registered.
3. If you choose to install a new component(s), click the Add Files button, choose the files that you want to install, and click Finish. If the DLL has a separate type library file (`.tlb`), you must select both the component and the type library to register the component correctly.

4. If you choose to install preregistered components, a dialog listing all the registered components will display. Select the ones you want and click Finish.

Using the Roles Folder The Packages folder also contains a Roles folder in which security roles are defined and assigned to the components within the package. A *role* is a group of users. By defining roles you identify a group of users who require access to a component. This is very helpful when moving the components to the production environment; instead of having to map users to a component, you can map them to a role. To create a new role, follow these steps:

1. Right-click the Roles folder and choose New ➢ Role.
2. Enter a name for the role and click OK to create a folder for the role. The name of the folder is the name of the role.
3. The newly created Role folder contains a folder called Users; right-click the Users folder and choose New ➢ User.
4. The standard Windows Discretionary Access List (DACL) displays, which you can use to grant rights to network accounts.

NOTE

The difference between the Identity and Roles assigned to a component is that the Identity is comprised of the credentials the component needs to present when requesting external resources, and Roles are comprised of the credentials of clients who are allowed to access the component.

Working with Individual Components The property page of a component has three tabs:

General This tab displays information about the component's file path and name, ClassID, and package name.

Transaction The settings on this tab determine how a component participates in a transaction. The options are:

- Requires A Transaction—The component must run in a transaction. If it is created by a component that is part of a transaction, then it is added to the active transaction. If it is created by a client or component that is not running under a transaction, it will start its own transaction.

- Requires A New Transaction—The component will always start a new transaction, even when created by a component with an active transaction.
- Supports Transaction—If created by a component with an active transaction, the component will join the transaction; otherwise, it runs without a transaction.
- Does Not Support Transactions—The component never runs under a transaction, even when created by a component with an active transaction.

Security The Enable Authorization Checking setting on this tab determines whether MTS enforces the security settings defined in the component's roles.

A component also has a child node called Role membership. This node allows you to grant security rights to roles defined in Package/Roles. Simply right-click the Role membership node, choose New ➢ Role, and select the appropriate roles from the dialog that displays.

Designing MTS Components

Using VB you can create components that run under MTS. MTS components must be apartment threaded ActiveX DLLs (the default).

When a client requests an instance of a component running under MTS, special Registry settings redirect the request to MTS. MTS instantiates the object and associates it with an object called ObjectContext. The ObjectContext is sort of like a wrapper around the object; all client communications with the object are transmitted through it. It maintains security and transactional information about the object. It also has a method called CreateInstance that allows you to instantiate other MTS components and add them to the current activity. Table 5.7 describes the methods of the ObjectContext object.

TABLE 5.7 Methods of the ObjectContext Object

Method	Description
CreateInstance (*ProgID*)	Instantiates the component specified by *ProgID* and adds it to the current activity.
IsInTransaction	Returns a Boolean value that indicates whether the current object is running in a transaction.

TABLE 5.7 *(cont.)* Methods of the ObjectContext Object

Method	Description
Security	Returns a SecurityProperty object that has several properties that allow you to programmatically identify who is accessing the current object. Its enumerations are: • GetDirectCaller • GetDirectCreator • GetOriginalCaller • GetOriginalCreator
EnableCommit DisableCommit SetComplete SetAbort	Described in the next section.

To programmatically access the ObjectContext of an object, select MTS Type Library (`mtxas.dll`) in the References dialog. The MTS type library exposes a global method (meaning you don't have to instantiate an object to call it) called GetObjectContext that returns the current object's ObjectContext:

```
Dim objContext as ObjectContext
Set objContext = getObjectContext
ObjContext.SetComplete

or

GetObjectContext.SetComplete
```

Understanding Transactions

As described previously, a transaction joins multiple objects into one unit of success or failure. This section explains how to develop components that take part in a transaction. First, however, you must understand MTS' transaction model.

As described earlier in the "Working with Individual Components" section, all MTS components have a transaction setting that determines how a component participates in a transaction. This property can either be set within MTS on a component's property page or in VB on an ActiveX DLL class module's property page under the MTSTransactionMode property. If the property is set within VB, then the MTS property page will reflect the VB settings. However, changes made in the MTS property page will override the VB settings. Visual Basic's naming of the valid settings differs somewhat from the options found on the MTS property page. Table 5.8 lists and describes the different syntaxes.

TABLE 5.8: VB Class Module and MTS Component Transaction Settings

VB Class Module	MTS Component	Description
NotAnMTSObject	N/A	Object does not support MTS.
NoTransactions	Does Not Support Transactions	Never runs under a transaction, even if created by a component with an active transaction.
RequiresTransaction	Requires A Transaction	Must run in a transaction. If it is created by a component that is part of a transaction, then it is added to the active transaction. If it is created by a client or component that is not running under a transaction, it will start its own transaction.
UsesTransaction	Supports Transaction	If created by a component with an active transaction, it joins, otherwise, it runs without a transaction.
RequiresNewTransaction	Requires A New Transaction	Will always start a new transaction, even if created by a component with an active transaction.

Every object in the transaction has the ability to indicate that its task has failed and thereby caused the transaction to abort. There are several flags maintained by MTS that indicate transaction status:

Transaction-Abort The transaction as a whole has an abort flag that by default is set to False. MTS uses this flag to determine whether to abort or commit the transaction.

ObjectContext-Commit The ObjectContext of each object in a transaction maintains a commit flag (otherwise known as a 'happy' flag) that by default is set to True. If an object calls either SetAbort or DisableCommit then the flag is set to False. When MTS evaluates the object's flag and finds it to be False, it switches the Transaction-Abort flag to True.

ObjectContext-Done The ObjectContext of each object in a transaction maintains a flag that indicates whether an object has completed its task, regardless of whether it was successful or not. When this flag is set to True through the SetComplete/Abort methods, MTS deactivates the object and evaluates the ObjectContext-Commit flag. When an object calls Enable/DisableCommit, it changes the ObjectContext-Commit flag but not the ObjectContext-Done flag. The object remains alive and the root object can continue to make method calls to the object in an attempt to have the object set its ObjectContext-Commit flag to True.

When the control returns from the root object to the client, MTS evaluates the Transaction-Abort and either commits or aborts the transaction. This control can return to the client for several reasons:

- When the root object calls SetComplete/Abort—At this point MTS evaluates the Transaction-Abort flag, which may have been set to True via the ObjectContext-Commit flag of any of the components in the transaction. A secondary object cannot affect the life of the transaction. When a secondary object calls SetAbort/Complete it only causes the object to be deactivated, and if SetAbort or DisableCommit was called, then the Transaction-Abort flag is set to True.
- When the root object finishes executing the method that the client called—At this point MTS evaluates the Transaction-Abort flag. It may have been left at False or switched to True by a DisableCommit call of the root object or by MTS when it found a secondary object's ObjectContext-Commit flag to be False.
- When the transaction exceeds the time limit set in the server's Transaction Timeout property, MTS aborts the transaction.

In summary, the typical life of a transaction looks like this:

1. The client instantiates an object that is either marked as Requires New or Requires Transaction and calls a method of the object. This object is known as the root object. The transaction has now begun.
2. The root object instantiates secondary objects using CreateInstance to take part in the transaction.

3. The secondary objects perform their work. If the secondary object is successful, it can either call EnableCommit, which allows the root object to make additional method calls to it, or it can call SetComplete, in which case it is deactivated. If it is not successful, then it can either call DisableCommit, which allows the root object to make additional calls to try to correct the problem, or it can call SetAbort, which deactivates the object and dooms the transaction.

Designing Objects for MTS

This section discusses several issues regarding designing objects for MTS.

Designing Stateless Objects

In traditional object-oriented programming, objects have properties that they maintain in memory. The client of the object rightfully expects the values of properties to be maintained throughout the life of the object. Such an object is said to be *stateful* because it maintains state between method calls. An alternative way of programming is to maintain state in the client and pass all required information to the object as method parameters.

The traditional method of stateful objects is cleaner and easier to work with. It also conserves network resources by limiting the amount of data that has to be transported across the network. However, there are circumstances in which a large number of clients maintaining state on the server would hinder scalability. All scenarios require individual analysis to determine which approach is the best.

An object that takes part in MTS transactions should be stateless. When a transaction is brought to a close because of the SetAbort/Complete methods, MTS deactivates all of the objects involved in the transaction. When MTS deactivates an object, it essentially destroys it and all the state maintained by it. MTS maintains the client reference to the object and performs just-in-time activation to bring it back alive the next time the client calls. However, the object does not have any of its state. MTS does this to ensure transaction isolation.

Pooling Resources

As described previously, MTS works together with the ODBC Resource Dispenser to pool database connections. When an object closes a connection the Resource Dispenser catches it and holds it open for the next object that requests a connection. To take advantage of connection pooling you must:

- Supply the same connection string for multiple connections. Multiple clients can use the same connection only if they provide the same connection string.

- Hold connections as briefly as possible. Acquire them late and release them early so that they are available to the pool.

Instantiating Objects

From within an MTS object there are three ways to instantiate other objects: the standard `CreateObject` and `New` statements and the ObjectContext's CreateInstance method. This section discusses when each should be used.

MTS components When instantiating objects from MTS components, regardless of whether they are part of the same DLL, use the CreateInstance method. This allows the object to be added to the same activity, and if necessary, to the active transaction. If you use the `CreateObject` or `New` statements, then MTS will think that a new client is requesting the object and it will start a new activity for it and possibly a new transaction. This will result in incorrect context information and poor performance. Note that if you use the `New` statement to instantiate an object from a class that is part of the same DLL, then VB does not use COM to instantiate the object. MTS will not know that the object exists.

External non-MTS components When instantiating non-MTS components such as ADO objects, it is safe to use any of the instantiation methods. If you use CreateInstance, the object is created but does not have an associated ObjectContext.

Debugging VB Code that Uses Objects from a COM Component

See Unit 7, "Testing the Solution," for full coverage of debugging client and server components.

Choosing the Appropriate Threading Model for a COM Component

Visual Basic performs threading services behind the scenes, thereby shielding developers from the complexity of allocating and managing threads. Visual Basic does allow for some control of a component's threading model.

> **NOTE** The threading concepts and terminology exposed to VB developers is somewhat different than those used by Win32 API developers, and therefore, may seem inaccurate outside of VB.

A component can expose multiple objects to multiple clients. Each client's request to run a procedure of an object is executed on a thread. There are two basic types of threading models: single threaded and multi threaded.

Single Threaded A single threaded component has only one thread with which to service requests; it must finish executing one request before servicing another. While one request is being serviced, other requests are blocked. Therefore, single threaded components are not scalable enough to be used as middle-tier components. However, they do provide several advantages not available with multi threaded components:

- An MDI form cannot be added to a multi threaded project because MDI parent and child forms must always run on the same thread.
- A modal form is only modal within its thread.
- Drag-and-drop functionality and DDE (Dynamic Data Exchange) communication can only be performed among forms within a thread.

If an ActiveX EXE requires the functionality listed above and must be multi threaded, then you can simulate multi threading by making the project single threaded (by setting its thread pool to 1, as described below) and setting the class module's Instancing property to *SingleUse*. This causes a new copy of the component to be loaded for each object requested. This option consumes a lot of memory.

Multi Threaded A multi threaded component can service a request for each one of its threads. It does not actually run two procedures at once; rather, through preemptive multi tasking, the processor allots time slices for each thread to execute. When it runs out of threads, clients are blocked until a thread becomes available. Each thread runs in its own *apartment*, which isolates it and its data from other threads. On single-processor machines, multi threading does not speed things up; in fact, it will probably slow things down because system resources must now be utilized to maintain and switch threads. The benefit of multi threading on a single-processor machine is that it enhances responsiveness or perceived performance by alternately servicing client requests instead of executing them on a first-come-first-serve basis.

Setting the Threading Model

The threading model of a project can be set on the General tab of a project's property page. The availability of the following options depends on the type of project:

ActiveX DLL The two valid settings are Single Threaded and Apartment Threaded (default). Apartment Threaded is equivalent to multi threaded. You cannot control the amount of threads an Apartment Threaded DLL uses because it runs in-process, and therefore, uses the threads supplied by the client application.

ActiveX EXE An ActiveX EXE doesn't have the Single Threaded/Apartment Threaded options; rather, it allows you to control how many threads are provided by the component. Its options include:

- Thread Pool—When you choose this option you must also specify how many threads should be maintained in the pool. Leaving the number of threads at the default amount of 1 makes the component single threaded. Any number greater then 1 makes the component multi threaded. When the component runs out of threads, clients have to wait until one becomes available. Creating more threads than the system can handle will hurt the performance of the entire system. Limiting the amount of threads will affect only clients accessing this particular component.
- Thread Per Object—This option causes the component to create a new thread for every object created by a client.

Using Visual Component Manager to Manage Components

The Visual Component Manager (VCM) is a graphical user interface built on top of the Microsoft Repository. The purpose of the VCM and the Microsoft Repository is to provide a mechanism to share information among developers. The Microsoft Repository provides a central location to store components and information about the components. The VCM is used to publish, find, and retrieve objects stored in the Microsoft Repository. Together, these tools provide developers with a mechanism to reuse components across development projects.

The term 'component' is used loosely throughout the literature of VCM. Any file that needs to be shared among developers is a component within VCM. The list of components can include:

Visual Basic Projects	Active Server Pages	ActiveX Controls
Visual Basic Forms	Word Documents	Java Classes
Code Modules	Visual Basic Project Groups	HTML Files
User Controls	Class Modules	Visual Modeler Models
COM Libraries	Property Pages	Help Documents
ActiveX Documents	COM Servers	Misc. Files
Java Applets		

The VCM is implemented as an add-in to the VB IDE. There are two components to the VCM: the VCM Explorer and the Publish Wizard.

Understanding the Microsoft Repository

Since the VCM implements services of the Microsoft Repository, you need to understand how the repository works. The Microsoft Repository is a metadata management utility. Its main function is to provide a centralized location to store components and information about the components. It is a nonvisual tool comprised of the Microsoft Repository Engine and a set of COM components called Tool Information Models (TIM).

The Microsoft Repository Engine is an object management layer built on top of a relational database. It controls information being stored and retrieved from the database. It is the link between the relational database schema and the object model of the TIM. A TIM defines the type of information that can be stored within the repository and the objects exposed by the Repository engine to tools like the VCM. VCM uses the Component Description Model (CDE) as its TIM. Any other application that also recognizes the CDE can share information with the VCM.

TIMs have been created to describe various aspects of the development process, including:

- object-oriented analysis and design

- component description and specification
- database schema and data warehousing

Together, the Microsoft Repository Engine and the TIMs act as an object-oriented database management system. The engine dynamically creates objects based on the type definitions of the TIM and the information stored in the database, and returns these objects to queries from applications like VCM.

The Microsoft Repository was designed to work with either Microsoft Jet databases or Microsoft SQL Server databases. Jet databases are used for smaller workgroups to share information among developers, while SQL Server databases are used for enterprise-wide development.

Using the VCM Explorer

The VCM Explorer is a simple user interface that is used to publish, find, and retrieve objects stored in multiple repository databases. The interface consists of three panes:

- the explorer pane
- the contents pane
- the properties pane

The explorer pane displays a hierarchical view of the folders in the repository database. The contents pane displays the contents of the selected folder, and the properties pane displays the properties of the object selected in the contents pane. The properties for objects stored in the VCM are described in Table 5.9.

TABLE 5.9: VCM Component Properties

Property	Description
Component Name	The name of the component.
Type	The component type. This property determines the handler that is assigned to the object as defined in the TIM.
Description	A textual description for the components, which is useful when searching for components.

TABLE 5.9: VCM Component Properties *(continued)*

Property	Description
Keywords	The primary search mechanism. The VCM stores a listing of possible keywords that can be edited by the user.
File Name	The name of the primary object file.
Author	The name of the person who wrote the object.
Date Published	The date when the component was published to the repository.
Usage Count	The number of times the component was added to a project.
Has Source Code	A logical operator that displays whether the component contains source code.
Has Documentation	A logical operator that displays whether the component contains documentation.
Has Help File	A logical operator that displays whether the component contains a help file.
Has Sample Code	A logical operator that displays whether the component contains sample code.

Publishing Components To publish components to the repository, use the Publish Wizard, as described later.

Finding Components The VCM Explorer contains a search utility to easily find components stored in multiple repositories. Searches can be performed on component names, keywords, component types, and text contained within descriptions and annotations. The author, the date the component was published, and the type of additional files contained in the component can also narrow the search.

Retrieving Components VCM provides several functions for retrieving components. The functions that are available depend on the component type that is being retrieved. A list of all of the functions is provided in Table 5.10.

TABLE 5.10: Functions for Retrieving Components from VCM

Function	Description
Add to Project	Adds the component to the current project or adds a reference to the COM server within the current project.
Add to Project Group	Creates a project group if one is not already loaded, and adds the project to that group.
Add to Toolbox	Adds an ActiveX control to the Toolbox of the current project.
Install on this Computer	Copies and installs files to the local computer; for instance, copying and registering ActiveX controls.
Load the Document/File	Opens a document within an associated application based on the file type.
Open	Loads the selected project.
Save to Disk	Copies the selected files to the local computer.

Using the VCM Publish Wizard

The VCM Publish Wizard is a tool used to publish components in a step-by-step manner. The Wizard collects information on the properties of the component. In the first step in the Wizard you select the repository database and folder where the component will be published. The final steps collect information for all of the properties described in Table 5.9. The Wizard also allows you to do the following:

- Add additional files that can be published along with the primary file.
- Set the property that allows COM components to be automatically registered when they are added to a project.

Registering and Unregistering a COM Component

The setup program created by the Package and Deployment Wizard registers all components included in a package. There are several ways to manually register and unregister a COM component depending on the type of component.

For an ActiveX DLL:

- On the development machine, register it by compiling it.
- Register it with `Regsvr32.exe` (ships with VB) by running `Regsvr32` followed by the component's file path and name:

```
Regsvr32 MyDLL/dll
```

- Unregister it by adding the `/u` switch before the filename:

```
Regsvr32 /u MyDLL/dll
```

For an ActiveX EXE:

- On the development machine, register it by compiling it.
- Run the EXE on a computer to automatically register it.
- Register it without running it by entering the component's file path and name followed by `/REGSERVER` at the command line. To unregister it, use the `/UNREGSERVER` argument.

STUDY QUESTIONS

Creating a COM Component that Implements Business Logic

1. If you need to create a component that determines whether a customer's order exceeds her credit limit, you should use a(n) __________ component.

2. If you want to create a stand-alone application that also exposes create-able objects, what kind of VB project should you choose?

   ____

3. True or False. An ActiveX control is out-of-process.

4. Why can't you implement object properties with public variables alone?

   ____

5. When do you use property set, and how is different from property let?

   ____

6. True or False. You implement a read-only property by supplying a property get, but not a property let or set.

7. When a property has multiple parameters, what is the relation between the get and let? Name three rules that apply.

   ____

   ____

   ____

STUDY QUESTIONS

8. When a property let has multiple parameters, which parameter is the actual value of the property? How does the user pass values to the other parameters?

____

____

9. If you declare an event that has a cancel parameter, how do you examine the value of the cancel parameter to see if the user wants to cancel?

____

10. What does declaring a procedure as Friend do?

____

11. If you have an `Order` class that is a child class of a `Customer` class, what Instancing setting should you use?

____

12. An ActiveX __________ component can be SingleUse.

13. ____________ and ____________ are the valid Instancing settings for an ActiveX control.

14. What is the most common Instancing setting for a create-able middle-tier component?

____

STUDY QUESTIONS

Compiling a Project with Class Modules into a COM Component

15. When implementing an object model that has parent and children classes, what is wrong with simply containing the children in a collection variable in the parent class? Give two reasons.

____

____

16. When implementing a wrapper collection class, how do you cause a compiler error if the developer attempts to add a non-child type to the class?

____

Creating ActiveX Controls

17. Which two UserControl events fire when a control is first placed on a form?

____

____

18. Which two UserControl events fire when a form that contains a control is closed during design time?

____

____

STUDY QUESTIONS

19. Which object is passed into the Read/WriteProperties events? Which of its methods should be used in these events?

____

____

20. When do control properties have to be persisted?

____

21. Which method of the UserControl should be called whenever a property is changed? What argument does it take?

____

____

22. The back color of a control's container is determined by examining the ________________ BackColor property.

23. UserMode is a property of which object? What does it indicate?

____

____

24. What must you do to provide a properties window with your control?

____

STUDY QUESTIONS

25. How do you set a property to be the default property highlighted in the properties window when it is first displayed?

____

26. How do you provide a dropdown list of enumerations for a property?

____

27. When creating a custom property page, do you have to add an Apply button? Why?

____

28. How do you determine from within your property page which controls the user currently has selected?

____

29. How do you notify the property page that a property has been changed, and why do you have to notify it?

____

____

30. How does a property page actually assign values to a control?

____

STUDY QUESTIONS

31. How do you connect a control to a property page?

____

32. How do you connect a single property to a property page?

____

33. True or False. To initialize a property page, you write code in the PropertyPage object's SelectionChanged event.

34. In order to make a single property of a control data-bound, what settings must you set?

____

35. In order to make multiple properties of a control data-bound, what settings must you set?

____

36. What does the Show In DataBindings Collection At Design Time setting do?

____

37. Is a data-bound property automatically displayed by the control? If not, where in the control do you write the code to display it?

____

38. What must you do to ensure that a data-bound property updates the data source?

____

STUDY QUESTIONS

39. Before telling the control to update the data source how do you check to see if a bound field is read-only?

____

40. Which property must you set to enable a control to be a data source, and what must you set it to?

____

41. In which event of a data source control do you return a recordset, and how is it returned?

____

____

____

42. When you set a control as a data source which data-aware procedure is automatically added to the code window?

____

Creating an ActiveX Document

43. The file type of a design time UserDocument is ________________.

44. ________________, ________________, ________________, and ________________ are the four properties you use to determine the visible portion of an ActiveX document.

STUDY QUESTIONS

45. How do you merge the help menu of an ActiveX document with its container's help menu?

____

46. During which event of a UserDocument should you persist data via a PropertyBag?

____

47. How do you determine what kind of container is hosting an ActiveX document?

____

48. If Internet Explorer is hosting your ActiveX document, how do you navigate to a different ActiveX document?

____

Designing and Creating Components that Will Be Used with MTS

49. MTS does *not* check security between which objects?

____

50. Does MTS perform resource pooling among components in different packages?

____

51. True or False. When an MTS object crashes, it can affect all the MTS components currently referenced by the client.

STUDY QUESTIONS

52. What does the Refresh All Components command do?

____

53. When should you use the Refresh All Components command?

____

54. What property is used for identifying the server to which the client configuration EXE will direct clients?

55. When should you use the Shut Down command of a package?

____

56. After MTS exports a package to a directory, what does the directory contain?

____

57. What does the Server Process Shutdown property affect?

____

58. How can you protect a package from accidental modification?

____

59. How are users added to a package's Role?

____

STUDY QUESTIONS

60. How are roles assigned to components?

____

61. How do you retrieve a reference to an object's ObjectContext?

____

62. What kinds of information are maintained by ObjectContext?

____

63. What is the difference between DisableCommit and SetAbort?

____

64. What is the difference between the Supports Transactions and Requires A Transaction settings?

____

65. How do you add a component to a transaction?

____

66. Why must MTS objects involved in a transaction be stateless?

____

67. What must you do to allow multiple clients to share a pooled database connection?

____

STUDY QUESTIONS

68. What happens if you use CreateObject to instantiate an MTS component from within an MTS component, and what consequences does it have?

____

69. Which methods of instantiation can you use when creating a non-MTS object such as ADO from within an MTS component?

____

Choosing the Appropriate Threading Model for a COM Component

70. How do multi threaded components enhance performance on a single-processor machine?

____

71. How do you set an ActiveX EXE component to be multi threaded?

____

72. What are the threading limitations of an MDI application, and how do you work around them?

____

Using Visual Component Manager to Manage Components

73. What is the relationship between Visual Component Manager and the Microsoft Repository?

____

STUDY QUESTIONS

74. True or False. VCM components have a property that indicates whether a component has associated source code.

____

75. What are two ways to use VCM to register a component?

____

____

____

Registering and Unregistering a COM Component

76. Name three ways to register an ActiveX EXE.

____

____

____

77. How do you unregister an ActiveX DLL without using the control panel?

____

SAMPLE TEST

5-1 If you want to create a word processor that also exposes create-able classes, what type of VB project should you use?

A. standard EXE

B. ActiveX EXE

C. ActiveX DLL

D. ActiveX control

5-2 In order for a user to run an ActiveX document within Internet Explorer, which file type must they navigate to?

A. `.dob`

B. `.dbx`

C. `.vbd`

D. `.vbx`

5-3 ActiveX controls are:

A. in-process and can be embedded in an ActiveX container.

B. out-of-process and can be embedded in an ActiveX container.

C. in-process and can execute asynchronously.

D. out-of-process and can be downloaded from the Web.

SAMPLE TEST

5-4 Which two statements about property get, let, or set are true?

A. The return value of the property get must always match the first parameter of the property let.

B. When a property let has multiple parameters, then the last parameter must be enclosed in parentheses on the left side of the equal sign next to the procedure's name.

C. When using property set, the client must use the set syntax to set the property.

D. To implement a read-only property, use property let without a get or set.

5-5 In order to raise an event from a class, what must you do?

A. Implement an event procedure in the class.

B. Declare the event and raise it using the `RaiseEvent` statement.

C. Events can only be raised from ActiveX controls.

D. Implement an event procedure in the class and raise it using the `RaiseEvent` statement.

5-6 A child class that depends on its parent class for its creation should be set to:

A. PublicNotCreatable.

B. Private.

C. MultiUse.

D. SingleUse.

5-7 A control's WriteProperties event fires:

A. whenever the control is destroyed.

B. whenever the control is created.

C. when the control is destroyed during design time.

D. when the control is created during design time.

SAMPLE TEST

5-8 How do you connect a control to a property page?

A. Choose the appropriate page in the Procedure Attributes dialog.

B. Set the PropertyPages property displayed in the control's properties window.

C. On the Control tab of the property page, choose the control.

5-9 Where are properties written during the WriteProperties event?

A. in the Property Bag object

B. in any external file

C. in the control's container

D. in the Extender object

5-10 Aside from Initialize, which property fires when a control is placed on a form?

A. ReadProperties

B. InitProperties

5-11 Which object provides information about a control's container?

A. Ambient

B. Extender

C. Parent

D. Propbag

5-12 If UserMode returns False, then the control's container is in:

A. run mode.

B. design mode.

SAMPLE TEST

5-13 In order to provide a standard properties window for your control you:

A. check the Use Property Page option in the Procedure Attributes dialog.

B. create it using a property page designer.

C. do nothing.

5-14 MTS facilitates the deployment of:

A. packages.

B. individual components.

C. individual components or packages.

D. interfaces.

5-15 In order to provide a dropdown list of enumerations for a property, what must you do?

A. Create an enumeration of the valid values and set the data type of the property let/get to the enumeration.

B. Include the valid values as parameters of the property let/get procedures.

C. Enumerations are only provided for predefined property types.

5-16 Where in a property page would you manually set the property values of a control?

A. SelectionChanged event

B. ApplyChanges event

C. Click event of the OK and Apply buttons

D. You don't set them manually, the property page does it automatically.

SAMPLE TEST

5-17 How do you make multiple properties of a control data-bound?

A. Mark one property as Property Is Data Bound and all additional properties as Add To Data Bindings.

B. Mark all the fields as Property Is Data Bound.

C. Mark all the fields as This Property Binds To Datafield.

5-18 Which of the following tasks are necessary when creating a data source control?

A. Check Property Is DataSource in the Procedure Attributes dialog. Set the data parameter of the GetDataMember event to a recordset.

B. Set the DataSourceBehavior property to `vbDataSource`. Connect to the data source in the Connect event. Set the data parameter of the GetDataMember event to a recordset.

C. Set the DataSourceBehavior property to `vbDataSource`. Set the data parameter of the GetDataMember event to a recordset.

5-19 What is the syntax for accessing an ActiveX document's container object model?

A. `UserDocument.Container`

B. `UserDocument.Parent`

C. `UserDocument.Host`

5-20 You can use the Visual Component Manager to store an ActiveX EXE in the Microsoft Repository and another developer can copy and register it on her machine.

A. True

B. False

SAMPLE TEST

5-21 If you have a data-bound property of a control called LastName that is bound to the Lname field and it is displayed in a text box called txtLastName, how would you ensure that the control updates the data source when the user enters new data into the text box?

A. In the Change event of txtLName, write the following code: `PropertyChanged "LName"`.

B. In the Change event of txtLName, write the following code: `PropertyChanged "LastName"`.

C. In the ApplyChanges event of the control, write the following code: `Property-Changed "LastName"`.

D. It's done automatically.

5-22 All ActiveX containers expose the same object model to the UserDocument.

A. True

B. False

5-23 MTS shields developers from multiuser issues with:

A. the concept of an activity.

B. just-in-time activation.

C. distributed transactions.

5-24 What kind of component can run under MTS?

A. any ActiveX component

B. apartment threaded ActiveX DLL or EXE

C. apartment threaded ActiveX EXE

D. apartment threaded ActiveX DLL

E. single threaded ActiveX DLL

SAMPLE TEST

5-25 You have a banking application that has two components: CreditAccount and DebitAccount. Sometimes they work alone. When they work together to transfer money between accounts, the CreditAccount first credits one account and then DebitAccount debits the other account. What transactional setting should each component have?

A. CreditAccount, Requires Transaction; DebitAccount, Supports Transaction

B. CreditAccount, Supports Transaction; DebitAccount, Requires Transaction

C. CreditAccount, Requires Transaction; DebitAccount, Requires Transaction

D. CreditAccount, Supports Transaction; DebitAccount, Supports Transaction

5-26 MTS checks security between:

A. all components.

B. all interfaces.

C. components in different packages.

5-27 Which one of the following is limited to components within a package?

A. transactions

B. resource pooling

C. activities

5-28 When you recompile an MTS component, what must you do in order for clients to access the component?

A. Export the component.

B. Shut down the component's package.

C. Set the Remote Server Name property.

D. Execute the Refresh All Components command.

SAMPLE TEST

5-29 What is a `.pak` file used for?

A. importing a package

B. exporting a package

C. compressing a package

D. re-creating a package

5-30 What is the name of the subdirectory created when an MTS package is exported, and what does it contain?

A. `Clients` subdirectory that contains an EXE that configures a client machine to access the package

B. `Clients` subdirectory that contains the setup program to install the client-side components

C. `Support` subdirectory that contains the files used to create the `.cab` file

5-31 What is the syntax for programmatically scrolling an ActiveX document?

A. `SetViewport x,y`

B. `ViewportLeft=x, ViewportTop= y`

C. `Scroll x,y`

D. `SetViewportLeft=x, SetViewportTop= y`

5-32 What do the Permission properties on the Advanced tab of a package's property page determine?

A. which users can access the package

B. whether a package can be deleted or modified

C. the identity of the components in the package

SAMPLE TEST

5-33 What steps must be taken to grant a user rights to an MTS component?

A. 1. Create a role for the component. 2. Add users to the `Users` subdirectory. 3. Add role(s) to the component's `Role Membership` subdirectory.

B. 1. Create a role for the computer. 2. Add users to the `Users` subdirectory. 3. Add role(s) to a component's `Role Membership` subdirectory.

C. 1. Create a role for the component's package. 2. Add users to the `Users` subdirectory. 3. Add role(s) to a component's `Role Membership` subdirectory.

5-34 Which of the following is a true statement regarding just-in-time activation?

A. Objects must be stateless because they lose their state between method calls.

B. MTS keeps discarded components running in order to have them readily available for subsequent instantiation requests.

C. If MTS detects that an object is not being used, then it deactivates it but maintains the client pointer in order to activate it when the client requests it.

5-35 Which threading model is appropriate for middle-tier components?

A. Apartment Threaded

B. Single Threaded

C. SingleUse

D. GlobalMultiUse

5-36 To implement a property for an object you should use:

A. property get and either set or let.

B. property get and either set or let or a public variable in a GlobalMultiUse class.

C. property get and either set or let or a public variable in any type of class.

SAMPLE TEST

5-37 Which of the following lines of code would conclusively abort a transaction?

A. `GetObjectContext.SetAbort`

B. `ObjectContext.SetAbort`

C. `GetObjectContext.DisableCommit`

D. `ObjectContext.DisableCommit`

5-38 What happens when you set an ActiveX EXE's thread pool to 1?

A. It makes the component multi threaded but limits the pool to one thread.

B. It makes the component single threaded.

C. One is not a valid setting.

5-39 Which one of the following lines unregisters an ActiveX EXE named `MyEXE.exe`?

A. `UnRegsvr32 MyExe.exe`

B. `Regsvr32 /u MyExe.exe`

C. `MyExe.exe /UNREGSERVER`

5-40 When a procedure is declared as Friend, it is:

A. only visible within the class.

B. visible within any ActiveX component.

C. only visible within the component.

D. only visible within the class and any child classes.

SAMPLE TEST

5-41 By looking at the properties pane of the Visual Component Manager Explorer, you cannot determine if a component:

A. has associated source code.

B. has an associated help file.

C. has associated documentation.

D. is currently in use.

UNIT 6

Creating Data Services

Test Objectives:

- **Access and manipulate a data source by using ADO and the ADO Data control.**
- **Access and manipulate data by using the Execute Direct model.**
- **Access and manipulate data by using the Prepare/Execute model.**
- **Access and manipulate data by using the Stored Procedures model.**
    - Use a stored procedure to execute a statement on a database.
    - Use a stored procedure to return records to a Visual Basic application.
- **Retrieve and manipulate data by using different cursor locations. Cursor locations include client-side and server-side.**
- **Retrieve and manipulate data by using different cursor types. Cursor types include forward-only, static, dynamic, and keyset.**
- **Use the ADO Errors collection to handle database errors.**
- **Manage database transactions to ensure data consistency and recoverability.**
- **Write SQL statements that retrieve and modify data.**
- **Write SQL statements that use joins to combine data from multiple tables.**
- **Use appropriate locking strategies to ensure data integrity. Locking strategies include read-only, pessimistic, optimistic, and batch optimistic.**

NOTE

Exam objectives are subject to change at any time without prior notice and at Microsoft's sole discretion. Please visit Microsoft's Training & Certification Web site (`www.microsoft.com/Train_Cert`) for the most current exam objectives listing.

This unit discusses creating data services for distributed applications using ActiveX Data Objects (ADO). In order to successfully create data services you must be able to do the following:

- Work with ADO objects and their properties and methods.
- Choose the appropriate ADO settings for the solution at hand.
- Write SQL statements that retrieve and modify data.
- Retrieve and modify data using Stored Procedures.
- Manage multiuser concurrency issues.
- Manage transactions in order to ensure data integrity.

Reviewing the ADO Object Model

Although full reference to the ADO object model is beyond the scope of this book, this section describes all the objects and their primary properties and methods. The sections that follow it will discuss how and when to use particular objects.

Understanding ADO

ADO is a set of ActiveX components that provides a standard interface for data access. Much like its predecessors, DAO (Data Access Objects) and RDO (Remote Data Objects), ADO exposes objects for connecting to data sources and manipulating and navigating them. Although ADO has greater flexibility and new features, these are not its primary advantage. Rather it is ADO's ability to connect to both relational databases and nonrelational data sources that makes it so useful. This feat is possible because of the OLE DB layer that sits between ADO and the data source.

The OLE DB specification allows for the creation of custom *Providers,* which can be written to access any data store. ADO interacts with the OLE DB Provider, and in turn, the Provider interacts with the data source. This ability to connect to diverse data stores is the goal of Microsoft's Universal Data Access (UDA) scheme. In an enterprise environment where an application may have to access data from many different sources such as SQL Server and Exchange, ADO is the right tool to use.

The ADO object model is very flexible. Its objects can be used both independently and interdependently. In addition, many of its properties can be set in multiple ways. Some properties can be set individually or as part of a composite property or as parameters of a method.

Understanding the Connection Object

The first task in retrieving data is to establish a connection with a data source. ADO accomplishes this with the *Connection* object. Table 6.1 describes its properties and methods.

TABLE 6.1: Connection Object's Properties and Methods

Property	Description

ConnectionString	Specifies the information required to connect to a data source. It is a concatenation of several values in a semicolon-delimited string. Its syntax is:
	`Provider="SQLOLEDB;Data Source=MyServer;Initial _`
	`Catalog=Pubs"`
	Note that Provider-specific values can be included in the ConnectionString. ADO ignores any values it doesn't understand and passes them to the Provider.
	Specifying the DSN (data source name) or Filename alone may suffice since they can contain all the information needed to connect to the data source.

TABLE 6.1: Connection Object's Properties and Methods *(continued)*

Property	ConnectionString Values	Description
ConnectionString (cont.)	Connection String can be comprised of the following values:	
	Provider	Name of Provider.
	Data Source	Name of server.
	User ID	Valid user ID.
	Password	User's password.
	Filename	File-based DSN.
	Initial Catalog	Default data source on the server to connect to.
	DSN	ODBC data source name.
Provider	Same as Provider in ConnectionString.	
DefaultDatabase	Same as Initial Catalog in ConnectionString.	
ConnectionTimeout	Sets or returns a long value that specifies how long to wait for the connection to open in seconds. Default is 15.	

Method	Description
Open	Opens the connection to the data source. Its syntax is: `Connection.Open [ConnectionString],[UserID], _ [Password], [OpenOptions]` The first three parameters are optional because they can be set as individual properties. ConnectionString — Same as ConnectionString property. OpenOptions — Set to adAsyncConnect in order to connect asynchronously.
Execute	Executes the specified command against the data source. Its syntax is: `Connection.Execute CommandText, [RecordsAffected],[Options]`

TABLE 6.1: Connection Object's Properties and Methods *(continued)*

Method	Description	
Execute (cont.)	CommandText	SQL statement or name of data source entity such as a table or stored procedure.
	RecordsAffected	A long variable to which the number of records affected by the Execute command will be returned.
	Options	See Table 6.9 for enumerations.
BeginTrans	Begins a new transaction.	
CommitTrans	Commits a transaction.	
RollBackTrans	Cancels all changes made during the transaction and closes the transaction.	

Understanding the Errors Collection

The Connection object contains an Errors collection that is populated by the Provider with errors returned from the data source. Working with the Errors collection is described in detail later in "Using the ADO Errors Collection to Handle Database Errors." It has the standard Collection properties and methods of Count and Item. It has a Clear method for clearing out the collection.

Understanding the Error Object

The Errors collection is populated with Error objects. The Error object has properties that provide information about the error, as described in Table 6.2.

Understanding the Command Object

The Command object is used to define a reusable operation against a data source. The Command object is also the only way to execute parameterized stored procedures and parameterized queries. The Command object's properties and methods are described in Table 6.3.

TABLE 6.2 Error Object's Properties

Property	Description
Number	Number that identifies the error.
Description	Description of the error.
Source	Name of the object (Object.Name) or application (ProgID) that raised the error. This will usually be an instance of an ADO object.

TABLE 6.3: Command Object's Properties and Methods

Property	Description
ActiveConnection	Either a Connection object or a valid ConnectionString.
CommandText	SQL statement or name of data entity such as a table or stored procedure.
CommandType	See Table 6.9 for enumerations.
Prepared	A Boolean value that specifies whether the Provider should save a compiled version of the command.
Method	**Description**
Execute	Executes a data action against a data source. Its syntax is: `Set recordset = command.Execute( [RecordsAffected], [Parameters], [Options])` RecordsAffected: A long variable to which the number of records affected by the Execute command is returned. Parameters: A variant array of values to be passed as parameter values. These values will override values stored in the Parameters collection. Options: See Table 6.9 for enumerations.

TABLE 6.3: Command Object's Properties and Methods *(continued)*

Method	Description		
CreateParameter	Creates a new Parameter object. The Parameter object must be manually appended to the Parameters collection. This method replaces the several lines of code that otherwise would be needed to create a Parameter object and set its properties. See "Understanding the Parameter Object" for a description of the method parameters. Its syntax is: `Set parameter = command.CreateParameter ([Name], [Type], [Direction], [Size], [Value])`		
	Type	See Table 6.9 for enumerations.	
	Direction	Indicates the direction of the parameter.	
		adParamUnknown	Not specified.
		adParamInput	Default. Input parameter.
		adParamOutput	Output parameter.
		adParamInputOutput	Both Input and Output parameters.
		adParamReturnValue	Return value.

Understanding the Parameters Collection

The Command object contains a Parameters collection, which is populated with Parameter objects that contain parameter information for the data entity (stored procedure or parameterized query) specified in the CommandText property. Table 6.4 describes the properties and methods of the Parameters collection.

TABLE 6.4 Parameters Collection's Properties and Methods

Property	Description
Count	Number of items in the collection.
Method	**Description**
Append	Adds a Parameter object to the collection. You must predefine the parameter before adding it. The syntax for appending is: `Command.Append Parameter`
Delete	Deletes an item from the collection. You can specify either a name or an ordinal position of a parameter.
Item	Retrieves an item from the collection. You can specify either a name or an ordinal position of a parameter.
Refresh	Populates the Parameters collection automatically instead of requiring Parameter objects to be appended manually.

Understanding the Parameter Object

The Parameter object contains parameter information required by either a stored procedure or parameterized query (see Table 6.5).

TABLE 6.5 Parameter Object's Properties

Property	Description
Direction	Specifies the direction of the Parameter object, whether it is input, output, or both. See Table 6.3 for enumerations.
Size	Sets the size if data type is of variant length.
Type	Data type. See Table 6.9 for enumerations.

Understanding the Recordset Object

The Recordset object contains rows of data that may either be the result set of a query or a programmatically built set of columns and rows (new to ADO). Table 6.6 describes its properties and methods.

TABLE 6.6: Recordset Object's Properties and Methods

Property	Description
ActiveConnection	Either a Connection object or a valid ConnectionString.
BOF/EOF	Beginning and End of File. Before the first record or past the last record.
CursorLocation	Location of the cursor engine. This may be either the client or server. See "Retrieving and Manipulating Data by Using Different Cursor Types" section for description and enumerations.
CacheSize	Tells the cursor how many records to fetch from the data source and store in local memory. Cached records will not reflect multiuser changes.
CursorType	Type of cursor. See "Retrieving and Manipulating Data by Using Different Cursor Types" section for description and enumerations.
Filter	A criterion by which the recordset is filtered to contain a subset of the entire recordset. It can be any valid WHERE clause of an SQL statement without the WHERE keyword.
LockType	Type of lock to place on the data source during editing. See "Retrieving and Manipulating Data by Using Different Cursor Types" section for description and enumerations.
Sort	Field(s) that the Recordset is sorted on. The list is comma-delimited and can have the Ascending or Descending keywords at the end.
Method	**Description**
AddNew	Adds a new record. New to ADO is a shortcut that allows you to pass an array of field names and array of values to populate the new record. The syntax is: `Recordset.AddNew [FieldList, Values]`
GetRows	Returns the recordset in a two-dimensional array. The array is automatically dimensioned. A field name or an array of field names can be specified for the Fields parameter to identify which fields to return. The syntax is: `Variant=Recordset.GetRows([Rows], [Start], [Fields])`

TABLE 6.6: Recordset Object's Properties and Methods *(continued)*

Methods	Description
GetString	Returns the recordset as a column and row-delimited string. Currently the string format can only be a delimited (adClipString) string using the RowDelimiter and ColumnDelimiter arguments. The row delimiter defaults to carriage return and the column delimiter defaults to tab. The syntax is: `String = recordset.GetString([StringFormat], [NumRows], [ColumnDelimiter], [RowDelimiter], [NullExpr])`
NextRecordset	Retrieves the next recordset where a stored procedure or compound SQL statement returns multiple recordsets.
Open	Opens a recordset. This method can be used several ways and is discussed in detail in "Accessing and Manipulating a Data Source by Using ADO." The syntax is: `Recordset.Open [Source], [ActiveConnection], _ [CursorType],[LockType],[Options]` The first four parameters are optional because they can be set as individual properties. For the last parameter, Options, see Table 6.9 for enumerations.
Resync	Refreshes the recordset with data from the data source. Discussed in detail in the "Using UpdateBatch Mode and Disconnecting Recordsets" section. The syntax is: `Recordset.Resync AffectRecords, resyncValues` AffectRecords: See Table 6.9 for enumerations. ResyncValues: adResyncAllValues — Refreshes the Value property resulting in lost updates. adResyncUnderlying Values — Refreshes the UnderlyingValue only. Updates contained in the Value property are preserved.

TABLE 6.6: Recordset Object's Properties and Methods *(continued)*

Methods	Description
Save	Saves the recordset to a file external to the data source: `Recordset.Save FileName`
Supports	Returns a Boolean value indicating whether the Recordset object supports any of the following functions: • Addnew • Bookmarks • MovePrevious • Resync • Update • UpdateBatch The syntax is: `Boolean=Recordset.Supports(CursorOptions)`
Update	Updates a record after an Addnew or an edit is performed. New to ADO is a shortcut that allows you to pass an array of field names and an array of values to populate the record. The syntax is: `Recordset.Update [Fields, Values]`
UpdateBatch	Writes pending updates when cursor lock is set to UpdateBatch mode. The syntax is: `Recordset.UpdateBatch AffectRecords`
AffectRecords	See Table 6.9 for enumerations.

Understanding the Fields Collection

The Recordset object contains a Fields collection that represents the columns of the result set. The Fields collection has the standard collection properties and methods of Count and Item.

A new feature of ADO is programmatic recordsets. This feature allows for a recordset to be built programmatically by appending fields to a closed recordset. The recordset must be closed while fields are added and must be opened before being used. Table 6.7 describes the methods used to build a recordset.

TABLE 6.7 Fields Collection's Properties

Property	Description
Append	Adds a new field to the collection. The syntax is: `Fields.Append Name, Type, [DefinedSize], [Attrib]` Type — See Table 6.9 for enumerations.
Delete	Removes an item from the collection. The syntax is: `Fields.Delete FieldName`

Understanding the Field Object

The Fields collection contains Field objects that represent the columns of the result set. The properties and methods of the Field object are shown in Table 6.8.

TABLE 6.8 The Field Object's Properties and Methods

Property	Description
Name	Name of the field.
OriginalValue	Value of the field originally obtained from the data source.
UnderlyingValue	Current value the recordset expects to find in the data source. If it finds a different value then an update will fail.
Value	Current value of field in recordset.

NOTE These properties are discussed in detail in the "Using UpdateBatch Mode and Disconnected Recordsets" section.

The common enumerations for ADO method arguments and object properties are shown in Table 6.9.

TABLE 6.9: Common Enumerations for ADO Method Arguments and Object Properties

Enumeration	Description
Options	Indicates how the Provider should evaluate the command.
adCmdText	Indicates a textual command such as an SQL statement.
adCmdTable	Generates an SQL statement to return all rows from a table.
adCmdTableDirect	Fetches all rows from a table.
adCmdStoredProc	Indicates a stored procedure.
adCmdUnknown	Provider evaluates unspecified type of command.
adCmdFile	Recordset only. Opens recordset from a persisted file.
adExecuteAsync	Executes command asynchronously.
adCmdFetchAsync	Fetches records asynchronously.
AffectRecords	Indicates the set of records to be affected by the command.
adAffectCurrent	Affects only the current record.
adAffectGroup	Affects all records in the current filter.
adAffectAll	Default. Affects all records, even those excluded by the current filter.
Type	Indicates the data type of a Field or Parameter object. (There are many types; only the most common are listed.) adBoolean adChar adCurrency adDate adDouble adInteger adSingle adVarchar

Accessing and Manipulating a Data Source by Using ADO

The ADO object model allows for unprecedented flexibility in accessing data. The objects can be used to access data interdependently or independently.

Using ADO Objects Interdependently

Each one of the primary ADO objects can access and modify data on its own. However, they provide special functionality when used in conjunction with each other. For instance, the Connection object is used to establish a connection to a database that can be used by other Command and Recordset objects. A Recordset can use the Command object to reuse a data action such as a parameterized stored procedure.

To use the ADO objects interdependently, follow these steps:

1. Use the Connection object to establish a connection to the data source.
2. Create a Command object that contains the information needed to perform an action against the data source, such as an SQL statement.
3. Set a Recordset object to the result set of the Command's Execute method. The syntax is:

```
Dim cnn as new adodb.Connection
Dim cmd as new adodb.Command
Dim rs as new adodb.Recordset
cnn.Open "Pubs"
Set cmd.ActiveConnection=cnn
cmd.CommandText="SELECT * FROM Authors"
Set rs=cmd.Execute
```

Each object can be used alone to perform an action against a data source. There are numerous ways to use each object.

Using the Connection Object Independently

In addition to establishing a connection with a data source, the Connection object can also directly execute a data action. In the following code snippet the Connection object opens a connection to a data source and then executes an SQL command:

```
cnn.open "Source:=Pubs" 'DSN
```

The following syntax does not return a result set:

```
cnn.Execute "DELETE * FROM AUTHORS"
```

but this syntax does:

```
Set rs=cnn.Execute("SELECT * FROM Authors")
```

NOTE Only Recordset objects opened using the Recordset's Open method can have various cursor and lock settings (see "Understanding Cursor Operations and Costs" later in this unit). Recordsets opened through the Command or Connection object's Execute method are ForwardOnly and ReadOnly.

Using the Command Object Independently

The Command object can also be used to open a data source and execute a command against it. You can connect a Command object to a data source in two ways: either by opening a new connection based on a Connection String or by using an existing connection opened by a Connection object. The following code also demonstrates how to execute a data action against the data source.

```
cmd.ActiveConnection="Pubs" 'DSN
'or
Set cmd.ActiveConnection=cnn
```

The following syntax does not return a result set:

```
cmd.CommandText=" DELETE * FROM Authors "
cmd.Execute
```

but this syntax does:

```
cmd.CommandText=" SELECT * FROM Authors "
Set rs=cmd.Execute
```

Using the Recordset Object Independently

The Recordset is the only object that can contain a result set; therefore, it is commonly used in conjunction with other ADO objects that return data. A Recordset can be used by itself to open a database connection and fetch data. The following code demonstrates that the easiest way to fetch data is by opening the connection and executing the command in one statement:

```
Rs.Open "SELECT * FROM Authors","Pubs"
'Or it can use the settings of a Command object
rs.Open cmd
```

Accessing and Manipulating a Data Source by Using the ADO Data Control

The ADO Data control allows you to easily open a Recordset from a data source and bind controls to the Recordset (see Table 6.10). The Property window of the data control is the easiest way to set the properties:

- Click the ellipses of the *ConnectionString* property and you are presented with a dialog that allows you to use a data link file, DSN (you can create a new one from the dialog), or connection string (you can build one from the dialog).
- Click the ellipses of the *RecordSource* property and you are presented with a dialog that allows you to choose a command type which may be a table, a stored procedure name, or an SQL statement.

NOTE

A new feature of the ADO Data control is the ability to bind controls to it at runtime. pes of cursors. Table 6.11 explains the features of each one.

TABLE 6.10: ADO Data ControlProperties

Property	Description
ConnectionString	Same as ConnectionString property of the Connection object.
RecordSource	Name of a table or SQL query.
Recordset	Sets or returns a reference to the Data control's Recordset. This property can be set to a valid Recordset object instead of setting ConnectionString and RecordSource properties.

Understanding and Using Cursor Types, Locations, and Locks

The ability to navigate, modify, and lock data is provided by the means of a mechanism called a *cursor*. There are several types of cursors that can be created, and each one consumes different types of resources in varying amounts. They can affect RAM, network bandwidth, and multiuser accessibility. Therefore, it is important to choose your cursor wisely. Inappropriate cursors will adversely affect performance and hinder scalability.

First we will look at various cursor options, and then you will learn how to decide which cursor to use.

Understanding Cursor Operations and Costs

Before you choose from the various cursor types, you must first understand the mechanics of a cursor and how the implementation of its mechanics affects resources.

Cursor population There are two ways a cursor can be populated. A cursor may be populated with the actual records of a result set or it may store pointers that it uses to fetch records as they are needed. Each population method consumes different resources. A cursor that populates with records is larger and consumes more memory. A population of pointers conserves memory; however, when the cursor moves to a new record, it must fetch it from the database.

Multiuser visibility When operating in a multiuser environment another user may make changes to the data after you have already fetched the data. Some cursors provide up-to-date data by querying the database for changes before moving to a new record. Constantly querying the database consumes server resources.

Ability to scroll Some cursors can only scroll forward through a recordset. A cursor that is able to also scroll backward requires more memory to be maintained.

Ability to be updated Some cursors are read-only; they don't allow you to modify the data. Cursors that can be updated contain additional metadata and consume more memory.

Locks Cursors place locks on the data rows or pages during updates in order to ensure data integrity. Locked data is not available to other users and thereby decreases throughput and scalability. In "Reviewing Cursor Locks," later in this section, locks are discussed in detail.

Maintaining data source connections Database connections are a limited, shared resource that should be conserved. Using disconnected recordsets conserves this limited resource (see "Using UpdateBatch Mode and Disconnected Recordsets" later in this section).

ADO has four types of cursors. Table 6.11 explains the features of each one.

TABLE 6.11: Cursor Types

Cursor Type	Population	Multiuser Visibility	Able to Scroll
ForwardOnly	Records. However, the cursor is populated with only one record at a time.	None	Forward only
Static	Records	None	Backward and forward
Keyset	Pointers	Edits, deletions, *not* additions	Backward and forward
Dynamic	Pointers	Edits, deletions, and additions	Backward and forward

Reviewing Cursor Locks

All database management systems must ensure that two users don't update the same data simultaneously, otherwise, there would be data corruption. The way databases ensure this is through locking other users out of the data while it is being updated. Locking the data upon updating is called *optimistic locking*.

Even when data is protected from corruption, there is still a chance of a data conflict. A *data conflict* occurs when a user opens a recordset and modifies a record, but before the user updates the data source, another user modifies the data in the data source. When the first user attempts to commit the changes, the cursor realizes that the underlying data is different from what was originally presented to the user and the cursor blocks the update, triggering a data conflict error. Data conflicts can only occur when updating through recordsets, not when updating through SQL. This is because SQL statements are not based on a previous read of the data, and therefore, don't have an original underlying value to trigger a conflict against.

One way of dealing with data conflicts is to lock the data immediately when the user reads it until she moves off the record. This is called *pessimistic locking*. Pessimistic locking is very detrimental to scalability because the data is locked indefinitely from when the user begins the edit.

Another way of dealing with data conflicts is to use ADO's *UpdateBatch* mode. The UpdateBatch will be discussed in detail in "Using UpdateBatch Mode and Disconnected Recordsets" later in this section. The four lock settings are described in Table 6.12.

TABLE 6.12: Lock Settings

Lock Setting	Description
adLockReadOnly	Data cannot be updated; no locks are placed.
adLockPessimistic	Data is locked upon editing in order to ensure that there will not be any data conflicts.
adLockOptimistic	Data is locked upon updating in order to protect from data corruption.
adLockUpdateBatchOptimistic	Updates are held pending until UpdateBatch is called.

In a multiuser environment where many records may be updated, you should carefully choose your lock setting in order to minimize the number of locks.

Using UpdateBatch Mode and Disconnected Recordsets When a cursor's lock type is set to UpdateBatch mode, all updates to the data are stored in the recordset and are held pending until the UpdateBatch method is called. ADO allows for the recordset to be disconnected from the data source while in UpdateBatch mode. The recordset is fully functional while disconnected. It can later be reconnected and used to update the data source. To disconnect and reconnect a recordset, follow these steps:

1. Set the recordset's ActiveConnection to Nothing.

   ```
   Set Recordset.ActiveConnection=Nothing
   ```

2. Modify data in the recordset.
3. Reconnect the recordset to the data source.

   `Recordset.ActiveConnection=`*`Valid Connection String`*

4. Update the data source.

   `Recordset.Update Batch `*`Affect Records`*

WARNING Do not call the Close method of the connection. Doing so will close the recordset.

The underlying data may have changed while the recordset was in UpdateBatch mode, causing subsequent updates to the record to trigger a data conflict. ADO provides several properties and methods to mitigate this problem (see Table 6.13). These properties allow you to determine which change to keep by comparing the other user's change, your change, and the original value of the record.

TABLE 6.13: Field Object's Value Properties and Resync Method

Property	Description
OriginalValue	The original value retrieved from the data source.
Value	Value currently in the recordset.
UnderlyingValue	Value that the cursor expects to see in the data source before updating it.

TABLE 6.13: Field Object's Value Properties and Resync Method *(continued)*

Method	Description
Resync	Refreshes the recordset with data from the underlying data source. The syntax is: `Recordset.Resync [AffectRecords],[ResyncValues]` AffectRecords — Determines the set of records to resync. This can be the current record, current filter, or all records, regardless of the filter. ResyncValues — Determines which property of the fields to refresh. This may be either the UnderlyingValue property or the Value property.

Here is a step-by-step description of how data conflicts can be handled:

1. UpdateBatch is called.
2. ADO checks the UnderlyingValue property of each field being updated against the actual data in the data source.
3. If the values don't match then the update for that record fails and the record is marked as conflicting.
4. In order to check for conflicting records, set the recordset's Filter property to `adFilterConflictingRecords`.
5. If there are conflicting records, then call the recordset's Resync method with the following settings:

   ```
   Recordset.Resync adAffectGroup, adConflictingRecords
   ```

   This will retrieve the current data in the data source and put it into the UnderlyingValue property of the fields in the recordset. If you specify `adResyncAllValues` as the second argument then the Value property of the fields will be refreshed, washing away any changes made to the recordset.
6. Compare the Value property of the record to the UnderlyingValue and OriginalValue properties, and based on business rules, decide whether to proceed with the update.

7. If you decide to proceed with the update, you can call UpdateBatch again since the UnderlyingValue has been resynced with the data source. The following line updates the current record:

```
Recordset.UpdateBatch adAffectCurrent
```

Reviewing Cursor Locations

ADO allows you to chose from two cursor libraries:

Server-side cursor The server-side cursor maintains the cursor on the server. The benefit of this is that the entire recordset does not have to be passed over the network to be maintained by the client, which may have limited resources. However, beware that the amount of resources consumed by server-side cursors increases with every additional user. Another benefit is that only server-side cursors can be Keyset or Dynamic type that provides multiuser visibility.

Client-side cursor The client-side cursor is maintained on the client machine. Client-side cursors are always Static type. They allow for more functionality than server-side cursors such as disconnected recordsets and sorting.

Making Good Cursor Choices

The key to high-performing and scalable applications is to conserve shared resources. Your choice of cursor directly impacts your shared resources. Here are some basic guidelines for working with cursors:

- Select as few rows as possible.
- Select only necessary columns.
- Refrain from using cursors that can be updated.
    - Fetch data as read-only and issue data modifications as individual SQL statements.
    - If you must have a cursor that can be updated, use a client-side cursor.
- Use cursors that can scroll only when absolutely necessary; consider using a forward-only cursor and scrolling through the recordset once and transferring the data to an array or a programmatic recordset.
- Be careful when choosing a server-side cursor because the amount of resources consumed increases with every additional user and can seriously hinder scalability.

- If the client requesting the data is a server (a shared resource), such as the middle tier in a distributed application, then there is no benefit in maintaining the cursor on the middle tier as a client-side cursor. The data server is better optimized to maintain cursors.
- Client side-cursors are always Static type, which is populated with records. Such recordsets must be small because client-side resources may be limited and transporting the records consumes network resources.
- Forward-only cursors do not consume a lot of memory because they are never populated with multiple records, rather, they fetch only the current record.
- Lock resources as briefly as possible.
  - Avoid using pessimistic locking as discussed in "Reviewing Cursor Locks" later in this section. It locks resources indefinitely from when a user begins to edit.
- Data source connections are a limited shared resource. Use client-side disconnected recordsets (discussed in "Reviewing Cursor Locks" later in this section) to preserve this resource.
- Use the Recordset's CacheSize property to set how many records to fetch at a time, in order to fine-tune when the cursor will have to make network trips to retrieve records.

As you can see from this list, there are pros and cons to even seemingly optimal cursor options. Therefore, managing shared resources requires you to carefully analyze the situation and weigh the options. Here are several scenarios that illustrate this point.

Scenario #1 You are developing for a client server application. You are forced to use a stored procedure that returns a large recordset; however, the user needs only some of the records. The user must be able to update the data. This data is needed only 5% of the time.

Solution Use a server-side, forward-only, read-only cursor. Execute updates with individual SQL statements.

Reason Because it is a large recordset it will be too expensive to transport across the network and to maintain on the client. However, since it is infrequently requested, keeping the connection alive and maintaining it on the server as a forward-only, read-only cursor should not cause a scalability problem.

Scenario #2 You are developing for a distributed application in which the data is accessed from the middle tier. You have a large list of items the user will work with for an extended period of time. The recordset must have the ability to be scrolled and updated. The data is required 85% of the time.

Solution Limit the data fetched as much as possible through the WHERE clause of your SQL statement. Use a client-side cursor in UpdateBatch mode (more on this later in "Using UpdateBatch Mode and Disconnected Recordsets"). After fetching the data, disconnect the recordset, send it to the front end, and close it. After the user finishes working with the data, send it back to the middle tier, reconnect it, and do a batch update.

Reason Since the data is required often, it should not be maintained on the server. By using a disconnected recordset, you preserve database connections and limit the amount of locks placed on the data during updating. By limiting the size of the recordset, you make it feasible to transport it to the front end.

Accessing and Manipulating Data by Using the Execute Direct and Prepare/Execute Models

When issuing SQL statements from code, the Provider must first compile the statement and then execute it. This can cause a performance hit every time the statement is used. The Command object's Prepared property solves this problem by saving a compiled version of the command before its first execution. This will slow down the first execution but will provide enhanced performance on subsequent executions. The syntax for setting the Prepared property is:

```
Command.Prepared = Boolean
```

Accessing and Manipulating Data by Using the Stored Procedures Model

A *stored procedure* is a body of code that can contain SQL statements (both data retrieval and modification), logic, and control flow statements. Stored procedures are stored in the data source; in addition, many database systems precompile stored procedures.

Stored procedures serve several purposes:

Fast execution of SQL When an SQL statement is executed from program code, it must first be parsed and compiled. Many database management systems precompile stored procedures, and therefore, provide better performance.

Enforce business rules Business rules ideally should be in the business tier as opposed to the data tier. However, there are times when it makes sense to put business rules in the data tier. This applies when the rules are simple and involve data actions such as Inserts, Updates, and Deletes. By putting them in the data tier, you increase performance and take advantage of some of the built-in capabilities of the data server.

Better security management In order to allow a user or component to issue a certain SQL statement, you may have to grant him or it write rights to several entire tables. A better way to do it from a security perspective is to put the SQL statement in a stored procedure and grant rights to the stored procedure alone.

Creating Stored Procedures

Stored procedures can contain SQL, logic, and control flow statements. In addition, they can contain *parameters*, which are values that can be passed into a procedure and/or values that are returned from a procedure. Here is the syntax for creating a stored procedure:

```
CREATE PROCEDURE procedure_name
[(parameter1 [, parameter2]
AS sql_statements
```

Parameters are declared with the following syntax:

```
@parameter_name datatype [= default] [Output]
```

- where `@parameter_name` is the name of parameter prefixed with the @ symbol

- `datatype` specifies the data type of the parameter
- `default` is the default value for the parameter; it allows the user to ignore the parameter
- `Output` contains a return value to be passed out of the procedure to the user

Here is a sample stored procedure that returns a recordset and value to the user:

```
CREATE PROCEDURE GetSales
@StoreID varchar, @OrderCount int
AS
SELECT * FROM Sales WHERE stor_id=@StoreID
SELECT @OrderCount=Count(stor_id) FROM Sales WHERE
 stor_id=@StoreID
```

You can create a new stored procedure from within the VB environment by following these steps:

1. Open the Data View window.
2. Create a link to the desired data source.
3. Expand the data link.
4. Right-click the Stored Procedures folder.
5. Choose New Stored Procedure.

A designer type window opens up with boilerplate code for a stored procedure.

Accessing Stored Procedures

Connection, Command, and Recordset objects can be used to execute stored procedures from within your code as follows:

Connection	`Set RS=Conn.Execute (CommandText:="GetSales", Options:= adCmdStoredProc)`
Command	`Cmd.CommandText="GetSales"` `Set RS=Cmd.Execute Options:= adCmdStoredProc`
Recordset	`Rs.Open Source:="GetSales", Options:= adCmdStored-Proc`

However, if the stored procedure requires parameters, then you must use the Command object. The next section describes several ways to pass parameters to the stored procedure.

Setting Values for Parameters

Stored procedures usually have parameters that allow you to pass data into the procedure that will be used as a criterion for the data action of the procedure. There are three ways to set values for parameters.

The first way to set parameter values is to create a Parameter object for each parameter that will be given a value and append it to the Parameters collection. The syntax is:

```
cmd.ActiveConnection = "pubs"
cmd.CommandText = "getauthor"
cmd.CommandType =adCmdStoredProc
Set p = cmd.CreateParameter(Name:="ID", Type:=adVarChar,
 Direction:=adParamInput, Size:=11)
cmd.Parameters.Append p
cmd.Parameters(0).Value = "000-36-5669"
Set rs = cmd.Execute
```

Instead of populating the Parameters collection manually, you may populate it automatically by calling the Refresh method. Although this is easier to code, it can hurt performance because ADO has to make a trip to the server to collect the parameter information. The syntax is:

```
cmd.ActiveConnection = "pubs"
cmd.CommandText = "GetAuthor"
cmd.CommandType = adCmdStoredProc
cmd.Parameters.Refresh
cmd.Parameters("@au").Value = "000-36-5669"
Set rs = cmd.Execute
```

In addition to setting values for each Parameter object, you can pass the values as an array to the Execute method. Values passed in this fashion override values set in Parameter objects. The syntax is:

```
Dim Values As Variant
ReDim Values(1)
cmd.ActiveConnection = "pubs"
cmd.CommandText = "GetAuthor"
```

```
cmd.CommandType = adCmdStoredProc
cmd.Parameters.Refresh
Values(0) = "000-36-5669"
Set rs = cmd.Execute(Parameters:=Values)
```

Using the ADO Errors Collection to Handle Database Errors

There are several types of errors that may be generated during the execution of an ADO operation.

ADO programmatic errors These are handled by the regular VB error handling mechanism.

Data-source–specific errors that are returned by the Provider These are added to the Errors collection. A single ADO operation can trigger several data source errors. Therefore, it is necessary to have a collection to contain them. Before ADO adds the first error for a given operation it clears out the collection. In addition to populating the Errors collection, a runtime error is raised.

Data source specific warnings that are returned by the Provider Warnings are added to the Errors collection; however, a runtime error is not always raised. Beware of warnings when issuing the recordset methods Resync, UpdateBatch, or CancelBatch, or setting its Filter property. If there is a data conflict with some of the records, warnings will then be returned by the Provider. If there is a conflict with all the records, then a runtime error is raised.

Managing Database Transactions to Ensure Data Consistency and Recoverability

If you are making multiple interdependent changes to a database, you will want to ensure the *atomicity* of the transaction. For instance, if you are transferring money between accounts, which involves crediting one account and debiting another, you want to ensure that both actions are successful or that both fail.

Transactions allow you to start a unit of work, perform several data operations, and decide whether you want to commit or abort the transaction.

Transactions can be performed with Microsoft Transaction Server (MTS), stored procedures, or through code with ADO. Generally, transactions that are closely related to data integrity should be put inside a stored procedure. Transactions that are based on complex business logic should be managed in code on the business tier, which is more suitable for programmatic logic. MTS' robust transaction services (see Unit 5 for more on MTS) allow for sophisticated transactions involving updating multiple databases. A simpler alternative where you don't need the power of MTS is an ADO transaction.

ADO transactions are managed with three Connection object methods: BeginTrans, CommitTrans, and RollbackTrans. Nested transactions (starting a transaction within another transaction) are supported by ADO, but may not be supported by the Provider. The BeginTrans method returns a long value that indicates the transaction level.

Writing SQL Statements that Retrieve and Modify Data

The following are commonly used SQL Data Manipulation Language (DML) statements.

To fetch data, use this syntax:

```
SELECT Column1,Column2 FROM Table
```

To modify data, use this syntax:

```
UPDATE Table SET Column1 = Column1 + (Column1 * .01)
```

To create new records, use this syntax:

```
INSERT Table (Column1,Column2) Values(Value1,Value2)
```

To delete rows, use this syntax:

```
DELETE Table WHERE Field = Value
```

The WHERE clause allows you to perform the SQL operation on records that match the specified criteria. The WHERE clause can be appended to the Select, Update, and Delete statements; for example:

```
WHERE Column1 = value
```

Writing SQL Statements that Use Joins to Combine Data from Multiple Tables

When selecting data from multiple tables you can use two different types of joins: inner joins and outer joins. *Inner joins* only return rows in which a matching record is found in both of the joined tables. *Outer joins* return all rows of one table and any matching rows from the other table. For example, if you have a Customer table and an Order table and you want to select only customers who have orders, you must perform an inner join. If, however, you want to select all customers and their orders and you also want to include customers who don't have orders, you must perform an outer join.

There are two ways to perform an inner join:

```
SELECT Customer.CustomerID, Order.OrderID FROM Customer,
 Order WHERE Customer.ID = Order.CustomerID
```

or

```
SELECT Customer.CustomerID, Order.OrderID From Customer
 INNER JOIN Order on Customer.CustomerID = Order.CustomerID
```

As mentioned earlier, an outer join selects all the rows from one table and any matching rows from the other table. Use the LEFT and RIGHT keywords to indicate which table should return all rows. To return all customers:

```
SELECT Customer.CustomerID, Order.OrderID From Customer LEFT
 OUTER JOIN Order on Customer.CustomerID = Order.CustomerID
```

If the Customer table is placed on the right side of the OUTER JOIN statement then use RIGHT OUTER JOIN instead of LEFT OUTER JOIN.

STUDY QUESTIONS

Reviewing the ADO Object Model

1. What is OLE DB?

2. Custom Providers are created for ____________.

A. ADO.

B. OLE DB.

3. List seven values that can be specified in the ConnectionString property.

____

____

____

____

____

____

____

4. True or False. A DSN can be passed as the ConnectionString in order to provide all the necessary connection information.

5. True or False. You can pass the ConnectionString as a parameter to the Open method of the Connection object instead of setting it as a separate property.

STUDY QUESTIONS

6. Which parameter of the Execute method can be set to an SQL statement?

____

7. Which data operations can only be performed with the Command object?

____

8. What are the two values to which the ActiveConnection property can be set?

____

____

9. Can an SQL statement be passed to the Execute method of the Command object?

____

10. True or False. The CreateParameter method creates a new parameter, set its values, and appends it to the Parameters collection.

11. Name two ways in which a connection can be set for a Recordset.

____

____

STUDY QUESTIONS

12. What does the Filter property do, and what is its syntax?

____

____

13. What are the two optional parameters of the AddNew and Update method, and what do they do?

____

____

14. What are the default values for the RowDelimiter and ColumnDelimiter parameters of the GetString method?

____

____

15. What does the NextRecordset method do?

16. What value can be passed as the Options parameter to the Open method of the Recordset object but cannot be passed as the Options parameter to the Execute method of the Connection and Command objects?

____

STUDY QUESTIONS

17. True or False. The Append method of the Fields collection fetches a field from the data source that is not selected in the SQL statement.

18. True or False. The Underlying value is the current value of the field in the data source.

19. What is the difference between the UnderlyingValue property and the OriginalValue property?

____

____

____

Accessing and Manipulating a Data Source by Using the ADO Data Control

20. True or False. The data source of bound controls can be set at runtime.

21. Which properties does the Recordset property of the ADO Data control replace?

____

22. How many objects can be used to open a recordset?

____

23. How is a recordset populated from the execution of a Command or Connection object?

____

STUDY QUESTIONS

24. What are two ways to use the Command object in conjunction with a Recordset object?

____

____

25. Name the four cursors and what they are populated with.

____

____

____

____

Understanding and Using Cursor Types, Locations, and Locks

26. What is the difference between the Keyset and Dynamic cursors?

____

27. Name the four types of locks and the one that locks the data the longest.

____

____

____

____

28. Are read-only cursors backward scrollable?

____

STUDY QUESTIONS

29. True or False. Only client-side cursors can be batch optimistic.

30. By default, a cursor is maintained on the____________.

31. True or False. Client-side cursors are always Static.

32. True or False. ForwardOnly cursors are populated with records, and therefore, should never be maintained on the server.

33. Why does pessimistic locking hinder scalability?

____

34. Why do server-side cursors have the potential to hinder scalability?

____

35. How can the CacheSize property enhance performance?

____

____

36. What is the difference between data corruption and data conflict?

____

____

STUDY QUESTIONS

37. Can a data conflict occur after an SQL update? Explain.

____

____

38. What is the purpose of using pessimistic locking? How does it achieve this purpose?

____

____

39. How does disconnecting a recordset conserve shared resources?

____

40. How would you commit an update on the current record to the data source while in UpdateBatch mode?

____

41. How do you check for conflicting records?

____

42. If there are conflicting records, how can you force an update?

____

STUDY QUESTIONS

Accessing and Manipulating Data by Using the Execute Direct and Prepare/Execute Models

43. What does the Prepared property of the Command object do?

____

Accessing and Manipulating Data by Using the Stored Procedures Model

44. How does the use of stored procedures allow for better security management?

____

45. When does it make sense to enforce business rules in stored procedures?

____

46. Which ADO objects can execute stored procedures?

____

47. When is it necessary to use the Command object to execute a stored procedure?

____

48. What are the two ways to populate the Parameters collection?

____

____

STUDY QUESTIONS

49. If parameter values are specified using the Value property of the Parameter object and by passing the values as an argument of the Execute method, which values will actually get passed to the procedure?

____

Using the ADO Errors Collection to Handle Database Errors

50. Which errors are added to the Errors collection, and which aren't?

____

51. What happens to the Errors collection when the first error for a given action is added?

____

Managing Database Transactions to Ensure Data Consistency and Recoverability

52. What are the three methods used to manage transactions with ADO?

____

____

____

53. When should transactions be managed from ADO as opposed to stored procedures?

____

STUDY QUESTIONS

Writing SQL Statements that Retrieve and Modify Data

54. ____________ is the SQL statement would you use to add a new record to a database table.

Writing SQL Statements that Use Joins to Combine Data from Multiple Tables

55. How would you write an SQL statement that retrieves all customers from the Customers table and any orders that they may have in the Orders table?

____

SAMPLE TEST

6-1 What is the relationship among VB, ADO, and OLE DB?

A. The VB runtime interacts with OLE DB, and OLE DB uses ADO to access the data source.

B. VB interacts with ADO, and ADO interacts with OLE DB, which in turn accesses the data source.

C. VB and ADO do not interact with OLE DB.

6-2 What are two ways to set the ConnectionString of a Connection object?

A. ConnectionString property and as an argument of the Execute method

B. ConnectionString property and as an argument of the Open method

C. ConnectionString property and as an argument of the Connect method

6-3 Which ADO objects can execute parameterized stored procedures?

A. Connection and Command

B. Connection, Command, and Recordset

C. Command

D. Recordset

6-4 An SQL statement can be passed to which method(s) as an argument?

A. Recordset's Open method and the Command object's Execute method

B. Recordset's Open method and the Connection object's Execute method

C. only to the Recordset object's Open method

SAMPLE TEST

6-5 What is or are the valid value(s) for the ActiveConnection property?

A. Valid ConnectionString

B. Connection object

C. Valid ConnectionString or a Connection object

6-6 Does the CreateParameter method automatically append the new Parameter to the Parameters collection?

A. Yes

B. No

6-7 Is it possible to connect to a database and execute an SQL statement with only the Recordset's Open method?

A. Yes

B. No

6-8 How is the UnderlyingValue of the Field object refreshed to reflect the current data in the data source?

A. The Provider does it automatically.

B. It is refreshed with the Resync method.

C. It cannot be refreshed.

6-9 The Recordset property of the ADO Data control can be used in place of which property?

A. ConnectionString property

B. Recordsource property

C. both a and b

D. neither a nor b

SAMPLE TEST

6-10 Cursors that are populated with record pointers:

A. consume more memory than cursors populated with records.

B. require more network trips than cursors populated with records.

6-11 Which cursor reflects multiuser additions?

A. Keyset

B. Multi

C. Dynamic

D. none of the above

6-12 Which cursor(s) cannot be scrolled backward?

A. ForwardOnly

B. ForwardOnly and Static

C. ForwardOnly and Pessimistic

6-13 What are valid settings for a cursor location?

A. client, server

B. client, middle tier, server

C. business tier, data tier

6-14 Which of the following cursors would be most detrimental to scalability?

A. Dynamic, Optimistic

B. Dynamic, Pessimistic

C. Static, Optimistic

D. Static, Pessimistic

SAMPLE TEST

6-15 How can you prevent data corruption?

A. Use a pessimistic lock.

B. Use an optimistic lock.

C. Trap the conflict with an error handler.

D. You don't need to do anything. The database automatically locks the record.

6-16 How can your application manage data conflicts and still remain scalable?

A. by using pessimistic locking

B. by using optimistic locking

C. by using UpdateBatch recordsets

D. by managing conflicts with the database

6-17 If you are working in a distributed environment in which you are accessing data from the middle tier and you have a very large result set, what cursor settings should you use?

A. client-side, forward-only, read-only

B. server-side, forward-only, read-only

C. client-side, static, read-only

6-18 To enhance performance while working with the Parameters collection:

A. use the Refresh method.

B. don't use the CreateParameter method.

C. manually populate the Parameters collection.

SAMPLE TEST

6-19 When is the Errors collection cleared?

A. Whenever you clear it manually.

B. Before the first error for a given operation is appended to the collection.

C. When the Count property exceeds the threshold set in the Threshold property.

6-20 If a transaction may be aborted based on complex business logic, where should it be managed?

A. stored procedure

B. from code using ADO

6-21 Which of the following methods aborts a transaction?

A. RollbackTrans

B. AbortTrans

C. EndTrans

6-22 How would you write an SQL statement that retrieves all customers from the Customers table and any orders that they may have in the Orders table?

A.
```
SELECT Customer.CustomerID, Order.OrderID From Customer LEFT OUTER
  JOIN Order ON Customer.CustomerID = Order.CustomerID
```

B.
```
SELECT Customer.CustomerID, Order.OrderID From Customer RIGHT OUTER
  JOIN Order ON Customer.CustomerID = Order.CustomerID
```

C.
```
SELECT Customer.CustomerID, Order.OrderID From Customer INNER JOIN
  Order ON Customer.CustomerID = Order.CustomerID
```

UNIT 7

Testing the Solution

Test Objectives:

- **Given a scenario, select the appropriate compiler options.**
- **Control an application by using conditional compilation.**
- **Set watch expressions during program execution.**
- **Monitor the values of expressions and variables by using the Immediate window.**
  - Use the Immediate window to check or change values.
  - Use the Locals window to check or change values.
- **Implement project groups to support the development and debugging processes.**
  - Debug DLLs in process.
  - Test and debug a control in process.
- **Given a scenario, define the scope of a watch variable.**

NOTE

Exam objectives are subject to change at any time without prior notice and at Microsoft's sole discretion. Please visit Microsoft's Training & Certification Web site (www.microsoft.com/Train_Cert) for the most current exam objectives listing.

Now that we have covered the major developmental tasks of creating user, business, and data services, we will discuss compiling and debugging an application.

Selecting the Appropriate Compiler Options

When compiling your application VB allows you to choose certain options that may optimize performance. Choose your options wisely. These options have the potential of hurting performance, and some of them can actually cause incorrect behavior, or even worse, fatal errors.

The compiler options can be found on the Compile tab of the Project Properties dialog (Project ➢ Properties ➢ Compiler tab) (see Figure 7.1).

Compiling Native vs. Interpreted Code

Source code can be compiled into either native code or interpreted code. When you compile to native code, the VB code is converted into binary code. This is the same format as executables compiled by C applications. When you compile to interpreted code, the VB code is compiled into p-code (pseudo code), which is a compressed form of the VB code. At runtime the p-code is converted to native code as it is executed.

Comparing Pros and Cons

The main difference between compiling to native code as opposed to p-code is that native code executes faster because it doesn't have to go through the intermediate step of converting to binary code. However, a p-code executable is smaller, and therefore, may run faster because it consumes less RAM. In addition, VB applications spend a lot of time calling external libraries, such as controls and DLLs. Compiling to native code will not significantly enhance these calls and the functionality they provide. Rather, native code is optimal for internal functions such as large calculations or loops. For a full listing of the pros and cons, see Table 7.1.

FIGURE 7.1
Compiler options dialog

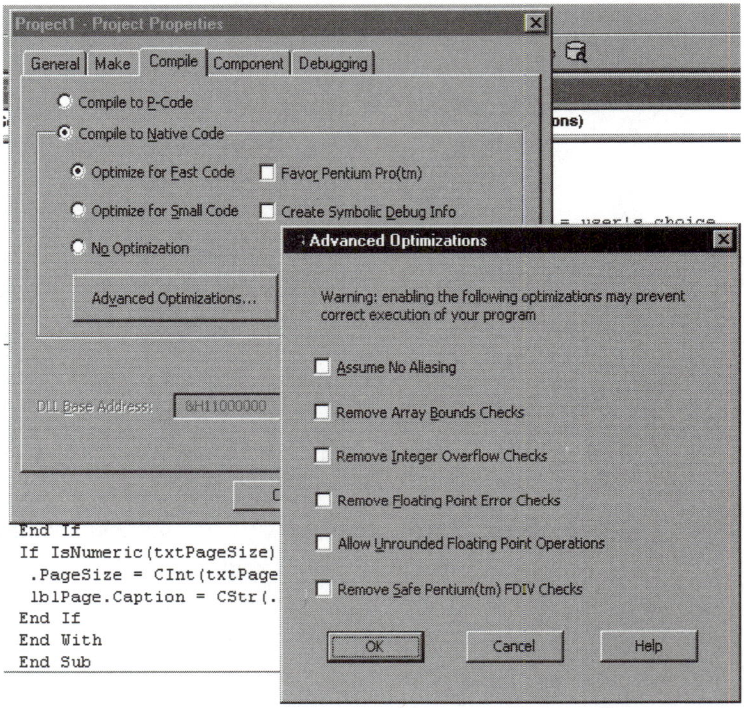

TABLE 7.1
Pros and Cons of Native vs. Interpreted Compilation

Feature	Native	Interpreted
Faster execution	✔	
Smaller EXE		✔
VB runtime DLL required in order to carry out execution of the EXE	✔	✔
Compiler optimization options available (described next)	✔	
Can debug compiled EXE using external debugging tools such as Microsoft's VC++ debugger	✔	

Understanding Compiler Options

The options on the Compile tab of the Project Properties dialog box are divided into two categories: standard (read: safe) and advanced (read: unsafe). Note that if you choose Compile To P-Code then all the options are disabled.

Choosing Standard Options

The standard options are the ones displayed directly on the Compile tab (see Figure 7.1). These options have the potential to enhance performance if chosen appropriately and to hurt performance if chosen inappropriately. However, these options are inherently safe—they won't cause incorrect behavior or crashes. Table 7.2 provides a full listing of the standard compilation options.

TABLE 7.2 Standard Compilation Options

Option(s)	Description
Optimize For Fast Code, Optimize For Small Code, No Optimization	The Optimize options instruct the compiler how to generate efficient binary code sequences by substituting VB code constructs with more efficient binary code sequences.
Optimize For Fast Code	Instructs the compiler to favor fast execution over the size of the compiled program.
Optimize For Small Code	Instructs the compiler to favor a smaller output over code that would execute faster.
No Optimization	This option may be useful if you suspect that the compiler's substitution is causing problems.
Favor Pentium Pro™	Some binary code can be optimized to run on this specific chip. Performance on other chips will be degraded.
Create Symbolic Debug Info	Used for debugging with external debuggers. Generates a .pdb file.

Choosing Advanced Optimization Options

The advanced optimization options are available when you click the Advanced Optimizations button on the Compile tab of the Project Properties dialog (see Figure 7.1). The resulting dialog is accompanied with a warning that reads, "Enabling the following optimizations may prevent correct execution of your program." Actually, some of the options may allow your program to attempt to write to restricted memory locations, which can result in system crashes. Table 7.3 describes each option and the risk it poses.

TABLE 7.3: Advanced Compilation Options

Option	Description	Risk	Safe to Use . . .
Assume No Aliasing	Allows the compiled application to make optimal use of memory storage. This can be invalid when one variable is passed ByRef to two different arguments of the same procedure and accessed by code within that procedure.	Invalid memory access by the application that can result in unexpected behavior.	If you only pass arguments by value (ByVal).
Remove Array Bounds Checks	During runtime, VB checks to make sure that all array access is within valid array bounds. Instructing the compiler not to check speeds up execution but no error will be raised if this rule is violated.	Invalid memory access by the application that can result in unexpected behavior and/or fatal exceptions.	If you are certain that you do not violate this rule.
Remove Integer Overflow Checks	During runtime, VB validates that all assignments to numeric (whole integer) variables are within range of the data type. Instructing the compiler not to check speeds up execution but no error will be raised if this rule is violated.	Incorrect results of numeric calculations.	If you are certain that you do not violate this rule.
Remove Floating Point Error Checks	Same function as integer overflow checks but applied to Floating Point data type.	Incorrect results of numeric calculations.	If you are certain that you do not violate this rule.
Allow Unrounded Floating Point Operations	During runtime, VB rounds off floating point calculation results to the correct precision before using them in comparisons. Instructing the compiler not to round off speeds up calculations.	Incorrect results of numeric calculations.	If you do not perform equality comparisons on the results of floating point calculations.
Remove Safe Pentium™ FDIV Checks	Instructs the compiler not to generate special code to perform valid floating point division (FDIV) so that it will work on Pentium™ processors that have the FDIV bug.	Incorrect results of numeric calculations.	If you are certain that none of your users use Pentium™ processors from the faulty batch.

Controlling an Application by Using Conditional Compilation

You may need to distribute specialized versions of your software depending on factors such as the user's nationality or hardware platform. In order to do so, you may need to alter segments of your source code. Visual Basic allows you to do this through *conditional compilation*. Conditional compilation instructs the VB compiler which pieces of source code to include in the compilation.

To perform conditional compilation, you must follow these three steps:

1. Define compiler constants.
2. Write conditional code based on the compiler constants that directs the compiler which code to include.
3. Set the desired values for the compiler constants and then compile.

For instance, let's assume that your application needs to reference different external files depending on the targeted user's nationality. You would include all of the nationality-specific code in an `If...Then End If` block. Your `If...Then` statement would be based upon the value of a compiler constant. Before you compiled for a specific audience you would set the constant to the appropriate value. The compiler would then only include the appropriate source code in the compiled program.

Defining Compiler Constants

Compiler constants are special constants that the compiler evaluates when reading conditional compilation statements. They can be defined in three different ways.

Defining Compiler Constants in Code

Compiler constants defined in code are modular in scope, which means they are always private to the module in which they are declared, regardless of where in the module they are defined. Compiler constants can be defined in code with the following syntax:

```
#Const Language=1
```

Defining Compiler Constants in the Project Properties Dialog

Compiler constants defined in the Project Properties dialog are global in scope. If a constant is declared in both the Project Properties dialog and in code, then according to the usual scope rules, modular constants override global constants.

To define compiler constants in the Project Properties dialog, follow these steps:

1. Click Project ➢ Properties.
2. On the Make tab of the Project Properties dialog, locate the Conditional Compilation Arguments field, and enter either a constant and its value or multiple constant/value pairs in a semicolon-delimited list; for example:

   ```
   MyConst1= Value1; MyConst2= Value2; MyConst3= Value3
   ```

Defining Compiler Constants from the Command Line

Compiler constants defined in the command line are global in scope. You can define compiler constants from the command line using the `/d` switch:

```
vb6.exe /make SomeApp.vbp /d EnglishVersion=1:
```

Writing Conditional Code

The only valid conditional compilation code is `If...Then End If` blocks prefixed with #:

```
#If Language=1 Then
 'English specific code
#Else
 'French specific code
#End If
```

Monitoring the Values of Expressions and Variables by Using the Debug Windows

Visual Basic has three debug windows you can work with: Immediate, Locals, and Watch. All the windows allow you to:

- view values of variables and object properties.
- change the values of variables and object properties.

However, each window has its own purpose and capabilities, as you will learn next.

Using the Immediate Window

The Immediate window allows you to execute code immediately without going into run mode. All the code must be on one line. You can enter one statement or multiple statements separated by colons.

You may use the Immediate window in both design and break modes. In break mode, it is commonly used to check or change the value of variables or object properties. In design mode, it is commonly used to test snippets of code.

Using the Locals Window

The Locals window functions only in break mode and displays the values for all variables and object properties in the current module or form. The Locals window is set up as a treeview. Local variables of the current procedure are displayed as top-level nodes of the tree. Values of modular scope are either children nodes of the Me variable for forms and class modules or children nodes of the *ModuleName* for standard modules. The multiple values of objects, control properties, and arrays are also displayed hierarchically in the treeview (see Figure 7.2).

You can change the value of a variable by clicking the Value column of the Locals window and entering a new value.

NOTE If you want to monitor a select set of values or if you want to monitor a specific value across multiple debugging sessions it is better to set up Watch expressions (explained next). The Locals window displays such a plethora of information that it may be difficult to navigate and view specific values.

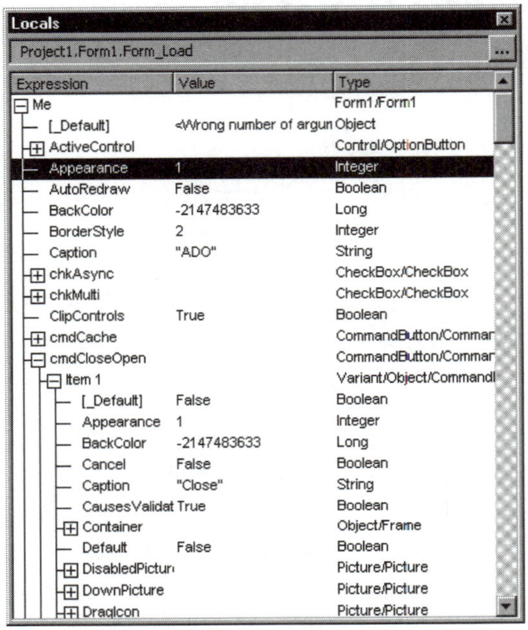

FIGURE 7.2

The Locals window

Using the Watch Window

A Watch expression is an expression that VB monitors during program execution. It allows you to debug complex code by analyzing a specific expression. Watch expressions do not have to be from the program code. They can include:

- variables
- object properties
- expressions (e.g., `strLname="Jones"`)

The Watch window can:

- display the value of the expression. You must manually go into break mode to view the value.
- break when the value of the expression changes. Visual Basic automatically goes into break mode and displays the Watch window.
- break when the value of the expression is True. Visual Basic automatically goes into break mode and displays the Watch window.

Setting Watch Expressions

Watch expressions can be set at both design time and break mode. To set up a Watch expression, follow these steps:

1. In the Debug menu, choose Add Watch. The Add Watch dialog displays, as shown in Figure 7.3.

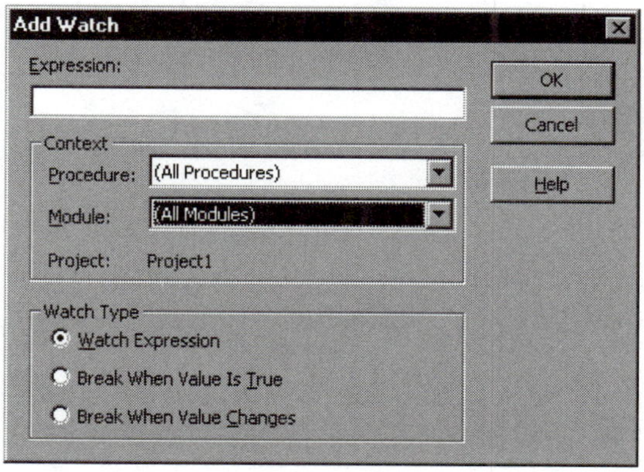

FIGURE 7.3
Add Watch dialog

2. Enter the Watch expression.
3. Choose a context (e.g., scope) for the expression. When you are outside of the specified context, the Watch window will display 'out of context' as the value of the expression. This allows you to limit the evaluation of an expression in case you have the same variable in different scopes or if you only want to monitor a value when it is in a certain procedure. There are two levels of scope that you may set:
   - Module—specifies the name of a module to monitor, such as a form or class; or you may set it to All Modules
   - Procedure—specifies the name of a procedure to monitor; or you may set it to All Procedures
4. Choose one of the following Watch types:
   - Watch Expression—in this setting you must manually go into break mode in order to monitor the expression
   - Break When Value Changes
   - Break When Value Is True
5. Click OK when you're done.

Alternately, use this method:

1. Highlight the desired expression in code window.
2. In the Debug menu, choose Quick Watch.
3. The Quick Watch dialog with the expression, current context, and type set to Watch Expression displays.
4. Confirm that you want to add this Watch expression by clicking Add.

NOTE: The Quick Watch dialog also displays the value of the highlighted expression.

Implementing Project Groups to Support Development and Debugging

ActiveX DLLs, EXEs, and controls supply objects to other applications, and in order to test them, you must have a client application to instantiate them. There are two things you should be able to do from the client application:

- Reference the server.
  - This allows you to declare variables of the server type (early-binding) as opposed to declaring them as Object (late-binding) and using the `CreateObject(ProgID)` method.
  - This also provides you with IntelliSense.
- Step into the server code as it is called from the client.

Using the References Dialog with VB Projects

In order to reference a server component from a client application, you must set a reference to it in the References dialog (Project ➢ References).

The References dialog searches the Registry and compiles a list of components that have type libraries. VB does not provide a way to directly create type libraries; rather, it creates the type library upon compilation of the component and embeds it into the component. This poses a problem with debugging when you want to set a reference to a component before it is compiled.

VB works around this problem by creating a temporary reference for ActiveX DLL and EXE projects. There are limitations to how these references can be referenced, as described later in this section.

NOTE

If the component you're looking for is not listed in the References dialog, you can locate it by using the Browse button. If you are trying to locate a reference to a running VB project, then point to the `.vbp` file.

Understanding Project Groups

The VB environment allows for one instance of the design environment to contain multiple projects of different types within a project group (`.vbg` extension). There are a few things you should know about project groups:

- After closing your projects, they can all be opened again by opening the project group.
- The VB menu and toolbar (aside from commands related to running the application) apply to the project that is highlighted in the Project Explorer.
- One project can be designated as the start-up project. This project will run when VB is put into run mode. To designate a project as the start-up project, right-click the project in the Project Explorer and choose Set As Startup.

Project groups play an important role in debugging ActiveX DLLs and controls, as we will examine next.

Debugging DLLs In-Process

A DLL is an in-process server, and therefore, it can be debugged in-process as part of a project group along with the client application. To create a project group, follow these steps:

1. Open the component project.
2. Add a Standard EXE by clicking File ➢ Add Project. Or click the Add Project button on the toolbar.
3. Choose Standard EXE. Visual Basic will automatically create a project group.

4. Set the Standard EXE as the start-up application by right-clicking the project in the Project Explorer and choosing Set As Startup. The Standard EXE should now be displayed in bold in the Project Explorer.

Now you must reference the server from the client. VB creates a server reference that is available in the References dialog of the client application. VB manages the reference for you; therefore, it will remain valid with the changes to the server.

5. Highlight the client application in the Project Explorer.
6. Click Project ➢ References.
7. Locate the listing for the server and check it.
8. Click OK.

You can now add code to the client application that instantiates and manipulates the server.

Debugging EXEs Out-of-Process

An EXE is an out-of-process server, and therefore, it should be debugged out-of-process in its own instance of the VB environment, separate from the client application. To do so, follow these steps:

1. Click Project ➢ Properties. In the Properties dialog, click the Components tab.
2. In the Version Compatibility field, choose Project Compatibility. This option helps maintain the GUID (Global Unique Identifier) for the type library across builds.
3. For Start Mode, choose ActiveX Component. This option starts the component as a server, as opposed to running it as a stand-alone application.

NOTE

If you run the component as stand-alone, and there isn't any state maintained upon start up (an example of a start-up state is when a form displays), the server will start and then shut down immediately.

4. Put the server component into run mode.

5. Open a new instance of the VB environment. (The temporary reference created by VB is only valid while the EXE is in run mode.)
6. In the client project, click Project ➢ References.
7. Locate the listing for the server and check it.

If during the debugging you receive one of the following error messages, then your reference is invalid:

- Connection to type library has been lost—press OK for dialog to remove reference
- Class does not support Automation or does not support expected interface
- Cannot instantiate ActiveX component

If you check the References dialog you may see the word 'MISSING' next to the listing for the server component. This may be for any one of the following reasons:

- The server component is not running. Put it into run mode and the reference should become valid.
- The GUID of the server's type library has changed, either because you compiled the server for the first time or because VB has changed it for some undocumented reasons. You cannot revalidate the reference, so you must remove it and add a new one, as follows:
  1. Click Project ➢ References.
  2. Locate the server listing and uncheck it.
  3. Click OK.
  4. Click Project ➢ References again.
  5. Locate the server listing and check it.
  6. Click OK.

Testing and Debugging a Control In-Process

An ActiveX control runs in-process, and therefore, it should be debugged in the same instance of the VB environment as the client project. Since the control has design and runtime behaviors you must also test the control while the client project is in design mode. To do so, follow these steps:

1. Open the control project.
2. Add a standard EXE to create a project group by clicking File ➢ Add Project or clicking the Add Project button on the toolbar.
3. Choose Standard EXE.
4. Set the standard EXE as the start-up project. Right-click the standard EXE in the Project Explorer and choose Set As Startup.

NOTE

If you leave the control as the start-up, then when you run the Project, the control will pop up in a browser. You will be able to debug it in process; however, you won't be able to test it in design mode or put code behind its events.

5. Close the control designer. (This activates the control. It should now appear enabled in the Toolbox.)

You can now place an instance of the control on the client form.

NOTE

Remember that the control designer must be closed in order for the control to be activated. If the control designer is open, then the control icon in the Toolbox and instances of the controls will be disabled.

STUDY QUESTIONS

Selecting the Appropriate Compiler Options

1. True or False. Compiler options are found on the Compile tab of the Project Properties dialog.

___

2. Why would you change the compiler options?

___

3. What is the difference between native code and interpreted code?

___

4. What are two reasons why compiling to native code doesn't always enhance performance?

___

___

5. True or False. VB runtime is needed to run programs that are compiled to native code.

6. When is it safe to choose Assume No Aliasing as a compiler option?

___

7. What does the advanced compiler option Remove Array Bounds Checks do, and what risk does it pose?

___

STUDY QUESTIONS

Controlling an Application by Using Conditional Compilation

8. True or False. You should use conditional compilation when you must change segments of code based on the version of the software.

9. What is a compiler constant?

____

10. Where can you define compiler constants?

____

____

____

11. What are the only valid conditional compilation statements?

____

Monitoring the Values of Expressions and Variables by Using the Debug Windows

12. Which two actions do all the debug windows allow you to perform?

____

____

13. __________ and __________ are the two modes in which you can use the Immediate window.

____

STUDY QUESTIONS

14. What kind of code can you execute in the Immediate window?

____

15. In which mode is the Locals window available?

____

16. What is the scope of variables displayed in the Locals window?

____

17. How are variables with form-level scope displayed in the Locals window?

____

18. How do you change the value of a variable in the Locals window?

____

19. The Add Watch dialog is available in which mode(s)?

____

20. What are valid Watch expressions?

____

____

____

STUDY QUESTIONS

21. What can the Watch window do when it evaluates an expression?

22. What are the two levels of scope that can be set in the Watch window?

Implementing Project Groups to Support Development and Debugging

23. Why is it necessary to have a separate test project when debugging ActiveX components?

24. What are the benefits of referencing the component from within the test project?

25. How should the VB environment be set up to test an ActiveX DLL?

26. How should the VB environment be set up to test an ActiveX EXE?

STUDY QUESTIONS

27. What is the most likely reason for the reference to an ActiveX EXE to be invalid and for the word 'MISSING' to be displayed next to it?

____

____

28. If the GUID for an ActiveX EXE has changed, how will it adversely affect your test project, and how can the problem be fixed?

____

29. Why must VB create a temporary reference for ActiveX components?

____

30. How do you set up the VB environment for testing ActiveX controls?

____

31. What do you have to do in order to enable the control to be used in the test project?

____

SAMPLE TEST

7-1 Which debug window is available during design mode?

A. Locals

B. Immediate

C. Watch

D. Monitor

7-2 Which debug window allows you to change the value of a variable?

A. Locals

B. Immediate

C. Watch

D. all of the above

7-3 If you are currently in break mode in the midst of a procedure in Form1 and you want to use the Immediate window to view a public variable called MyName in Form2, what code would you write?

A. None; it can't be done.

B. `?Form2.MyName`

C. `Print MyName`

7-4 If you want to view a global variable named MyName in the Watch window so you can monitor it to see when it changes in a Form1, how should you set the scope?

A. Set Procedure to All Procedures and Module to Global.

B. Set Procedure to All Procedures and Module to Form1.

C. Set Module to Form1; there is no setting for Procedure.

D. Set Procedure to All Procedures; there is no setting for Module.

STUDY QUESTIONS

7-5 Conditional compilation is used to:

A. cause compilation to abort if specified criteria are not met.

B. conditionally compile segments of code.

C. compile the most optimized executable by automatically choosing the appropriate compiler option(s).

7-6 Which of the following are two *invalid* ways of defining compiler constants?

A. in code

B. in the Project Properties dialog

C. in the Package and Deployment Wizard

D. from the command line

E. in the Registry

7-7 Which of the following statements are *not* valid conditional compilation statements?

A. `#IF #End If`

B. `#Select Case #End Select`

C. Neither A nor B is valid.

D. Both a and b are valid.

7-8 In order to debug an ActiveX control you must add a standard EXE to the control project and set a reference in the test project to the control.

A. True

B. False

SAMPLE TEST

7-9 In order for an ActiveX control to be enabled in a test project the:

A. control designer must be open.

B. control designer must be closed.

C. control must be manually put in run mode.

7-10 If a reference to an ActiveX EXE has the word 'MISSING' displayed next to it, what is the most likely reason why?

A. The ActiveX EXE is not open.

B. The ActiveX EXE is not in design mode.

C. The ActiveX EXE is not in run mode.

D. The test project has not been compiled.

7-11 Your application will be running on a machine with limited RAM and the application does a lot of automation using Excel. Will compiling to native code enhance performance?

A. Yes

B. No

7-12 Which one of the following compiler options is always safe to choose?

A. No Optimization

B. Assume No Aliasing

C. Allow Unrounded Floating Point Operations

D. Remove Array Bounds Checks

UNIT 8

Deploying an Application

Test Objectives:

- Use the Package and Deployment Wizard to create a setup program that installs a distributed application, registers the COM components, and allows for uninstall.
- Register a component that implements DCOM.
- Configure DCOM on a client computer and on a server computer.
- Plan and implement floppy disk–based deployment or compact disc–based deployment for a distributed application.
- Plan and implement Web-based deployment for a distributed application.
- Plan and implement network-based deployment for a distributed application.

NOTE

Exam objectives are subject to change at any time without prior notice and at Microsoft's sole discretion. Please visit Microsoft's Training & Certification Web site (www.microsoft.com/Train_Cert) for the most current exam objectives listing.

After your application is created, debugged, and compiled, it's time to distribute it. This unit discusses using the Package and Deployment Wizard to distribute an application. We will also cover configuring client machines to access DCOM components.

Using the Package and Deployment Wizard

The Package and Deployment Wizard (PDW), a member of Microsoft Visual Studio, helps you easily perform all the tasks needed to distribute an application. All packages distributed with PDW can be uninstalled from the Control Panel using Add/Remove Programs. In order to successfully distribute an application you must do the following:

- Assemble all of the required application files such as the EXE/DLL, runtime files, server components, and ActiveX controls.
- Depending on the method of distribution, create a setup program that installs and registers the application and its components.
- Depending on the method of distribution, copy the application files onto distribution media.
- Depending on the method of distribution, publish the application to a Web site from where it can be downloaded.

The following sections explain how to use the PDW to perform these tasks.

Packaging Application Files

PDW helps you collect all the files required by your application. After you're done putting them all together, PDW compresses the files into one or more cabinet files (`.cab`). There are two types of packages that you can create: a standard package or an Internet package.

Creating a Standard Package

A *standard package* is distributed either via disks (floppies or CDs) or a network directory. The package includes a setup program generated by PDW called `setup.exe`. The user runs `setup.exe` to install the application. The following files are included in a standard package:

Application files These files are compressed into the .cab file.

`Setup1.exe` This is the setup program generated by PDW that installs and registers the application. This file is also compressed into the `.cab` file.

`Setup.exe` This program is generated by PDW, and it is the one that the user runs on the target computer. It prepares the files for installation and automatically runs `Setup1.exe`.

`Setup.lst` This file is used by the install programs to provide information about which files to install and where to install them.

Support directory This directory contains the files that make up the `.cab` file and the `.ddf` (Diamond directive file) file that uses the Diamond compression utility (`Diamond.exe`) to create the `.cab` file. You can modify the `.ddf` file to create a modified `.cab` file.

The PDW allows you to do the following when creating a standard package:

- Add and remove files from the package. PDW automatically includes the main application file, server components referenced by the application, and required runtime files. You may need to add other files such as a database, graphics files, or documentation.
- Choose if you want to generate one `.cab` file (typically used for distribution from a network share or CD-ROM) or multiple `.cab` files (for distribution with floppy disks). If you select the floppy disk option, you may choose from several sizes, including 1.44MB, 2.88MB, 1.2MB, or 720KB.
- Indicate Start menu program groups and items that will be created on the target machine.
- Set the install location for the files to be installed on the target machine. PDW allows you to enter a path or choose from predefined constants that point to common locations such as the `Windows`, `System`, or `Program Files` directories. You can add a slash and the name of a folder to point to a subdirectory of one of the predefined constants.

- Mark components as shared files. Shared files are not removed during an uninstall unless there are no other programs using the component.

Planning and Implementing Web-based Deployment

Internet packages are used to distribute ActiveX components (DLLs, EXEs, controls, and documents) and DHTML applications via a Web page. PDW packages the component files only (not the HTML pages) into a `.cab` file. When a browser accesses a Web page that references a component, it downloads the `.cab` file; verifies that it is safe; and unpacks, installs, and registers it. The files that can be included in an Internet package are:

- The `.cab` file that contains the application components.
- The secondary `.cab` file that contains the runtime components such as the VB runtime DLL. If the user already has it on his machine, then this file is not downloaded. Optionally, PDW allows you to point to a Web site to download external components. For instance, you may point to Microsoft's Web site to download the VB runtime components.
- An INF file that contains installation and Registry information. It also references any secondary `.cab` files or external sources for components such as a Web site.
- A sample HTML file that contains the HTML required to reference the components in order to trigger a download.
- A `Support` directory. Same as the one in the standard package.

When you create an Internet package, PDW allows you to do the following:

- Add or remove files from the package.
- Choose whether to place components such as runtime components or ActiveX controls in a secondary `.cab` or to fetch them from a Web site (PDW allows you to choose Microsoft's Web site or to enter a URL of another Web site).
- Mark components as safe for initialization and for scripting. By marking it safe for scripting you are guaranteeing that your components do not and cannot be used to write to or delete arbitrary files on the end user's machine.

NOTE You must have your files digitally signed in order for some browsers to accept your components.

After you have created your Internet package, you can place it on a Web site and distribution will occur via browser download when a user accesses an HTML file that references the components.

Deploying Packages

PDW can assist you in deploying an existing package to floppy disks, CD-ROMs, a network directory, or a Web site. The deployment really can be done manually through copy and paste; however, PDW provides some other tips and shortcuts. When you click Deploy on the opening screen of the PDW, you are presented with three choices:

Floppy Disks This option is only available if you choose the multiple `.cab` option during the packaging. PDW asks you if you want to format the disks before copying to them (if they are already formatted then you don't need to). You must use blank disks.

Folder This option copies files to a local or network directory. Use this option to deploy to a CD-ROM.

Web Publishing This option allows you to add files and directories to be published to a Web site. This is useful for publishing additional HTML and graphical files. PDW will maintain the directory structure when publishing the files. You must specify a Web site to deploy to and the Web publishing protocol (either Post or FTP).

Installing and Registering DCOM Components

DCOM (distributed COM) allows a client application to instantiate and run a COM object on a remote machine. In order for a DCOM connection to work, there are several settings that must be set on both the client and the server:

- client-side Registry settings that point to the remote components on the server
- server-side security settings that allow a client to access the server component
- server-side security settings that give the client application an identity to be used when running processes on the server

Configuring Client-side Settings for DCOM

The first thing that you have to do is make sure that the client supports DCOM. For Windows 95, you must install DCOM for Windows 95, which is available for download from Microsoft's Web site. Later versions of Windows 95 and Windows NT ship with DCOM support.

As you will learn next, there are four ways to configure client-side settings for DCOM.

Using PDW

You can use PDW to configure the client as follows:

1. On the Component tab of the Project Properties dialog, check Remote Server Files. This option instructs VB to generate a `.vbr` file when the component is compiled. The `.vbr` file contains all the Registry keys that have to be added to a client of the server.
2. Run PDW for the client application.
3. On the Included Files screen of PDW, replace the reference to the server component with a reference to the server component's `.vbr` file.
4. After including the `.vbr` file, PDW displays the Remote Servers screen where you can enter the name or IP address of the server that will host the server component. If you leave it blank, then the user will be prompted for the machine name during setup. On this screen verify that DCOM has been chosen for Connection instead of Remote Automation.
5. Run the setup program generated by PDW on the client machine.

Running `CliReg32.exe`

Another method of configuring the client using the `.vbr` file generated by PDW is to run `CliReg32.exe`, which ships with VB. In fact, PDW uses this program for client configuration.

You can run `CliReg32.exe` from the command line, and pass it a `.vbr` file as an argument. `CliReg32.exe` will prompt you for the server name and ask if you want to use DCOM or Remote Automation.

Using DCOMCNFG.exe

DCOMCNFG.exe can be used to configure a client without a .vbr file. DCOMCNFG.exe can be found on computers that support DCOM. You can use it as follows (see Figure 8.1):

1. Run DCOMCNFG.exe from the command line.
2. On the Applications tab select the server application from the Applications list.
3. Click Properties.
4. On the Location tab, select Run Application On The Following Computer.
5. Enter the location of the server computer or browse to locate it.

FIGURE 8.1
Using DCOMCNFG.exe to configure a client

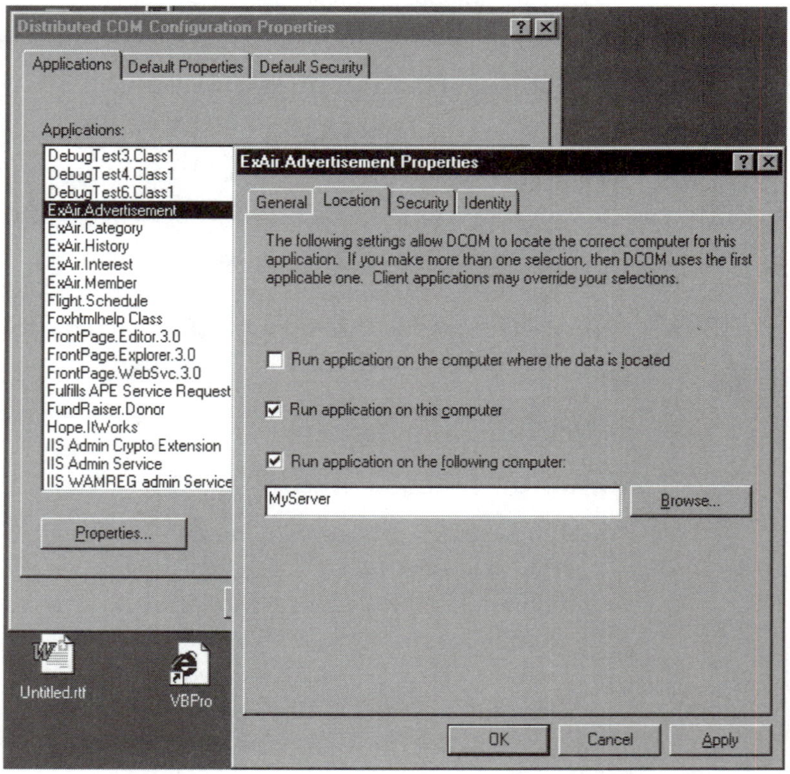

Configuring MTS Clients

Clients of MTS components are the easiest to configure. Here's how to do it:

1. Export the MTS component to create an MTS Package.
2. Locate a subdirectory of the exported package called `Clients`.
3. On the client machine, run the EXE file found in the `Clients` directory.

Configuring the Server

The server for a non-MTS component is configured using `Dcomcnfg.exe`. Configuring MTS components is discussed in Unit 5, "Creating and Managing COM Components."

Setting Default Properties

The machine-wide DCOM settings found on the Default Properties tab of `DCOMCNFG` dialog include (see Figure 8.2):

Enable Distributed COM On This Computer If this option is unchecked then clients will not be able to launch any DCOM servers.

Default Authentication Level This setting determines how often a client's credentials are checked. They can be checked during the connection, with every single communication, or with the transmission of every packet (there are also varying degrees of security packets).

Default Impersonation Level This setting is used to protect the client. When a server authenticates a client, it has access to the client's credentials. This setting determines what a server can do with the client's credentials. The server can use them for authentication only (Identify), access local resources (Impersonate), or access local and remote resources (Delegate). The anonymous setting is not supported and is automatically upgraded to Identify.

Setting Security Rights

In order for a client to access a component on the server he must have the right to do so. There are three levels of permissions that can be assigned:

Access permissions Determines who has the right to access the server component once it is running.

FIGURE 8.2
DCOMCNFG Default Properties tab

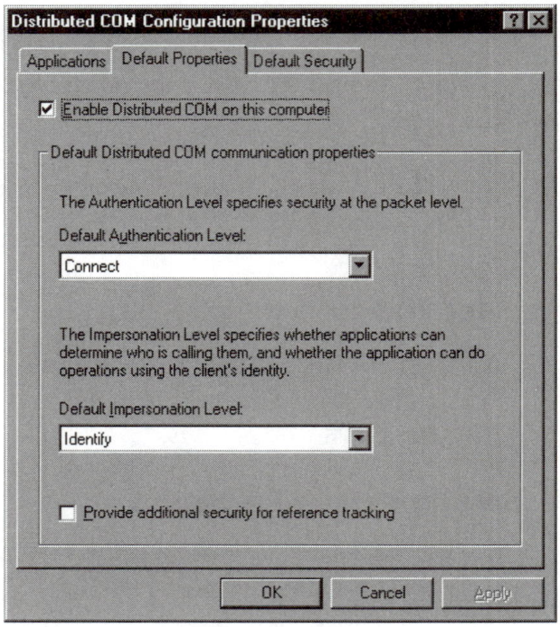

Launch permissions Determines who has the right to start the server component if it is not already running.

Configuration permissions Determines who has the right to change the first two security settings.

These three settings can be set either at the machine level (default permissions), which affects all components on the machine that don't have custom settings, or for each component. Default permissions can be set on the Default Security tab. To set customized settings for a specific component, select the component in the list on the Applications tab, click the Properties button, and click the Security tab. Each one of the permissions can be set individually by clicking its Edit button, which will bring up the standard Windows Discretionary Access List (DACL) that allows you to grant rights to network accounts (see Figure 8.3). On the Security tab of an individual component you can choose Use Default for any one of the three permissions.

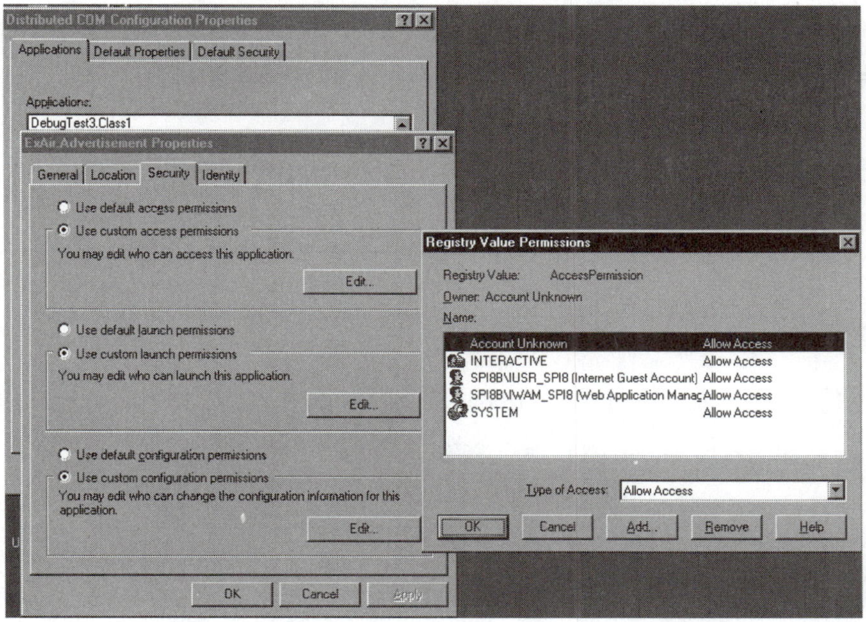

FIGURE 8.3
DCOMCNFG custom security settings

Setting Identity

The Identification tab (available only on an individual component's property page) allows you to set the identity to be used by the server component when running processes on the server. The available settings are:

Interactive User The server component assumes the identity of the user who is currently logged on to the server. It rarely makes sense to use this setting. You usually wouldn't want to leave the component's identity up to chance. In addition, if the server is running with nobody logged on, then the component won't run. You may want to use this setting when you want the component to display messages for debugging purposes. Only a user who is logged on can display messages on the server.

Launching User Default. The component assumes the identity of the client who activates it. This setting can hinder scalability because users with different accounts will cause multiple instances of the component to run.

This User When choosing this option, you must specify a valid user account. This option makes the most sense; it makes managing security much easier if the component always assumes a given identity.

STUDY QUESTIONS

Using the Package and Deployment Wizard

1. How is an Internet package installed on a user's machine?

2. When creating a standard package, how do you indicate that a certain file should be installed in the `Windows\System` directory?

3. What is a multiple `.cab`, and what is it used for?

4. How do you create a package that allows itself to be uninstalled from the user's machine?

5. How would you distribute a component in an Internet package without including the actual component file in your package?

6. What are three choices for deploying with PDW?

STUDY QUESTIONS

Installing and Registering DCOM Components

7. How is a `.vbr` file created, and what is it used for?

____

8. True or False. You configure a DCOM client using PDW by removing the reference to the server component and adding a reference to the server's `.vbr` file.

9. What happens if you don't specify the DCOM server's name when you create a DCOM client package?

____

10. How do you use `CliReg32.exe` to configure a DCOM client?

____

11. How do you use `Dcomcnfg.exe` to configure a DCOM client?

____

12. How do you configure an MTS client computer to use DCOM?

____

13. True or False. If you are using `DCOMCNFG` to configure a server, the Authentication level setting determines how often a client's credentials are checked.

STUDY QUESTIONS

14. If you are using DCOMCNFG to configure a server, what does the Impersonation Level setting do?

____

15. When are the default security settings found in DCOMCNFG used?

____

16. What happens if a component is not running and a client who has access permission attempts to access the component?

____

17. For which setting is Interactive User a valid option, and what does it mean?

____

18. Which Identity setting is the most scalable, and why?

____

SAMPLE TEST

8-1 Multiple `.cabs` are used for:

- **A.** floppy disks.
- **B.** deploying to multiple Web sites.
- **C.** distributing two applications at once.
- **D.** DCOM components.

8-2 A `.vbr` file is generated when compiling:

- **A.** a server component with the Remote Server Files property chosen.
- **B.** all ActiveX server components.
- **C.** a client component with the Remote Server Files property chosen.
- **D.** all ActiveX clients.

8-3 What happens if a user has access permission only and attempts to access a component that is not currently running?

- **A.** The attempt fails.
- **B.** The component runs.
- **C.** The component runs, but under default security settings.

8-4 What is a `.vbr` file used to configure?

- **A.** a DCOM client
- **B.** a DCOM server
- **C.** both a and b

SAMPLE TEST

8-5 Which one of the following is a valid way of distributing components via an Internet package?

A. Compress all components into the package's main `.cab` file.

B. Compile the component as an ActiveX download component.

C. Use PDW to indicate that the component should be downloaded from a specific Web site.

8-6 DCOMCNFG has an option that disables any components on the server from being activated with DCOM.

A. True

B. False

8-7 Using PDW, how can you specify that a file should be installed in a subdirectory of the `Windows` directory?

A. It can't be done.

B. On the Install Locations screen, choose the Windows constant and add a slash followed by the subdirectory name.

C. Place the file in the desired directory before packaging, and PDW will maintain the directory structure.

8-8 When configuring a server using DCOMCNFG, which option determines the setting that is used to protect the client?

A. Authentication level

B. Impersonation level

C. Identity

SAMPLE TEST

8-9 Which one of the following functions does the Package and Deployment Wizard (PDW) *not* do?

A. Register components on the target machine.

B. Compress application files into a `.cab` file.

C. Set up security rights for DCOM clients.

D. Publish packages to Web sites.

8-10 When are default security settings used for a server component? Choose two.

A. when the component is set to use default security

B. when the component does not have customized security settings

C. when Identity is set to Interactive User

D. when Authentication level is set to packet

8-11 Which Identity setting may cause many instances of the component to run and thereby hinder scalability?

A. Interactive User

B. This User

C. Launching User

8-12 Which one of the following options is *not* a method you should use to configure a DCOM client?

A. `CliReg32.exe`

B. `Dcomcnfg.exe`

C. setup program generated by PDW

D. `DcomClient32.exe`

E. MTS client EXE

UNIT 9

Maintaining and Supporting an Application

Test Objectives:

- **Implement load balancing.**
- **Fix errors, and take measures to prevent future errors.**
- **Deploy application updates for distributed applications.**

NOTE

Exam objectives are subject to change at any time without prior notice and at Microsoft's sole discretion. Please visit Microsoft's Training & Certification Web site (`www.microsoft.com/Train_Cert`) for the most current exam objectives listing.

After deploying an application you are far from done. Now it is time to maintain and support the application. This includes enhancing performance as the user base grows. In addition, there are always unexpected errors and requests for additional functionality. In order to provide bug fixes (service packs) or enhanced functionality (new versions), you will have to do some additional development on your components and recompile and distribute them to your existing clients. This unit discusses the issues involved in providing these services.

Implementing Load Balancing

In client server architecture, the availability of the server is critical to application functionality. *Load balancing* enhances server availability by joining multiple machines into a cluster so they act together to provide the required services. This section discusses using Microsoft Cluster Server to provide load balancing.

Using the Microsoft Cluster Server

Microsoft Cluster Server (MSCS) is currently available as part of Windows NT Server Enterprise 4. MSCS provides two types of clusters:

Two-server clusters for availability Two-server clusters are used to protect against server unavailability due to a system crash or down time for maintenance. MSCS' two-server cluster architecture allows for multiple servers to assume ownership over one set of hard disks. When the primary server is unavailable, the backup assumes ownership of the disks and acts as the server.

Multiple-server clusters for enhanced processing power Multiple-server clusters are used to enhance performance by distributing processing across multiple servers.

The following sections discuss how servers and applications can take advantage of MSCS' services.

Ensuring Server Availability

MSCS can detect server failure and automatically respond by transferring ownership of cluster resources to a backup server. MSCS can also detect application failure and either attempt to restart the application on the same server or on a backup server. MSCS can ensure the availability of a server machine and its applications by providing the following *failover* services. There are two types of applications that can benefit from this service:

NT services Built-in NT services, such as file shares, print queues, Internet Information Server (IIS), Microsoft Message Queue Server (MSMQ), Microsoft Transaction Server (MTS), can be restored by MSCS to their last known state before the failover.

Well-behaved applications In order for an application to benefit from a failover, it must be able to restore itself to its last known state before the failure occurred. A *well-behaved application* maintains its state externally and is able to restore itself to its last known state after a failure occurs. For example, Microsoft SQL server maintains a transaction log from which it can restore itself after a failure. In addition, the client application must be able to handle the temporary unavailability of the server while the failover is taking place.

Balancing Server Workload

The current release of MSCS, phase 1, allows for manual load balancing. An administrator can monitor server workload by using the MSCS' performance monitor and manually distribute processing across the cluster by pointing and clicking in the MSCS console. Phase 2 of MSCS will automatically distribute processing across the cluster when it detects server overload. MSCS will base its automatic load balancing on thresholds and settings set by an administrator.

Designing Cluster-Aware Applications

Cluster-aware applications are designed to intelligently distribute processing across a cluster. For instance, if a component has two resource-intensive processes, a developer can design the component to allocate the processes to two different servers. Cluster-aware applications are developed using the COM components exposed by the Microsoft Cluster Automation Server (`MSCLUS.DLL`). For more information, see the Microsoft Cluster Server SDK.

A future version of MTS will be cluster-aware and thereby provide free cluster-aware functionality to all MTS components.

Fixing Errors, and Taking Measures to Prevent Future Errors

For coverage of this see Unit 7, "Testing the Solution," and Unit 4's "Implementing Error Handling in Distributed Applications" section.

Deploying Application Updates for Distributed Applications

In a component-based architecture, enhancing or fixing the functionality of your application does not require you to replace the entire application; instead, you can update the functionality of discrete components and distribute them to your users.

In a component-based application, the client expects the server component to have a certain interface (properties and methods). If an updated component exposes a different interface than the client expects, then the application will not function and will very likely crash. In order to prevent such occurrences, the COM specification has versioning regulations that require that any change to a component's interface render the component as a new version, and therefore, keep the client applications bound to the old version from being disturbed.

Only changes to the existing interface require a new version. Changes to the interface might include changing property/method names, parameters (even optional parameters), and return values. Changing the implementation of a property/method does not require a new version. Visual Basic also allows you to add methods and properties to an interface without changing the version (existing clients will only have access to the old interface, while new clients can take advantage of the new properties and methods).

In order to understand how VB enforces COM versioning, you must first understand a little bit about how COM works. Under COM, a component is identified by its GUID, which is stored in the Registry. Actually, a component has several GUIDs for its type library, classes, and interfaces. When a client application references a COM component, COM looks up the component based on its GUIDs. A new version of a COM component has new GUIDs, and therefore, cannot be referenced by pre-existing clients.

Note that COM versioning only applies to early-bound clients that reference the component from the References dialog. Late-bound clients that use the `CreateObject` function based on the component's progID do not maintain any reference to the component's GUID, and therefore, they are not regulated by COM versioning regulations. If a late-bound client accesses a component whose interface is not compatible with the way the client is accessing it, then the client will crash. However, interface compatibility is quite lax. Optional parameters can be added to procedures, and return values of functions can be changed to return smaller values.

Visual Basic enforces COM versioning when compiling or running the component in the VB IDE based on the Version Compatibility setting found on the Component tab of the Project Properties dialog. The three settings are:

Binary Compatibility When choosing binary compatibility you must specify an existing compiled version of the component against which binary compatibility will be enforced. When compiling, VB checks whether every existing property and method is the same as the existing compiled version. If it finds a difference it will warn you and present you with the following options:

- Cancel—Cancel the compile by clicking the Cancel button.
- Break Compatibility—This option compiles a new version of the component that will be incompatible with existing clients.
- Preserve Compatibility (Advanced)—This option does not generate a new version; however, existing clients will crash when referencing the component. As the dialog says, only use this option if existing clients will not be used anymore and you want to maintain the same interface definitions.

Project Compatibility This option is used during development to allow you and other developers to maintain a reference to the component throughout changes to the interface. Visual Basic does change some of the GUIDs, and therefore, components compiled with this option will not be compatible with existing clients.

No Compatibility If you select this option, VB generates all new GUIDs for the component. Components compiled with this option cannot be used with existing compiled clients or with existing projects that reference the component (a new reference must be set).

When distributing component updates, you probably will want existing clients to be able to work with the updated component. Therefore, you must choose Binary Compatibility and be sure not to make any changes to the component's existing properties and methods.

STUDY QUESTIONS

Implementing Load Balancing

1. What is a cluster?

2. What are the two basic services provided by Microsoft Cluster Server?

3. What is a cluster-aware application?

Deploying Application Updates for Distributed Applications

4. What kind of component changes cause a client application to crash?

5. What does COM accomplish with component versioning?

6. Why aren't late-bound clients regulated by COM component versioning?

STUDY QUESTIONS

7. How do late-bound clients deal with component interface changes?

8. When distributing component updates, which version compatibility setting should you choose, and why?

SAMPLE TEST

9-1 Does component versioning take effect when running a component project in the VB IDE?

A. Yes

B. No

9-2 How can you design VB components to take special advantage of Microsoft Cluster Server's services?

A. Use the COM components exposed by Microsoft Cluster Automation Server.

B. VB components cannot be designed to take special advantage of Microsoft Cluster Server.

9-3 Load balancing is used to:

A. enhance client-side performance.

B. automatically protect against runtime errors.

C. enhance server-side performance.

D. integrate components with MTS.

9-4 When compiling component updates, which component versioning setting should you choose?

A. Binary Compatibility

B. Project Compatibility

C. No Compatibility

D. Maintain Compatibility

SAMPLE TEST

9-5 Does adding a method to a component that is set to Binary Compatibility make it a new version?

A. Yes

B. No

9-6 What kinds of clients are affected by the component versioning?

A. late- and early-bound

B. late-bound

C. early-bound

D. all

9-7 Does adding an optional parameter to a component's method that is set to Binary Compatibility make it a new version?

A. Yes

B. No

UNIT 10

Final Review

FINAL REVIEW

This unit presents you with a series of questions similar to those you will encounter on the actual exam. The real exam will have about 50-55 questions with a 90-minute time limit. Currently you have to score about 71.5 percent or better to pass. The 55 questions in this unit are representative of what you will see on the exam.

1 To design an object that raises an event, what steps must you take?

- **A.** 1. Add the Event procedure to the class module. 2. Call the RaiseEvent method in a procedure of the class module.
- **B.** 1. Declare the Event in the General Declarations section. 2. Add the Event procedure to the class module. 3. Call the RaiseEvent method in a procedure of the class module.
- **C.** 1. Declare the Event in the General Declarations section. 2. Call the RaiseEvent method in a procedure of the class module.

2 You are asked to design an application that retrieves a customer order consisting of data from Microsoft Exchange and SQL Server. The data is fetched based on an Order ID. The application then processes the order based on the customer's credit limit and sends an e-mail message to the customer informing him that the order has been carried out. What would be the best design for this application?

- **A.** Create two middle-tier components: GetOrderInfo and ExecuteOrder. Use GetOrderInfo to fetch the data from Microsoft Exchange and SQL Server, combine it into a recordset, and return it to ExecuteOrder, which would then process the order and send the e-mail confirmation.
- **B.** Create two middle-tier components, ExecuteOrder, which fetches the data and executes the order, and NotifyCustomer, which sends the e-mail confirmation.
- **C.** Create one data tier component that fetches the data from Microsoft Exchange and SQL Server and combines it into a recordset, which is returned to a middle-tier component called ExecuteOrder that processes the order and sends the e-mail confirmation to the customer.

FINAL REVIEW

3 You can use the Fields collection's Append method to:

A. build an ADO recordset programmatically.

B. fetch fields from the data source not specified in the original Open statement.

C. build a recordset before fetching the data in order to enhance performance.

4 You are designing a system that accesses data from multiple data sources, and you want to use MTS transactions. Which of the following tool(s) and technology or technologies must you use?

A. ADO

B. Microsoft Cluster Server

C. databases that support the OLETX or XA standards

D. SQL Server on a dedicated data tier

5 What threading model must be used for MTS components?

A. apartment

B. single

C. thread pool

D. thread per object

6 A business rule states that the all new customers must provide their Social Security number for use as the primary key for the customer record. Where is the best place to enforce this rule?

A. front tier

B. middle tier

C. data tier

D. front tier and middle tier

FINAL REVIEW

7 Which event of a WebClass is the right place to collect a user's name to be used throughout the session?

A. Start

B. BeginRequest

C. Initialize

D. BeginSession

8 You find that whenever you recompile VB components installed in MTS, they can no longer be accessed by client applications. What should you do?

A. Make sure the MTSTransactionMode property of the class modules are set to a value other than 0 (`NotAnMTSObject`).

B. Use the MTS add-in within the VB environment to refresh MTS-specific Registry settings.

C. Install service pack 3.

9 How would you use the Menu Editor to create a submenu of a menu called File?

A. Insert a menu after File and indent it.

B. Create a menu and check its IsChild property.

C. Create a menu and enter File as the Parent property.

10 An ActiveX EXE server should be debugged with a client project:

A. in a project group.

B. running in a separate instance of VB.

FINAL REVIEW

11 How do you dynamically add menus at runtime?

A. Create a menu array at design time and use the standard Load method to add additional items.

B. Use the Add method of the Menus collection.

C. Menus cannot be added at runtime.

12 How do you programmatically display a pop-up menu?

A. Pass any menu that has a submenu as the parameter of a Form's PopupMenu method.

B. Mark the menu as 'Popup' in the Menu Editor and call its Show method.

C. In the Right-click event of the menu, set its Popup property to True.

13 After reviewing the requirements of an application you've identified several entities, two of them are Category and Product. Category has name, description, and shelf number attributes. Product has name, price, and category attributes. Which statement is true regarding designing the database schema for this scenario?

A. Product would be a table with a primary key 'Product_ID' and a foreign key 'Category_ID'.

B. An associative entity would need to be created to link Product to Category.

C. The attributes of the Category entity would become columns in the Product table.

14 After reconnecting a disconnected recordset and updating the database you should:

A. 1. Call the recordset's Resync method to check for conflicts. 2. If there are conflicts, examine the Underlying Value and Value properties of the Field object to determine whether to force the updates.

B. 1. Set the recordset's Filter property to `adConflictingRecords` to check for conflicts. 2. If there are conflicts, call the recordset's Resync method. 3. Examine the Underlying Value and Value properties of the field object to determine whether to force the updates.

FINAL REVIEW

15 Which of the following is common functionality of the TreeView, ImageList, ListView, and StatusBar controls?

A. They are all common Windows controls that can be set to automatically display common Windows dialogs such Open/Save and Windows Explorer.

B. They are all lightweight controls.

C. They all have an Add method that can optionally return a reference to the newly added item.

16 When a ListItem's View property is set to `ivwList`, the ListSubItems are:

A. not displayed.

B. displayed as attributes of the ListItem.

C. displayed as the caption of the ListItem.

17 Your application loads an MDI form and three of its children, but only displays two. In addition, it displays a regular form. The user attempts to close the MDI parent form, and you cancel the unload in the QueryUnload of the second MDI child form. How many forms will the Forms collection have?

A. two

B. five

C. four

D. three

18 How do you design a VB application to allocate processing across multiple servers?

A. Use the COM components exposed by Microsoft Cluster Automation Server.

B. It can't be done

FINAL REVIEW

19 You have a Div tag that displays 'My Home Page' and you want to it to display 'Welcome to My Home Page' with 'Welcome' in bold. Which one of the following lines should you use?

A. `dvHomePage. InsertAdjacentText "AfterBegin", "<b>Welcome</b> to"`

B. `dvHomePage. InsertAdjacentHTML "AfterBegin", "<b>Welcome</b> to"`

C. `dvHomePage.OuterHTML= "<b>Welcome</b> to"`

D. `dvHomePage.InnerHTML= "<b>Welcome</b> to"`

20 In Visual Basic 6, a text box can be bound to an ADO recordset at runtime.

A. True

B. False

21 What happens if a user presses F1 while the focus is on a control that does not have a HelpContextID, but the frame and form that the control is situated on have HelpContextIDs?

A. No help is displayed.

B. The help topic associated with the Frame is displayed.

C. The help topic associated with the Form is displayed.

D. The default help topic of the application is displayed.

22 You have several top-level menus on a form and some of the menus have submenus. How are the Click events of the individual menus handled?

A. All menus share the same Click event.

B. Each top-level menu has its own Click event, and submenus share their parents' Click event.

C. All menus, including submenus, have their own Click event.

D. Menus don't have a Click event.

FINAL REVIEW

23 Help files created with the HTML Help Workshop compile into:

A. `.chm` files.

B. `.hlp` files.

C. `.chp` files.

D. `.htm` files.

24 You are developing a server component. How do you link the server's help topics to the Help button of a client's error message box?

A. Call the Err.Raise method in the component and pass it the help file and help context ID as arguments.

B. Set the component's HelpFile and HelpContextID.

C. It can't be done.

25 You have a form that has TreeView control and a ListItem control that will share many icons. What is usually the best way to manage the icon files?

A. Store the filenames of the icons in constants, and set the appropriate properties to the constants.

B. Store the icon files in an ImageList control, and set the TreeView and ListItem's ImageList property to the ImageList control.

C. Store the icon files in a database, and use a data control to bind the controls to the database.

FINAL REVIEW

26 If you have the following property declaration inside a class module, how should a client developer set the property?

A. Public Property Let Color (Shade as integer, Value as String)

B. *Object*.Color(3)="Red"

C. *Object*.Color= 3,"Red"

D. Set *Object*.Color(3, "Red")

27 How does a client application usually access a class set to PublicNotCreatable?

A. The client application accesses it through the property of another object in the component that instantiates the PublicNotCreatable class and returns a reference to it.

B. The client application declares a variable of the PublicNotCreatable class type and uses the New keyword to instantiate it.

C. A client application cannot obtain a reference to a PublicNotCreatable class.

28 `Dcomcnfg.exe` can be used to configure:

A. the client machine.

B. the server machine.

C. both the client and the server.

29 Which properties of an ActiveX control have to be persisted in a PropertyBag?

A. properties set by a client developer during design time

B. properties set by a user during runtime

C. properties set during client design time and runtime

FINAL REVIEW

30 What syntax would you use to determine whether a control is in client design mode or client run mode from within an ActiveX control's code?

A. `UserControl.UserMode`

B. `Extender.UserMode`

C. `Ambient.UserMode`

31 The front tier and middle tier of an application will be separated by a WAN. One of the business entities has numerous attributes. What is the best way to implement the business entity?

A. as a business component on the middle tier that has its attributes implemented as properties

B. as a business component on the middle tier with its attributes passed in the form of a disconnected ADO recordset between the middle and front tier

C. as a business component on the front end that directly communicates with the data tier

32 In order to roll back a compiled component to a previous version you can use:

A. Visual SourceSafe.

B. Visual Component Manager.

C. Microsoft Cluster Server.

D. Visual Basic 6, Enterprise Edition.

33 Which one of the following is *not* defined by a Microsoft Transaction Server (MTS) package?

A. unit of distribution

B. process boundary

C. resource pooling

D. trusted security domain

E. administrative rights

FINAL REVIEW

34 If you pin a file stored in Visual SourceSafe and then share it among multiple projects, what happens?

A. No one is able to modify it.

B. Everyone is able to edit it.

C. VSS does not allow you to share pinned files.

D. VSS will automatically branch the file.

35 What happens when an MTS transaction times out?

A. The transaction is aborted.

B. The outcome depends on the state of the transaction's abort flag.

C. The transaction is committed.

D. The package's processes shut down.

36 You want to allow only certain developers to modify MTS packages. What must you do?

A. Set the Permission options on the computer's property page.

B. Set the Permission options on the package's property page.

C. Assign users to the System package's Administrator role.

D. This cannot be done.

37 How would you add an MTS component called Bank.DebitAccount to a transaction started by a component called Bank.CreditAccount?

A. from the CreditAccount object, call
`GetObjectContext.CreateInstance("Bank.DebitAccount")`

B. in the Initiate event of the DebitAccount object, call
`GetObjectContext.BeginTrans`

C. from the CreditAccount object, call:
`GetObjectContext.JoinTrans("Bank.DebitAccount")`

FINAL REVIEW

38 How do you add a Node to a specific position in the hierarchy of a TreeView control?

A. by specifying an existing node in the Relative parameter of the Add method

B. by specifying the Index parameter of the Add method

C. by using the Add method of an individual Node

39 You have a component called AccountTransfer that both debits and credits accounts. Sometimes the component alone is used to transfer money from one account to another. And sometimes it used as the tail-end of a sales order that begins with the SalesOrder component updating a database and the SalesOrder component calling the AccountTransfer to allocate the funds for the sale. Which transactional setting should the AccountTransfer component have?

A. Requires A New Transaction

B. Requires A Transaction

C. Supports Transaction

D. Does Not Support Transactions

40 Parameterized stored procedures can be executed by the:

A. Command object only.

B. Connection object only.

C. Recordset object only.

D. Connection and Command objects.

E. Connection, Command, and Recordset objects

FINAL REVIEW

41 Choose the valid setting(s) for the ActiveConnection property.

A. Connection object

B. Valid connection string

C. Connection object and valid connection string

42 The application you're designing has a user interface that is very much subject to change. What kind of UI would be best to use?

A. VB-form–based UI

B. Browser-based–HTML UI

C. none of the above

43 How do you handle events of nonreferenced controls that are added to the Controls collection at runtime?

A. Declare a variable as VBControlExtender using the WithEvents keyword, and write event-handling code in the ObjectEvent event routine.

B. Declare a variable as Object using the WithEvents keyword, and write event-handling code in the ObjectEvent event routine.

C. Write event-handling code in the event routine shared by all the controls in the array.

44 To absolutely abort an MTS transaction from within a secondary object (that did not start the transaction) call:

A. DisableCommit.

B. SetAbort.

C. RollBackTrans.

D. EnableAbort.

FINAL REVIEW

45 Which one of the following is *not* a valid value for the Source parameter of a recordset's Open method?

A. command object

B. filename of a persisted recordset

C. connection string

D. SQL statement

46 If a user wants to start an ActiveX document application, to which file type should they navigate?

A. `.dob`

B. `.vbd`

C. `.dox`

D. `.htm`

47 Which ADO cursor reflects multiuser additions?

A. Keyset

B. Dynamic

C. Public

48 In which debug window(s) can you change the value of a variable in break mode?

A. Immediate

B. Locals

C. Watch

D. all of the above

FINAL REVIEW

49 Which one of the following tasks *cannot* be performed by Visual Component Manager?

A. retrieving a class module and adding it to a VB project

B. retrieving a MS Word document and opening it

C. retrieving a component, copying it to disk, and registering it

D. importing components into MTS packages

50 If you have an application that has a portion of code that must be different based on user configurations, you should:

A. use conditional compilation.

B. create separate versions.

C. use the `Alias` function of the Windows API.

51 How is an Internet package created with the Package and Deployment Wizard (PDW) installed on a user's machine?

A. When the user accesses the ASP page generated by PDW, the Peer Web Services receives the package and installs it.

B. When the user accesses the Web page that references the package, the browser downloads it and installs it.

52 Which of the following lines of code would you use to determine what kind of application is hosting your ActiveX document?

A. `TypeOf(UserDocument.Parent)`

B. `UserDocument.Parent`

C. `TypeName(UserDocument.Parent)`

FINAL REVIEW

53 How should a client computer be configured to call an MTS component over DCOM?

A. Run `Regsvr32.exe` on the client computer.

B. MTS generates an EXE that can be run on the client computer to configure it.

C. Export an MTS client package to the client computer.

54 What kind of clients don't need the protection of COM versioning?

A. early-bound

B. late-bound

C. MTS clients

D. none of the above

55 An MTS object that takes part in transactions should be stateless because:

A. the object is deactivated when the transaction is finished.

B. MTS pools objects and a client application never knows which object it will get.

APPENDIX A

Study Questions and Sample Test Answers

Unit 1 Answers

Study Questions

Designing a Database

1. logical design
   physical design
2. tables
3. kernel
   associative
   characteristic
4. one-to-one
   one-to-many
   many-to-many
5. NOT NULL
   CHECK
   UNIQUE
6. an attribute

Designing Services

7. user interface
   business
   data
8. data components

9. direct access

   stored procedures

10. Win32 front ends in Visual Basic

    ASP pages serving Web pages

11. COM DLL

Keeping Tabs on Performance Issues

12. stored procedures

13. Apply any rules before beginning a transaction that changes data.

14. True

Sample Test

1-1 B

1-2 B

1-3 D

1-4 C

1-5 A, C

1-6 A

1-7 C

1-8 D

1-9 B

1-10 A

Unit 2 Answers

Study Questions

Choosing a Data Tier

1. optimized SQL processing on the server side
   ability to handle many users
   sophisticated security schema
   support for MTS transaction

Designing the Middle Tier

2. Modifications to the business components only have to be made to the set of components on the server as opposed to redistributing the components to all the users.

3. if the user expects immediate validation of the business rule and the rule is seldom changed

4. if the rule involves a lot of data access

5. Abstract the data access code into separate components in order to provide a standard data access method for business components.

Choosing a Front Tier

6. HTML front ends, because modifications to HTML file do not require any recompilation or redistribution

7. Remote activation through DCOM requires special client-side Registry settings that are difficult to configure and maintain for many users.

8. HTML front ends are easiest because there is no installation necessary; the user only has to access the Web page.

9. DHTML can dynamically change the user interface without making a trip to the server.

10. The application code is compiled into DLLs which must be downloaded and installed on the user's machine.

Sample Test

2-1 D

2-2 A

2-3 C

2-4 C, D

2-5 C, D

Unit 3 Answers

Study Questions

Establishing the Environment for Source-Code Version Control

1. source code control
   version tracking

2. default security level that applies to all VSS projects
   security for an individual project

3. It locks out other users from modifying the file and copies the file to the developer's working folder.

4. Sharing links a file to multiple projects; changes in one project are seen by all projects. Branching copies the file to multiple projects; changes in one project are not seen in multiple projects.

5. Project A is unable to make changes to the file. Project B's changes are seen by Project A.

6. version number

   date/time stamp

   label

7. Differences between files cannot be shown.

   Files cannot be merged.

   Multiple checkouts are not permitted.

Installing and Configuring VB for Developing Distributed Apps

8. service pack 3

9. B

10. It allows the user to browse and reverse-engineer class diagrams created with Visual Modeler.

11. SQL Server service pack 3

12. A, B

13. Check the Enable Authorizing Checking option on the Security tab of the System package's property page.

14. by assigning users to the Administrator or Reader roles of the System package

Sample Test

3-1 D

3-2 B, D

3-3 C

3-4 A

3-5 D

3-6 A

Unit 4 Answers

Study Questions

Implementing Navigational Design

1. Use the Menu Editor's arrow keys to indent the menu.

2. In a MDI application, it automatically lists all open children forms.

3. They must be on the same level of the menu hierarchy.

   They must be adjacent to each other.

4. True

5. `Load mnu(2)`

6. True

7. Any menu that has a submenu. Only the submenu is displayed.

Creating Data Input Forms and Dialog Boxes

8. It is used as repository for images.

9. `ImageList.ListImages.Add [index], [key], picture`

10. It is used to set the Picture property of a ListImage object: `Set ImageList.Listimages(0).Picture=LoadPicture (FileName)`

11. with the Add method of the Nodes collection

12. Use the Relative and Relationship arguments of the `Nodes.Add` method.

13. Position the focus at a specific Node by setting its Selected property to True, and then move to the Nodes around it by using the Next, Previous, Parent, and Child properties.

14. `Set NewNode =TreeView.Nodes.Add()`

15. List, Report

16. Five. The ListItem and each of the ListSubItems require a column head.

17. Set the SortKey property to the index of a ColumnHeader, and set the Sort property to True.

18. In the ButtonClick event, examine the Button parameter to determine which button was clicked.

19. Set the button to tbrDropDown, and add ButtonMenu objects to the ButtonMenus collection.

20. Simple and Normal. When set to Simple, the Panels collection is not used and the value of SimpleText property is displayed. When set to Normal, the Panels collection is used.

21. Its name is Form1. Forms are retrieved from the Forms collection by a numeric index. To identify a new instance of a form, either set its Tag or Caption to a unique identifier.

22. True

23. `If TypeOf Controls Is ControlType Then`

24. True

25.
```
Load cmd(1)
Unload cmd(1)
```

26. on top of the first control in the array

27. `Set NewControl=Controls.Add (ProgID, name, [container])`

28. Declare a variable as `Dim WithEvents NewControl as VBControlExtender`. Handle the controls' custom events in the ObjectEvent event.

29. It is the parameter passed into the ObjectEvent event.

    It has a Name property that identifies the event raised and an EventParameters collection that provides information about parameters.

Writing Code that Validates User Input

30.
```
If KeyAscii < Asc("0") Or KeyAscii > Asc("9") Then
 KeyAscii=0
End If
```

31. It causes the Validation event to fire when a user leaves a control.

Writing Code that Processes Data Entered on a Form

32. Initialize

33. False

34. when the form is unloaded and explicitly set to Nothing.

35. QueryUnload event of the owned form

    QueryUnload event of the owner form

    Unload event of the owned form

    Unload event of the owner form

36. All child forms unloaded prior to this one are unloaded, but all child forms that have not yet been unloaded and the MDI parent form are not unloaded.

37. UnloadMode. It tells you why the form is being closed.

Adding an ActiveX Control to the Toolbox

38. Project ➢ Components

    Ctrl+T

    Right-click the Toolbox and choose Components

Creating Dynamic Web Pages by Using ASP and WebClasses

39. BeginRequest

40. Start event

41. HTML templates have an associated HTML file that can be used to connect elements to WebItem events. WebItems only contain code.

42. VB adds code to the HTML element which causes the browser to fire the event to which it is connected.

43. Elements that have an attribute that can contain a URL

44. A WebItem object. It causes the associated HTML template to be written to the browser.

45. After the WriteTemplate method is called, the WebClass searches for specially marked replacement tags in the HTML template. If it finds any, it fires the ProcessTag event to replace them.

46. It takes a WebItem and an Event and returns the URL of the specified event.

47. The UserEvent event procedure has a parameter that describes the specific event that was fired.

48. with the `Request.Form` collection

49. `Response.Write HTML`

50. IIS will manage the instantiating and threading of the object.

51. `Session(VariableName)=Value`

Creating a Web Page by Using the DHTML Page Designer

52. Save the HTML in an external file.

53. Regular positions the element in the regular flow of the document. Absolute positions the element outside the flow of the document at a specific x/y-coordinate.

54. ID

55. BaseWindow

56. `ElementID.Style.BackgroundColor= Color`

57. InnerHTML processes tags to display the HTML effects, while InnerText displays the actual tags.

58. The element is destroyed.

59. `dvWelcome. InsertAdjacentText "BeforeEnd", "John"`

60. It must be absolutely positioned.

61. by increasing the element's Style.PosLeft property

Using Data Binding to Display and Manipulate Data from a Data Source

62. Retrieve individual DataBinding objects by passing the name of the property to the Item method of the control's DataBindings property, and set its DataSource property to a valid data source.

63. ADO Data control and ADO recordset

Instantiating and Invoking a COM Component

64. By reading the type library, VB is able to compile more efficient code.

65. Because late-bound components are declared as Object and the WithEvents keyword only works with objects declared as a specific type.

66. Select the component in the References dialog, declare an object of the components type, and instantiate it.

67. Variables declared with WithEvents cannot use the New keyword.

Creating Call-Back Procedures between COM Components and VB Client Applications

68. The client instantiates it and passes it to the server, and the server calls one of the call-back objects that is designated as the call-back procedure.

Implementing Online User Assistance in a Distributed Application

69. `App.HelpFile=HelpFile` or set the Help properties available in the Project Properties dialog.

70. frame's

71. WhatsThisHelpID and WhatsThisButton of the control and form have to be set so that they don't display Max/Min buttons.

72. Help Topics, Help Index, Help Contents

73. Topic

74. `.chm`

75. Return an error code as a value of the function.

Raise an error using `Err.Raise`

76. `On Error Goto 0`

77. As arguments of the `Err.Raise` method

78. Write `On Error Resume Next` before the error-prone line. Check for errors after the error-prone line.

Sample Test

4-1 D

4-2 B

4-3 A

4-4 B

4-5 A

4-6 A

4-7 B

4-8 A

4-9 B

4-10 B

4-11 B

4-12 B

4-13 C

4-14 C. When an MDI child form is loaded, the MDI form must also be loaded.

4-15 C

4-16 A

4-17 A

4-18 A

4-19 C

4-20 C

4-21 A

4-22 C

4-23 A

4-24 B

4-25 A

4-26 B

4-27 A

4-28 C

4-29 B

4-30 D

4-31 A

4-32 A

4-33 B

4-34 A

4-35 A

4-36 client

4-37 B

4-38 A

4-39 C

4-40 A

4-41 B

4-42 A

4-43 C

4-44 B

Unit 5 Answers

Study Questions

Creating a COM Component that Implements Business Logic

1. ActiveX DLL

2. ActiveX EXE

3. False

4. because variables cannot be part of a public interface

5. when a property contains an object; the client must use the Set syntax to set the property

6. True

7. Let always has one more parameter than get.

   All the parameters must have the same name and type.

   The return value of the get must match the last parameter of let.

8. The last parameter is the actual value. The user places values for the other parameters in parentheses on the left side of the equal sign next to the property's name.

9. Examine the argument passed to the event with the `RaiseEvent` statement.

10. It makes the procedure visible only within the component.

11. PublicNotCreatable

12. EXE

13. Private, PublicNotCreatable

14. MultiUse

Compiling a Project with Class Modules into a COM Component

15. If the developer adds a non-child type to the collection, you cannot stop him with a compiler error. The client does not have access to the Item and Count methods of the collection.

16. by declaring the parameter of the Add method as the child class' type

Creating ActiveX Controls

17. Initialize, InitProperties

18. WriteProperties

    Terminate

19. Property Bag

    ReadProperty and WriteProperty

20. whenever the control is destroyed during design time

21. PropertyChanged

    PropertyName

22. Ambient's

23. AmbientProperties

    It returns True if the control is on a container that is in run mode as opposed to design mode.

24. Nothing. A properties window is automatically provided for a control.

25. In the Procedure Attributes dialog, check the User Interface Default option.

26. Create an enumeration for the property values, and set the data type for the property let/get procedures to the enumeration.

27. No. The OK, Cancel, and Apply buttons are provided for free.

28. by examining the SelectedControls collection

29. Set the Changed property to True, in order to tell the property page to raise the ApplyChanges event when the user clicks OK/Apply and to enable the Apply button.

30. It doesn't do it automatically. You have to manually assign properties to controls contained in the SelectedControls property in the ApplyChanges event.

31. In the control's properties window, click PropertyPages and choose the appropriate page.

32. In the Procedure Attributes dialog, choose the property page in the Use This Page In The Browser list.

33. True

34. In the Procedure Attributes dialog, check Property Is Data Bound and This Property Binds To Datafield.

35. Check Property Is Data Bound for all the properties.

36. It allows the user to bind the property during design time using the DataBindings dialog.

37. No. You write code to display it in the property let procedure.

38. When the user changes the property, pass the property name to the PropertyChanged method.

39. Pass the property name to the CanPropertyChange method.

40. `DataSourceBehavior=vbDataSource`

41. in the GetDataMember event

    It is returned by setting the data parameter to a recordset.

42. GetDataMember

Creating an ActiveX Document

43. `.dob`

44. ViewportHeight, ViewportWidth, ViewportLeft, ViewportTop

45. Name it 'Help,' and set its NegotiatePosition property to Right.

46. WriteProperties

47. by checking the TypeName of the Parent property

48. `UserDocument.Parent.Navigate`
    `SomeUserDoc.vbd`

Designing and Creating Components that Will Be Used with MTS

49. between components in the same package

50. no

51. False

52. It writes the Registry settings that direct component requests to MTS.

53. After you recompile a component that causes the special MTS settings to be overwritten.

54. the Remote Server Name property

55. when you want to modify a component that MTS is keeping alive

56. the component DLLs, `.pak` file, and `Clients` subdirectory which contains the client configuration EXE

57. the amount of time MTS keeps a component alive after it is released by a client

58. by setting the Disable Changes, Disable Deletion properties on the Advanced tab of a package's property page

59. by right-clicking the `Role's Users` subdirectory and choosing New User

60. by right-clicking the `Role Membership` subdirectory of a component and choosing New Role

61. with the GetObjectContext method

62. transactional and security

63. Both set the ObjectContext's commit flag to False, but only SetAbort also sets the Done flag to True, causing MTS to deactivate the component.

64. Both of them are added to the current transaction, but only Requires A Transaction starts a new transaction if there is no current transaction.

65. with the CreateInstance method

66. When the transaction is completed with the SetAbort/Complete methods, MTS destroys the object and its state.

67. All the clients should supply the same connection string.

68. MTS starts a new activity for the new object, causing the object to have incorrect context information and poor performance.

69. CreateObject, New, and CreateInstance

Choosing the Appropriate Threading Model for a COM Component

70. by allowing a thread to begin execution before the current thread is finished

71. Set the amount of threads in the thread pool to greater than 1.

72. MDI applications must be single threaded. Multi threaded functionality can be simulated by setting the class module's Instancing property to SingleUse.

Using Visual Component Manager to Manage Components

73. The Repository stores the information and surfaces it as objects to VCM.

74. True

75. When retrieving a component, choose Install On This Computer.

    When publishing a component with the Publish Wizard, choose the COM registration option that causes the component to be automatically registered when added to a project.

Registering and Unregistering a COM Component

76. Compile it.

Run it.

Run it from the command line followed by `/REGSERVER`.

77. Run `Regsvr32` from the command line followed by `/u` and the component's filename.

Sample Test

5-1 B

5-2 C

5-3 A

5-4 C, D

5-5 B

5-6 A

5-7 C

5-8 B

5-9 A

5-10 B

5-11 A

5-12 B

5-13 C

5-14 A

5-15 A

5-16 B

5-17 B

5-18 C

5-19 B

5-20 A

5-21 B

5-22 B

5-23 A

5-24 D

5-25 A

5-26 C

5-27 B

5-28 D

5-29 A

5-30 A

5-31 A

5-32 B

5-33 C

5-34 A

5-35 A

5-36 A

5-37 A

5-38 B

5-39 C

5-40 C

5-41 D

Unit 6 Answers

Study Questions

1. OLE DB is the technology that interacts with the actual data source.
2. B
3. Provider, Data Source, User ID, Password, Filename, Initial Catalog, DSN
4. True
5. False
6. CommandText
7. parameterized stored procedures and queries
8. Connection object and valid ConnectionString
9. No, it must be set using the CommandText property.
10. True
11. ActiveConnection property and ActiveConnection parameter of the Open method
12. It filters the recordset to contain a subset of the entire recordset. It has same syntax as the WHERE clause of an SQL statement without the word WHERE.

13. FieldList and Values. They provide a shortcut for updating and adding in one line of code.

14. RowDelimiter = Carriage Return

    Column Delimiter = Tab

15. A: It retrieves the next recordset where a stored procedure or compound SQL statement returns multiple recordsets.

16. A: adCommandFile

17. False

18. False. The Underlying Value is the value originally retrieved from the data source and is what the cursor expects to find in the data source when executing an update.

19. The OriginalValue property will retain its value throughout the life of the recordset. The Underlying Value, which is the value the cursor expects to be in the data source, can be updated using the Resync method.

Accessing and Manipulating a Data Source by Using the ADO Data Control

20. True

21. ConnectionString and Recordsource

22. three: Connection, Command, and Recordset

23. `Set rs= Object.Execute`

24. `Set recordset.ActiveConnection = command`

    `recordset.open command`

25. ForwardOnly, Records

    Static, Records

    Keyset, Pointers

    Dynamic, Pointers

Understanding and Using Cursor Types, Locations, and Locks

26. Dynamic cursors reflect multiuser additions; Keyset cursors don't.

27. ReadOnly, Optimistic, Pessimistic (locks the longest), Batch Optimistic

28. Yes, they can be. A cursor's ability to scroll is not dependent on its readability.

29. True

30. True

31. True

32. False. Although they are populated with records as opposed to pointers, ForwardOnly cursors only contain one record at a time.

33. because it indefinitely locks data resources from the time an edit begins

34. Each additional user consumes more server-side resources.

35. It controls how many records are stored in local memory, thereby affecting how often the cursor will have to make network trips to retrieve data.

36. Data corruption occurs when two users update the same record simultaneously, resulting in bad data. A data conflict arises when a user updates a record after it already has been changed by another user.

37. No. SQL statements are not based on a previous read of the data, and therefore, don't have an original Underlying Value to trigger a conflict against.

38. It ensures that updates do not encounter conflicts by locking out other users from the data while it is being edited.

39. by freeing a data source connection

40. `Recordset.UpdateBatch adAffectCurrent`

41. Set the Recordset's Filter property to `adFilterConflictingRecords`.

42. `Recordset.Resync adResyncUnderlyingValues` will refresh the UnderlyingValue property to reflect the current data in the data source and allow the cursor to update the data source.

Accessing and Manipulating Data by Using the Execute Direct and Prepare/Execute Models

43. It instructs the Provider to save a temporary compiled version of the command before its first execution.

Accessing and Manipulating Data by Using the Stored Procedures Model

44. They allow you to grant security to specific tasks instead of to entire tables.

45. when the rules are simple and involve many data actions

46. Connection, Command, and Recordset

47. when you are working with parameterized stored procedures

48. manually creating and appending parameters to the collection
    calling the Refresh method

49. the values passed in the Execute method

Using the ADO Errors Collection to Handle Database Errors

50. Data-source–specific errors are, ADO programmatic errors aren't.

51. The collection is cleared.

Managing Database Transactions to Ensure Data Consistency and Recoverability

52. BeginTrans, CommitTrans, and RollbackTrans

53. when transactions are based on complex business logic

Writing SQL Statements that Retrieve and Modify Data

54. INSERT

Writing SQL Statements that Use Joins to Combine Data from Multiple Tables

55.
```
SELECT Customer.CustomerID, Order.OrderID From Customer LEFT OUTER JOIN
Order on Customer.CustomerID = Order.CustomerID
```

Sample Test

6-1 B

6-2 B

6-3 C

6-4 B

6-5 C

6-6 B

6-7 A

6-8 B

6-9 C

6-10 B

6-11 C

6-12 A

6-13 A

6-14 B

6-15 D

6-16 C

6-17 B

6-18 C

6-19 B

6-20 B

6-21 A

6-22 A

Unit 7 Answers

Study Questions

Selecting the Appropriate Compiler Options

1. True

2. to enhance performance

3. Native code is in binary format, ready to be executed. Interpreted code is converted to binary as the program runs.

4. Compiled native code is bigger than interpreted code, and therefore, consumes more memory. Functions executed in external libraries such as OCXs and DLLs are not enhanced by compiling to native code.

5. True

6. when you do not pass any arguments ByRef

7. It instructs the compiler not to check if assignments to arrays are beyond the bounds of the array. It poses the risk of invalid memory access that may cause a system crash.

Controlling an Application by Using Conditional Compilation

8. True

9. a special constant that the compiler will evaluate when reading conditional compilation code

10. in code using the `#Const` statement

    in the Conditional Compilation Arguments field in the Project Properties dialog

    from the command line when compiling

11. `#IF...Then`
    `#Else`
    `#End If`

Monitoring the Values of Expressions and Variables by Using the Debug Windows

12. view values of variables

    change the values of variables

13. design mode, break mode

14. any valid VB code

15. break mode

16. modular

17. under the Me variable

18. Click the value and type in the new one.

19. design and break modes

20. variables
    object properties
    expressions (e.g., *variable=value*)

21. Break when the value changes.
    Break when the value is true.
    Display the value of the expression.

22. Module
    Procedure

Implementing Project Groups to Support Development and Debugging

23. because ActiveX components supply objects that are instantiated by a client application

24. You have the ability to declare variables of the component's type.
    You are provided with IntelliSense.

25. Add a standard EXE project to the component project, thereby creating a project group. Set a reference in the test project to the component project. Set the test project as the start-up project.

26. Put the component project into run mode. Open a new instance of the VB environment. Choose a standard EXE for the test project. Set a reference from the test project to the running component.

27. The ActiveX EXE is not in run mode.

28. The reference to the ActiveX component will become invalid. It can be fixed by unchecking the reference in the References dialog, closing the dialog, reopening it, and checking the reference.

29. because the References dialog lists references to type libraries, which are only created upon compilation in VB components

30. Add a standard EXE project to the component project, thereby creating a project group. Set the test project as the start-up.

31. Close the control designer.

Sample Test

7-1 B

7-2 D

7-3 B

7-4 B

7-5 B

7-6 C, E

7-7 A

7-8 B

7-9 B

7-10 C

7-11 B

7-12 A

Unit 8 Answers

Study Questions

Using the Package and Deployment Wizard

1. When the user accesses a Web page that references the components, the browser downloads the `.cab` file, unpacks it, and installs it.

2. When you use the PDW, you are provided with predefined constants for common directories.

3. PDW can break a package's `.cab` file into multiple files so that the package can be distributed via floppy disks.

4. All packages created by PDW can be uninstalled from the Control Panel via Add/Remove Programs.

5. PDW allows you to indicate that a file should be retrieved from a Web site. The `.inf` file generated by PDW indicates where the file is stored.

6. Floppy Disks

   Folder

   Web Publishing

Installing and Registering DCOM Components

7. A `.vbr` is created by compiling a server component that has the Remote Server Files option chosen as one of the project properties. It is used for configuring a DCOM client.

8. True

9. The user is prompted during setup for the server's name.

10. Run it from the command line, and pass it the server's `.vbr` file as an argument.

11. On the Applications tab choose the server, click Properties, choose Run Application On The Following Computer, and enter the name of the server computer.

12. Run the EXE found in the `Clients` subdirectory of an exported package.

13. True.

14. It determines to what extent the server can use the client's credentials.

15. If a component doesn't have customized security settings or if the component has been set to use default security

16. The component is not activated. Starting a component requires launch permission.

17. For Identification. When set to Interactive User, the server component assumes the identity of the user who is currently logged on.

18. This User allows multiple clients to use the same instance of the component and simplifies security management.

Sample Test

8-1 A

8-2 A

8-3 A

8-4 A

8-5 C

8-6 A

8-7 B

8-8 B

8-9 C

8-10 A, B

8-11 C

8-12 D

Unit 9 Answers

Study Questions

Implementing Load Balancing

1. A cluster is a group of machines joined together by clustering software that allows the servers to work together to provide server functionality.

2. availability and load balancing

3. It is an application that is designed to allocate processing across a cluster using the Microsoft Cluster Automation Server's COM components.

Deploying Application Updates for Distributed Applications

4. changes to the component's interface

5. It ensures that components that have had interface changes are rendered as a new version, and therefore, will not be referenced by existing clients.

6. Component versioning is based on the component's GUID, and late-bound clients don't maintain a reference to a component's GUID.

7. If the client accesses the interface in a way that is not compatible with the new interface, then the client crashes.

8. You should choose Binary Compatibility because this ensures that the updated version will maintain the same GUIDs as the old component, and therefore, will work with existing clients.

Sample Test

9-1 A

9-2 A

9-3 C

9-4 A

9-5 A

9-6 C

9-7 A

Unit 10 Answers

Study Questions

1. C

2. A

3. A

4. C

5. A

6. D. Since this rule is not likely to change and a user would expect immediate validation, such as a text box on the UI that restricts input to the Social Security number format, you want it on the UI tier, but you also want it on the middle tier so that future UI's aren't forced to implement the rule.

7. A

8. B
9. A
10. B
11. A
12. A
13. A
14. B
15. C
16. A
17. B
18. B
19. B
20. A
21. B
22. C
23. A
24. A
25. B
26. A

27. A

28. C

29. A

30. C

31. B

32. A

33. E

34. A

35. A

36. C

37. A

38. A

39. B

40. A

41. C

42. B

43. A

44. B

45. C

46. B

47. B

48. D

49. D

50. A

51. B

52. C

53. B

54. B

55. A

APPENDIX B

Strategies for Successful Test Taking

This book is written for the express purpose of helping readers pass Exam 70-175, Designing and Implementing Distributed Applications with Microsoft Visual Basic 6.0. This book focuses on the specific content material covered on the exam. Most of us have had the unfortunate experience of doing poorly on an exam, even after many long hours of study. To that end, we are including this appendix. Our aim here is to focus attention on the skills that can make your studying more effective and maximize your chances of passing the exam. We will cover two general classes of these skills in this appendix:

- Effective study techniques
- Test-taking skills

Remember, our point in this discussion is not to encourage you to take shortcuts in your preparations. We cannot overemphasize the necessity of a solid mastery of the exam content. The goal of this section is to make sure that you are studying effectively and that poor habits or other circumstances do not interfere with your chances of passing the exam.

Learning Effective Study Techniques

Microsoft designs its certification exams to be difficult to pass. The reason for this is not to fail qualified individuals (though it may feel that way sometimes). All certification programs are by definition designed to certify competence. In the case of Microsoft, the driving goal is to certify that an MCP or MCSD is an experienced professional in the credentialed areas. The exams are written with this objective in mind. Exam objectives assess both a detailed knowledge of relevant technologies and a working knowledge of software usage patterns. Your study, then, should give you both a knowledge of important facts and specifications as well as the ability to relate to the tools like they are old friends.

There are several skills that can assist in your efforts to memorize important technical facts. We begin our discussion with coverage of these techniques.

Using Mnemonics

One of the most powerful (and least used) aids to memorization is the use of mnemonics, or individualized memory prompts. The key to mnemonics is to use word or visual associations that are unusual enough to remember easily. For memorizing lists, acronyms can be a useful prompting tool. A phrase or sentence that contains the key words can also be helpful. Perhaps the most famous instances of these techniques are from the music pedagogy camp. Practically every new piano student is taught that "Every Good Boy Does Fine" to represent the notes that fall on the lines of the treble clef, and F-A-C-E, the acronym that gives the notes that fall between the lines. Similarly, the list of Active Server Page Intrinsic Server Objects (Session, Application, Request, Response, and Server objects) can be remembered by finding a unique acronym like ASP-ARRSS. A phrase to aid recall of these objects might go something like this, "In a Web *application*, the browser *requests responses* from a *server*, simulating a *session*."

NOTE

There are no right or wrong mnemonics; the key is that the cue have some sort of personal meaning that you can recall.

You may have been forced into using mnemonics by an over-vigilant system administrator. Many multi-user systems have such restrictive constraints on the selection of passwords that users must find a way to combine numbers, letters (in different cases), and punctuation in some way that they can remember.

TIP

The numbers 2 and 4 are particularly handy in making mnemonics. You can build sentences around their similarities to the words "to" and "for." For instance, a graduate of Florida State University might select went2FSU as a password string. This particular string will never show up in a dictionary of common passwords, yet the user is likely to remember it because it has a personal meaning.

Using Repetition

Why is it that you have no trouble remembering your Social Security number or the Pledge of Allegiance? How about your credit card, frequent flyer, or checking account numbers? These pieces of information may have little daily use or intrinsic personal meaning, but we retain them for years because of chronic exposure. In fact, you can tell a lot about a person and their life by the types of information they have committed to memory through repetition. If you have committed large portions of the Visual Basic language to memory from consistent use, you are probably on the path to passing the exam with ease. If this statement does not accurately describe you, your job is to make it so.

If you want to become familiar with Visual Basic and the elements of distributed application development and you don't work with Visual Basic regularly, find ways to expose yourself to these tools. Some of the means at your disposal for increasing your exposure to Visual Basic development include:

- working your way through the study questions in this book
- working through the exercises given in the Microsoft courses
- working through practice exams

This book is written to provide you with a review of the information likely to appear on your exam. Work through each of the study questions, and make sure you feel comfortable with the solutions. One of the ways this relatively brief exposure can aid in recall is by providing you with a visual experience.

Using Visualization

Studies of learning styles have shown that different people learn best through different means. For some, optimal learning comes through the use of mnemonics. For others, hands-on experience is essential for any meaningful recall. Still others rely on simple repetition to embed information in their minds. Educational psychologists have found that learning is tied to our physical senses. If we listen to a certain piece of music while studying a topic, for instance, that information is recalled much more easily if we again listen to that piece of music. Multimedia presentations are especially effective in teaching, as multiple senses are used simultaneously.

NOTE

Multimedia is not just a fancy use for technology. Based on sound, sight, and interaction, multimedia helps us learn faster and more thoroughly because we learn best when multiple senses are used.

One effective technique that you can use in the course of your study is to take advantage of visual aids whenever possible. Additionally, if your experience is that you learn well through visual experiences or hands-on practice, you should use that knowledge to your advantage while studying. As you read through example procedures, close your eyes and visualize the sequence of events as they transpire. If you then sit at your keyboard and actually work through the procedure, you are now reviewing what you have learned. It may also be helpful to examine the various elements of the user interface. By following the changes in state of the user interface, visually cued learners can master complexities that are otherwise difficult to grasp.

Thinking Critically

Mnemonics, repetition, and visualization will aid you in storing and retrieving bits of data. However, the Microsoft certification exams are written to test your facility with the software, not just your ability to memorize static facts. In other words, the exam will also examine skills like problem solving, software development, and your understanding of which tools to apply to which jobs. If your brain is like a computer, you must do more than write a large amount of data to a text file on your hard disk. To pass the exam (and be an effective developer of distributed applications), you must also be able to take in information, process it, and store it in data structures that allow for future context-sensitive retrieval. These data structures can then, in turn, be used in the processing of future incoming information. In the realm of computer science, this is similar to neural networks or artificial intelligence.

The key to processing what you learn in this way is to consistently ask yourself the following questions while studying:

- How is this topic connected to the rest of the information in this chapter or book?
- How might I implement this feature or technology in a development project?
- How does this relate to my past experiences? Could I have used this in an earlier project? How did developers perform similar tasks before this particular technology was available?

Introducing this level of processing will definitely slow your acquisition of the information contained in this book. The lost efficiency, however, will be insignificant compared to the depth of understanding you will achieve. If you want to master the material and pass the exam, this type of rigorous effort will make the difference.

Why bother with this extra effort? Because when you incorporate information this way, you grasp the "big picture." When you know what the big picture looks like, you can make educated guesses about aspects of the picture you haven't explicitly studied. In an effort to assess your level of familiarity with their various developer tools and operating systems, Microsoft has created exam questions that probe the darker and more obscure areas of the image. In the first two chapters of this book we have attempted to lay out the major aspects of the big picture. We encourage you to read these chapters carefully. As you read the later chapters, push to see how each topic fits within the larger context.

If you want to be very thorough in your preparation, read this entire book twice. The first time through, you will only understand each chapter within the context of the previous chapters. During a second read-through, however, you can consider the entire book as you read—how all the features relate and what they do within those relationships.

Once you've reviewed the material contained in this book, you are ready to create a plan of attack for successfully passing the exam. The remainder of this appendix will deal specifically with ways to leverage what you have learned and maximize your exam score.

Mastering Test-taking Skills

There are two important aspects of test preparation, the steps you take before beginning the exam and the little tricks that help you successfully recognize correct exam responses. While it may be tempting to skip to the section on selecting correct answers, we encourage you to review the "Before the Exam" items and use them as part of a comprehensive exam strategy.

Preparing Yourself before the Exam

These pre-exam strategies may not directly *improve* your test score. We have included them here because of the potential *not* using these strategies has to *lower* your score. It is truly unfortunate when a person studies diligently for an exam and is then unable to perform to potential because of avoidable circumstances. Failing Microsoft certification exams is costly both financially and personally. Take full advantage of the effort you have spent in your studying by avoiding common obstacles.

Knowing Yourself

A little self-evaluation can go a long way toward preventing exam difficulties. The saddest sort of mistakes are the ones we make repeatedly. Think back over your past experience with test taking. If you have previously taken Microsoft certification exams, these experiences should be given special attention. What types of experiences have you had in prior exams? How successful have you been? Did you run out of time? Did you arrive late? Were you fully prepared? What can you learn from those past experiences that may help you prepare for a successful exam this time?

Your answers to the questions above will be individual. We encourage you to carefully plan ways to avoid any problems you may have previously had. Careful study and the techniques previously above may help with many problems. There are two relatively common test-taking challenges, that merit some specific mention.

Test anxiety has profoundly impaired millions of careers. Its symptoms are those associated with a "fight or flight" instinct: rapid heartbeat and breathing, sweating, general nervousness, and in more severe cases, an overwhelming sense of panic. If you suffer from mild to moderate anxiety when you take exams, try some of the following techniques to control your anxiety while testing:

- Remember that some anxiety is a normal reaction to the situation.
- Prepare well for the exam. The better prepared you are, the easier it will be to remain calm.
- Breathe slowly and deeply before and during the exam.
- Ensure you get adequate rest prior to the exam. If your body is fatigued, it will have a more difficult time responding well to the stress of the exam.
- Avoid consuming caffeine and nicotine. These chemicals are stimulants that act to increase the anxiety symptoms you feel.
- If you are so inclined and have a few weeks until you take the exam, a regular pattern of prayer or meditation is often helpful in learning to calm your body's reactions.

If your anxiety is more severe, you may want to seek assistance from a qualified psychotherapist. Alternatively, you may want to talk to your physician about medications that can help you cope with these brief and specific episodes of anxiety.

Another personal trait that sometimes keeps people from doing their best on exams is self-doubt. If you find that you tend to approach tests with an optimistic attitude but then midway through an exam you begin to doubt yourself and feel overwhelmed by the difficulty of the questions, there are some strategies that can help.

- Prepare well, including gaining a solid understanding of the topics to be covered and the level of detail you will need to know.

- Remind yourself before and during the exam that most tests beyond high school are written to assess students who vary significantly in their abilities. This includes students at the high end of the range of abilities. Some questions are quite difficult, but only seasoned professionals are expected to know the answers. Perfect scores on Microsoft exams are relatively uncommon. Remind yourself that not knowing all of the answers immediately is the way the test designers intended it to work. It does not automatically mean that you will fail the exam. Stay focused and use the knowledge you have acquired from study and the strategies given below to answer as many questions correctly as you can.

- Work smart. Since all questions are worth the same number of points, don't linger on difficult questions. Select your best guess, then mark the question for review after you have completed the easier questions. This will have two positive effects: you won't use up time on hard questions that you could use more efficiently on easier questions, and you'll feel less frustrated as you move through the exam.

Finally, the last 24 hours before the exam can make a big difference in your performance. The next topic will cover some ways to take full advantage of those last hours.

Setting the Stage for Success: The Last 24 Hours

The essential element you should attend to in the final hours before the exam is concentration. Several factors can hamper your ability to concentrate, and you should do what you can to prevent any impairment. These concentration-reducing factors include fatigue, agitation, anxiety, and distractions. Below are some rules to help you avoid the most common of these:

- If you have not been to the testing site before, make a trip there prior to the testing day so you'll know where to park and how to get into the testing facility.

- Get a good night's sleep the night before the exam. If your style is to spend hours cramming just before the exam, schedule your exam for the afternoon. After a solid night of sleep, study for most of the morning and then go to the testing center. If this is difficult because of your work schedule, many larger cities have centers that are open on Saturdays. Don't underestimate the importance of good sleep. It may not explicitly improve your score, but without it your brain won't work as well, and on Microsoft exams that will hurt you.

- Arrive early. Go out of your way to arrive early at the testing center. A delay in travel can leave you arriving late and feeling flustered. Plan ahead. It's better to arrive early and spend a few moments relaxing or reviewing than to run in at the last moment and have to immediately begin concentrating. If you were unable to make a prior visit to the testing center, or if you are traveling to a different city to take the exam, this item is especially important. Before you begin the exam, prevent any distractions by visiting the restroom or getting a drink of water if needed. Don't let minor annoyances become big headaches.

- See "Things to Know about Taking Microsoft Exams" for other details of the testing experience. Knowing what to expect will make the whole experience go more smoothly and allow you to focus all of your energies on the exam itself.

Things to Know about Taking Microsoft Exams

- You will need to present two forms of ID.
- You will be asked to agree not to tell others about the content of the exam.
- These are closed-book exams. Don't bring notes or other aids into the exam.
- You will be given scrap paper to use while taking the exam, but you will have to give it back when you complete the exam.
- You may be monitored with audio or video equipment while taking the exam.

Selecting the Right Answer

Microsoft certification exams intend to measure the degree to which you have mastered the subject matter, and they do that quite well. However, the exams (like most exams) also indirectly test how well you have mastered the art of test taking. The remainder of this appendix will focus directly on techniques that can improve your general test-taking abilities.

The effect of test-taking skills is being able to test above your actual ability. The basic skill involved in effective multiple-choice testing is guessing well which answer is correct. We will present some basic practices, or good habits, for test taking. You should learn to apply these practices every time you answer an exam question, whether it's from Microsoft or anyone else.

Later, we present some more sophisticated strategies that may apply in certain circumstances.

Establishing Basic Practices

Six good habits for test taking are covered here. These basic practices generally should help you identify correct responses and avoid errors, while the advanced tools are primarily to help you guess effectively when you can't identify the correct answer directly. The basic practices covered below are:

- Read questions twice—watch for "not," "un-," and double negatives.
- Guess the correct answer yourself before reading the given responses.
- Always read all of the responses before selecting one.
- Eliminate obviously wrong choices.
- Don't spend too much time on hard questions.
- Never change an answer unless you are sure it is wrong.

TIP: Jot this list on a small card, and review these items just before taking any practice exams. Also, review these just before taking your certification exam.

Read Questions Twice Carefully read each question. Watch for words that may reverse the meaning of the question with prefixes like "un-" or "im-." Other ways meanings can be reversed are with words like "not" or the use of double negatives. Double negatives can be particularly difficult, as the second negative may arise in a response.

If a particular question is overly complex or initially confusing, you may want to diagram the question on your scrap paper, noting the crucial elements of the question. You may question the extra time it will take to read the questions twice, but we recommend this method because with only one reading, the full meaning of the question is often not apparent. For example, consider the following question:

Which principle of object design states that the implementation detail of the way an object works should be hidden from the developer?

At first glance, you may interpret this question, incorrectly, to be asking about hidden objects. The second time through, you may notice the crucial phrase of the question is, "Which principle of object design…" Reading the sentence twice enhances the accuracy of your understanding. Misinterpreting a question is more common in testing situations, because you are rushed and under pressure.

NOTE Some questions may have more than one correct response, and you will be asked to select a certain number of correct responses. Because there is no partial credit given, selecting only one response will be a wrong answer. Read directions carefully!

Guess the Answer Yourself Before Reading Response Options If you are able to answer the question yourself, and your response is one of the listed options, the likelihood is very good that you have answered correctly. If you don't try to guess before seeing the given options, you may be misled by one of the incorrect responses. The main benefit to guessing early is this opportunity to bypass potential error.

Read All of the Responses Before Marking Your Choice Your goal is to get as many questions correct as possible. Don't miss anything by answering a question without considering all of the possible responses. Some exam questions include two essentially correct responses, and you must select the one that is *most* correct. If you don't read them all, you may bypass the most correct response.

Eliminate Obviously Wrong Choices If you cannot figure out the correct response, it is to your clear advantage to make an educated guess. This often means eliminating false options, and choosing among the remaining options. If you know the answers to half the questions on an exam, and guess randomly at the other half, you would on the basis of probability, get a score of 62 percent (50 percent for the answers you knew, and 12 percent or so for the ones you got right by guessing randomly). If you are able to eliminate just one wrong response choice from each of the unknown questions, you will raise your score to 67 percent. If you reduce the pool by two on each question, your score increases to 75 percent. These figures are assuming that you select from the remaining responses randomly. Using a well-reasoned comparison of remaining responses using the tactics discussed next, you may be able to do even better.

Don't Spend Too Much Time on Hard Questions As stated earlier, your score and your personal experience will be better if you are able to manage the inevitable difficult questions. Pick an answer, mark the question for review, and come back to it later, when you have completed the easier questions.

Never Change Your Answer Unless You Absolutely Know It Is Wrong Several studies (and a huge collection of anecdotal evidence) have shown that when answers are changed, correct answers are changed to incorrect ones far more often than the other way around. About the only time you should feel comfortable in changing a response is if you find solid evidence in a subsequent question that your choice was wrong. There may be other times when you recognize problems and change answers, but you should always do so cautiously.

Using Advanced Strategies

So, now you've learned good habits for avoiding unnecessary errors. You will encounter some questions in your exam that you don't know the answers to. Good habits won't get you far on these questions. There are techniques, some of which we will present here, that can improve your chances of a correct response on these more difficult questions. To their credit, Microsoft puts great effort into their test-creation process, and these techniques will not always work.

The key to these techniques lies in an analysis of the response options given. In creating questions, the Microsoft staff has one basic goal, to create questions that will discriminate between testers with solid knowledge and experience and those without. There are a few types of questions that may discriminate in this way.

- A question with a series of response options that are only finely distinguished from each other or that fall into clusters.
- A question with response options that are largely unique from each other.
- Some combination of the previous two.

These types of questions are handled differently. Your first task is to determine which type of question it is. You can quickly determine which type of question you are facing and then use the correct choice-selection strategies.

Analyzing Clustered Responses As noted above, some questions contain response sets with similar or clustered response options. The following question illustrates this type of question:

1. If HTML form contains a text input field called Name, how would the value of that field be read in an Active Server Page (assuming that the method of the form is POST)?

   A. `Request.QueryString("Name")`

   B. `Response.QueryString("Name")`

   C. `Request.Form("Name")`

   D. `Response.Form("Name")`

The key to improving your success rate with this type of question is to look for the variation patterns in the response options. By giving a series of responses that differ systematically, the test developers are indirectly prompting you to remember certain issues relevant to the question. These questions are much easier to answer correctly than similar questions with random response options. This assumes, of course, that you have at least a basic knowledge of the subject matter.

In the previous example, the four responses vary in two ways: half begin with a reference to the Request object, and half with the Response object. Additionally, two items reference a QueryString collection, and two reference a Form collection. In other words, by selecting these particular response options, the test creators are hinting that some combination of these two is the correct choice. The trick then, lies not so much in figuring out the syntax as it does in figuring out which structural elements are involved.

If the responses given for this question were more random, then you would get fewer hints. In that case, you must be aware of many interacting issues, disproving three incorrect choices (including syntax or other meta information). When the only hope you have is to recall *anything* from a study guide, this reduction of noise is a great advantage.

Other examples of these "variations on a theme" questions are given below. Examine the available responses, and practice identifying the variance issues.

1. A CGI application is:

A. interpreted code running in a separate address space from the Web server.

B. interpreted code running in the same address space as the Web server.

C. compiled code running in a separate address space from the Web server.

D. compiled code running in the same address space as the Web server.

2. Which code statement would allow you to point the user's browser to a page called `newpage.html`?

A. `Request.Redirect newpage.html`

B. `Request.Navigate newpage.html`

C. `Response.Redirect newpage.htm`

D. `Response.Navigate newpage.html`

3. Which code sample would set a reference of the variable called EngObj to a running instance of the Truck.Engine object?

A. `EngObj=CreateObject("Truck.Engine")`

B. `Set EngObj=CreateObject("Truck.Engine")`

C. `EngObj=Server.CreateObject("Truck.Engine")`

D. `Set EngObj=Server.CreateObject("Truck.Engine")`

For Question 1, the crucial differences are the type of code being run (interpreted or compiled) and the location of the code processing (in-process or out-of-process). Question 2 focuses on the essential differences between the Request and Response objects and the Navigate and Redirect methods. Question 3, in contrast, focuses attention on the syntax of the code rather than the objects or methods called.

Identifying Unique Responses When test responses do not have overlapping content, the strategies at your disposal are quite different. In this situation, there are more techniques available, but they are less reliable, and are not used on all unique-response questions.

The main advantage you have with this type of question is that the responses still have to be uniquely correct, so the alternatives can be more obviously unrelated. These answers are also frequently shorter and simpler than their overlapping cousins. The downside to these questions is that you get less information to aid you in extrapolating the correct answer.

The tools you have for these types of questions are as follows:

- These questions, especially if the responses are short and simple, are typically looking for recognition of a significant term. If one term looks like it might be related to the question and the others mean nothing to you, pick the one that rings a bell, even if it is a small bell.
- Unlike the overlapping-type responses, in the case of unique responses, a response that stands out from the group is likely to be the correct one.
- Watch for specific details. The more descriptors in use, the more likely this is the correct answer. Consider the following:

  1. In a typical two-tier application, the database engine will reside on a:

  A. NetWare server

  B. central database application server

  C. client workstation

  D. Windows NT computer

  In this case, the “B” answer is distinguishable from the “D” by its extra defining adjectives.

- Watch for qualifiers. In other words, “always” and “never” are difficult standards to match, so correct responses will often contain words like “usually” or “typically.”

- Some response sets will contain only a list of numbers. In general, test creators rarely choose one of the extremes for the correct answer. If you have no idea and are guessing, select one of the central responses. Consider the following example:

  1. How many different types of class objects can a collection hold?

     A. 0

     B. 1

     C. 2

     D. 3

The answer to this question is 1, but if you don't know this at exam time, you can at least guess that A and D are probably not the correct responses. Using this technique, your chance of being correct improves from 25 percent to 50 percent.

A final comment on an old wives' tale: many students have picked up the habit of always selecting "C" when the correct answer is not known. The rationale for this tactic is a fear that guessing at random may cause them to miss all correct responses and selecting "C" guarantees 25 percent probability on these guessed items (assuming four response options are given).

The "select C" logic has two flaws. First, it denies the laws of probability. If you select from four items randomly, you should consistently get approximately 25 percent correct. The more questions guessed randomly, the more narrow the range of variation around that 25 percent mark.

The second flaw in this logic is that by taking this conservative approach, potential opportunities are lost. As noted earlier, ruling out a few clearly false responses along the way raises your chances of guessing correct responses.

If you have previously used this method, we hope that reading this appendix will discourage you from its use. You can do much better without necessarily knowing any more basic information.

NOTE The Microsoft certification exams are constructed by professionals trained in test creation procedures. Questions and response sets have been designed to reduce the effectiveness of these techniques. Using them is still likely to improve your scores, but these strategies will not compensate for inadequate study and preparation. The best approach to certification exams is a combination of thorough study, applied experience, and skilled test taking.

Glossary

Abstraction The ability of an object to provide a virtual representation of a physical object or process. Using the concept of abstraction, you can reference an object without needing to describe in detail every individual attribute of the object.

Active Server Pages An ISAPI extension that allows HTML Script tags to execute on the server. HTML is placed in an Active Server Page. Script is marked for server-side execution and the executing script creates an HTML response to send back to the browser.

ActiveX An implementation of COM that defines the structure of components and object models.

ActiveX Data Objects (ADO) A set of programmable objects designed to interface with OLE DB. The ADO object model showcases a more simplified hierarchy than its predecessors. The ADO object library is currently available from Microsoft free of charge in the OLE DB SDK.

Aesthetics The elements on an application interface that provide a visually pleasing environment. Fonts, complementary colors, and graphics can all provide aesthetic elements to an application interface.

Application Programming Interface (API) A set of functions or component interfaces that are available to other applications to provide programmability for a component or service. There are two major types of API interfaces. They are traditional call-level interfaces that are implemented as function calls in a DLL, or COM interfaces that are implemented as objects.

Atomic The attribute of a transaction that defines it as all-or-none. If a data modification is guaranteed to be atomic, then every element of the modification must succeed or the entire modification must be reversed.

Attribute A property or description of an entity used in database design. If the entity you are describing is a car, the attributes might be color, weight, etc. Attributes are represented in a database as the columns or fields in a table.

BackOffice A collection of Microsoft client/server applications bundled in a single package. BackOffice products include SQL Server, Exchange Server, SMS, SNA, and MSCS.

Bandwidth The capacity of a network link to transmit data at a certain rate. Usually expressed in bits per second, 10 Mbps (megabits per second) is a common bandwidth for Ethernet networks. Bandwidth can either describe the total capacity of the network or the remaining capacity after all existing network traffic is taken into account.

Bidirectional Character Set A character set that supports writing from both right to left and left to right. Middle Eastern languages in particular require bidirectional character sets. Although the native text is written from right to left, numbers and other European words that may be incorporated into the Middle Eastern language are written from left to right.

Business Services Functionality in an application that defines business logic. Data validation rules and other business rules make up the business services of an application.

Class The formal definition of an object. When an object is instantiated, the instantiation is based on the defining class. This class defines the interfaces (its methods, properties, and events).

Class ID A unique 128-bit value (GUID) that identifies a given COM interface as unique across all COM interfaces. This value is stored in the windows registry under CLSID subkeys. In an HTML object tag, the class ID identifies the object that is being inserted into the Web page.

Client/Server A database application architecture that divides the processing tasks of the application between the server and a workstation. Other servers on the networks may also provide additional processing. There are two general forms of client/server architecture: two-tier and multiple-tier.

Codepage A set of characters assigned to code points that is intended for a locale-specific implementation. ANSI code pages provide support for multiple characters by assigning each a number from 0 to 255. The computer stores the number internally and the character translation occurs through the code page.

Code Point A single point in a code page or character set that identifies a single character. ANSI code pages define 256 code points. Each code point represents a single character that is rendered by a font written explicitly for that code page.

Collection A group of one or more objects. A collection is an object that provides containership for other objects. All collections should support at least one property called *Count*, which returns the total number of objects in that collection.

Common Gateway Interface (CGI) An application that runs on a Web server designed to provide services and/or return HTML to a browser through the Web server. In IIS 3, CGI applications run in a separate process address space from the Web server process itself.

Component An object or group of objects compiled into a binary file (usually COM-compliant) that can be accessed from applications.

Component Object Model (COM) A specification that defines binary standards for object interfaces and specifies how objects relate and work with each other. Object Linking and Embedding (OLE) and ActiveX are both implementations of the Component Object Model.

Consistency An attribute of a user interface to provide the same visual cues for the same actions without deviation. For example, if an opening file folder is used in one screen to symbolize a file open operation, the same metaphor should be consistently applied throughout the application. This includes all applications in a suite of which this application may be a member.

Console Interface A legacy command window interface most commonly used for batch executions, emulations, and utility configurations.

Cookie A small file hosted on the browser that allows the Web developer to store information concerning the preferences of the Web user making the connection. The cookie can also be used to maintain persistence of variables and other data across pages.

Cryptography API The component of WOSA that provides support for cryptography services running under Microsoft Windows through a common API. Service providers that are Crypto API–compliant will operate with any client application written to the Crypto API standard.

Data Access Objects (DAO) The proprietary COM interface to Microsoft's JET database engine version 3.5 and earlier. The Data Access Objects provide support for JET databases, other ISAM databases through installable ISAM drivers, and ODBC databases.

Data Services Functionality in a database application that interacts directly with the data storage. The data engine in a database application represents the data services interface.

Decision-Support System A database that is used primarily as a reporting system. Decision-support databases are responsible for returning data to clients based on data selects, but rarely have any data modifications or insertions issued against them. Decision-support systems are often good candidates for denormalization.

Denormalization The process of deliberately violating the rules of normalization in order to improve performance in a database.

Deployment The process of installing applications on all the clients and servers that will run an application.

Device In SQL Server 6.5, a preallocated unit of storage used to create databases. SQL Server 7 no longer uses devices.

Directness The ability of an interface to give the user visual cues that indicate a direct response to an action taken by the user. For example, if a user double-clicks an icon, the mouse pointer will change to an hourglass. The hourglass is a direct result of the user's action.

ECMAScript Defined by the European Computer Makers Association, ECMAScript defines a standard for JavaScript implementation in a Web page.

Encapsulation The ability of an object to hide its implementation details from the object's consumers. The object becomes a "black box," where a set of interfaces is known, but how the interfaces are implemented is not known or needed by those calling the object.

Entity An object or process that a database describes. In an inventory database system, an entity might be a customer or a product. Entities are represented in relational database structures as tables.

Event A notification fired by an object altering the system of a condition that has occurred. In event-driven programming, events are the code catalysts. Nothing happens until an event fires. An event can be triggered by the user as in a Click event of a command button, or it may be fired by the system, as in the Load event of an HTML page.

Exchange Server Microsoft BackOffice product that provides e-mail and groupware services. The e-mail services can be for the local network and also for Internet mail.

Feedback The ability of an application to provide constant information to the user about application state and program flow. For example, when you press a toggle button, its shadowing changes, making the button appear to be pressed down. This informs the user that the feature symbolized by that button is engaged.

File-Server Database A database architecture in which a data engine that resides on a client workstation accesses data stored in data files on a network file server. This approach is different from a client/server database in that the entire application and data engine resides on the client workstation. The server stores the file for shared access.

File Transfer Protocol (FTP) A protocol used to transfer files (upload or download) over the Internet or intranets. The FTP interface is typically text-based, and WWW protocols are GUI-based.

Flat File A data storage format in which all of the data is stored in few large tables rather than broken up into smaller tables and related together. Flat-file storage structures suffer from the disadvantage of storing a significant amount of redundant data.

Globalization The process of developing software with international distribution in mind. The globalization process becomes part of the initial planning phase. There is virtually no difference between a domestic distribution and an international distribution where the code is concerned.

Groupware Software that allows groups to collaborate on projects. Tracks multiple accesses and changes to files so all the members of a group can see what other group members have done on the project.

HTML Form An HTML structure that allows input to be received from a user and sent back to a process residing on a server. This server-side process might be a CGI application or an ISAPI application such as Active Server Pages.

HTML Tag An identifier in a text file used to instruct Web browsers about how text should be formatted and displayed. Some tags are browser-specific as to their interpretation, while others will look the same displayed in almost any browser.

HTTP Response The response to an HTTP request. The HTTP response usually contains the Web page requested by the browser, but it can also be a custom-created HTML page generated by an Active Server Page or some other server-side process.

HTTP Request The message sent from the browser to the Web server when a page is requested or a form is submitted. The HTTP request message may contain values captured in an HTML form. These values can then be processed by a server-side process.

Hyperlink Text marked by an anchor tag in an HTML page that, when clicked, points the browser to another location. Hyperlinks usually appear in another color, such as blue, when rendered on a Web page.

Hypertext Markup Language (HTML) The language of the World Wide Web. HTML is not a programming language; it is a text markup environment like RTF in which tags that are used to mark the text are interpreted by the Web browser that loads the HTML file.

Inheritance The ability of one class to define the interfaces, properties, and methods of another class. A class can be created based on another class. The new class will have the same properties and methods of the original base class, but the new class can add its own or take away from the base class behaviors. Not currently supported by Visual Basic.

Internationalization A generic term that refers to the process of preparing software for international distribution. A developer can accomplish internationalization in one of two distinct ways. The developer can either localize the application or globalize the application.

Internet Server API (ISAPI) An API set that allows the Web developer to create applications that run on the Internet Information Server in response to browser requests. ISAPI applications can provide services to a browser such as data connectivity or return HTML to the browser.

Intranet The use of Internet protocols and programming within a local area network. An intranet works the same way as the Internet; however, only local users are allowed to access intranet content.

Internet Information Server (IIS) Microsoft BackOffice product that provides Web publishing, FTP publishing, and on older versions Gopher publishing capabilities on an intranet or the Internet.

Java A programming language developed by Sun Microsystems. Java is an object-oriented language very similar to C++ in structure. It can be used to create small applets that run in a Web browser and can be incorporated as part of a Web site. It can also be used to create stand-alone applications that run independently from the Web. The interest in Java is primarily due to the fact that it can run on any hardware platform that supports a special interpreter called a Java Virtual Machine.

Java Applet A small compiled Java class designed to run inside a Web browser. Applets are created with the Java language and are marked in an HTML file with an applet tag. The codebase attribute of the applet tag identifies the source of the applet's code. Applets are not permanently installed on the user's system and must be downloaded every time the Web page is accessed.

JavaScript A programming language created by Netscape Communications that can be used inside of script tags on a Web page. JavaScript was formerly called LiveScript in its initial releases. It is usually added to a Web page to provide interaction with the user and other dynamic features in an internet application.

Java Virtual Machine A Java interpreter used to execute Java bytecode on a host machine. A Java Virtual Machine can be created for any hardware platform, thereby enabling the bytecode to be cross-platform.

Joint Engine Technology (JET) Microsoft's single-tier data engine. JET runs locally on each user workstation. Data can be stored locally or on a network server. JET ships as the native database engine in Microsoft Access, and it also ships with Microsoft Visual Basic.

JScript In Internet Explorer, JScript is the Microsoft version of JavaScript. JScript is included with Microsoft Internet Explorer 3 and higher.

Keep Alive The Keep Alive extension added to HTTP 1.1 allows a TCP connection to be maintained when the Web server would normally close it. This provides more responsiveness between the browser and the Web server, but it also increases the overhead on the Web server to maintain the open connection.

Key Folders in the Registry that hold values. Also referred to as subkeys.

License Service API (LSAPI) The WOSA component that provides support for licensing services running under Microsoft Windows through a common API. Service providers that are LSAPI-compliant will operate with any client application written to the LSAPI standard.

Locale A specific language and sublanguage implementation. A locale is defined by its language, not by its geographical location.

Localization The process of creating software for a specific locale. This means designing the application for implementation only in that locale and creating other distributions for alternate locales that the distributor wants to support.

Logo Compliance Adherence to Microsoft's regulations allowing an ISV to include a Microsoft Logo on their products. Logo programs include Windows 95/NT–compatible, Microsoft Office, and Microsoft BackOffice.

Many-to-Many Relationship A method of relating two tables together such that one record in the first table relates the potentially many records in the second table and the reverse is also true. This approach requires a third table to act as an intermediary between the two related tables.

Messaging API (MAPI) The WOSA component that provides support for e-mail and messaging systems through a common API. Service providers that are MAPI-compliant will operate with any client application written to the MAPI standard.

Method A behavior of an object that is defined in the class from which the object is instantiated. Methods cause things to happen in an object-based application.

Multiple Document Interface (MDI) An application interface in which the main window is a container window that can hold multiple documents at the same time. Microsoft Word is an example of a multiple document interface application.

Multiple-Tier A client/server database architecture that divides processing responsibility among many computers on the network. While the data engine resides on the application server and the client application resides on the client, there may be other servers that host business objects designed to process business rules.

Normalization The process of removing data redundancy in data storage by following a set of rules known as the normal forms. A normalized database is the opposite of a flat-file database.

Object An object is the implementation of a class. It is something that you initiate and control through code. An object supports properties and methods that define how the object appears and behaves.

OLE DB A set of low-level COM interfaces designed to provide common support for database access. Similar in purpose to ODBC, OLE DB provides a COM interface and ODBC provides a traditional call-level interface.

One-to-Many Relationship A method of relating two tables together such that one record in the first table relates to potentially many records in the second table. This type of relationship is the most common in relational database structure.

One-to-One Relationship A method of relating two tables together such that one record in the first table can relate to a maximum of one record in the related table.

Online Transaction Processing System A database that is used primarily to accept data modifications in the form of inserts, updates, and deletes. Online transaction processing systems are rarely used for heavy reporting. They are usually poor candidates for denormalization.

Open Database Connectivity (ODBC) A component of the Windows Open Services Architecture that defines a generic standard for accessing databases. ODBC defines a call-level API set and a SQL grammar conformance requirement.

Persistence The ability of a variable or other piece of information to maintain its value across the destruction and re-creation of its container, such as a Web page or a VB UserControl.

Polymorphism The ability to implement interfaces generically in your applications without regard to the code in the class that implements the interface. In other words, you can have multiple classes that define the same interfaces; however, the actual code behind these interfaces may perform different tasks depending on which class is used. Visual Basic uses the Implements keyword to provide polymorphism.

Property An attribute or description of an object that is defined in the class from which the object was instantiated.

Proxy Server Microsoft BackOffice product that provides a firewall to protect local resources from unauthorized Internet access and also controls Internet access of local users.

Pull Installation A method of deploying applications over the network where the deployment process is initiated by the client by connecting to a server that contains the application. The application is pulled to the client.

Push Installation A method of deploying applications over the network where the deployment process is initiated at a central server and is pushed down to the clients.

Record An instance of an entity used in database design. Every record is a unique observation of an entity, complete with information regarding all attributes of that entity. Records are represented in a database as rows in a table.

REGEDIT The Registry editing tool provided with Windows 95. Also can be used in Windows NT 4 to edit that Registry.

REGEDT32 The Registry editing tool provided with Windows NT.

Registering Applications The process of notifying the operating system about installed applications. This information must be written to specific locations in the Registry.

Registry A database used by Windows 95 and Windows NT operating systems to store system configuration information. Applications written for these platforms also store configuration information in the Registry. Replaced `.ini` files under older Windows platforms.

Relationship Commonality between two or more entities in a relational database. Relationships between entities allow data to be extracted from multiple sources and related together. There are three types of relationships: one-to-one, one-to-many, and many-to-many.

Remote Data Objects (RDO) Developed by Microsoft, RDO is a thin, component layer that sits on top of the ODBC API. The RDO object model provides an alternative to the ODBC API for the database developer who must access ODBC data sources. RDO 2 is the last version of RDO available from Microsoft.

Scalability The ability of a software component to handle very large amounts of traffic. For example, a component object that can handle a large number of requests coming from the Internet as easily as it handles a single request from one user is said to be scalable.

Scope The defined visibility of an object, variable, or procedure. For example, if a variable is declared to be visible to all procedures in an application, it is said to have public scope.

Shell Extension An extension to the operating system interface that provides additional functionality that would be defined at the operating system level rather than the application level. Modifying or customizing system elements is usually accomplished through shell extensions.

Simplicity The ability of an interface to be accessible to users at all levels of sophistication. Interacting with a Windows application should be instinctive and simple.

Single Document Interface (SDI) An application interface in which all of an application's windows are stand-alone and are not contained by one another.

Single-Tier An application architecture that places the entire responsibility for processing on a single computer. File-server databases are single-tier databases because the data engine resides on the workstation while the data used by the engine resides on a file server. Single-tier applications can also exist completely on a single computer as a stand-alone system.

SMS Installer An add-on product to Microsoft's SMS that allows you to package applications together in a single self-extracting executable for easy installation.

SNA API The component of WOSA that provides support for IBM System Network Architecture, allowing connectivity to IBM mainframe and AS/400 computers. The SNA API works with Microsoft SNA Server to provide gateway services to these systems without placing any of the implementation complexities in the client application.

System Network Architecture (SNA) Server Microsoft BackOffice product that provides connectivity between a Windows NT network and IBM AS/400 or mainframe computers.

Speech API The WOSA component that provides support for speech engines and text-to-speech services running under Microsoft Windows through a common API. Service providers that are Speech API compliant will operate with any client application written to the Speech API standard.

Structured Query Language (SQL) Server The Microsoft BackOffice product that provides database capabilities. Many BackOffice products, such as SMS, use SQL Server to store their data. Programmers can also write custom databases by using Transact-SQL, the programming language of SQL Server.

Subkey Folders in the Registry that hold values. Also referred to as keys.

Subtree The largest subdivision of the Registry. The Windows NT Registry has five subtrees; the Windows 95 Registry has six subtrees.

Systems Management Server (SMS) Microsoft BackOffice product that provides network management services. With SMS, the administrator can inventory network clients, remote control clients, and distribute software to clients.

Task Help A help window that provides a user with step-by-step instructions to complete a task. The task help window is a pop-up, meaning that it remains on top of all other windows at all times so that it can be visible to provider instructions when needed.

Telephony API (TAPI) The WOSA component that provides support for modems and other telephone equipment operating under Microsoft Windows through a common API. Service providers that are TPI-compliant will operate with any client application written to the TPI standard.

Thunking The process of converting a DLL call such that a 16-bit application can call a 32-bit DLL or the reverse. Windows 95 supports thunking in both directions, but Windows NT supports thunks only from 16-bit to 32-bit.

ToolTip A small yellow window that appears when the mouse pointer is paused over an object, most commonly a button on a toolbar. The window contains a one or two-word description of the function of the tool.

Transaction Log In SQL Server, the log portion of a SQL database. Modifications to SQL databases are usually first written to the transaction log and then written to the database.

Two-Tier A client/server database architecture that divides processing responsibility between the client workstation and a networked application server. In this scenario, the data engine resides on the server, while the client application resides on a workstation. Business rules can be implemented on the server, workstation, or both.

Unicode A character set that stores characters as two bytes rather than one. This allows up to 65,535 characters to be referenced from the character set rather than 256. The mission of Unicode is to provide a single character set under which all of the world's characters can be referenced.

User Services Functionality in an application that interacts directly with the user. User services include receiving user input, formatting, and reporting.

Values The configuration parameters in the Registry. Values have three components: the name, type, and setting.

VBScript A programming language created by Microsoft that can be used inside of script tags on a Web page. VBScript is based on the Microsoft Visual Basic programming language and is usually added to a Web page to provide interaction with the user and other dynamic features in an Internet application.

Windows Open Services Architecture (WOSA) A set of APIs that provide a single system-level interface to enterprise computing environments, while hiding the complexities of heterogeneous environments from end users and developers.

World Wide Web (WWW) A graphical method of publishing content over the Internet or intranets. Often referred to as the Web.

Index

Note to the Reader: Throughout this index **boldfaced** page numbers indicate primary discussions of a topic. *Italicized* page numbers indicate illustrations.

A

B

C

D

E

F

G

H

I

J

K

L

M

N

Q

R

S

T

U

V